"*The Quiet Millionaire* is loaded with valuable strategies for maintaining and growing wealth throughout one's life." —CPA Wealth Provider

The
Quiet
Millionaire

A Concise Guide for Accumulating and Keeping Your Wealth
to Eliminate Financial Stress and Enjoy a Lifetime
of Security and Independence

Brett Wilder
Certified Financial Planner™

Axiom Book Award Winner for Personal Finance
Revised and Updated!

WHAT PEOPLE ARE SAYING ABOUT THE QUIET MILLIONAIRE

"Tackling complex topics in plain terms, The Quiet Millionaire *is thoroughly accessible to readers of all financial backgrounds and highly recommended."*
—Midwest Book Review

"This book contains many valuable insights, and Wilder does an excellent job of facilitating a more informed advisor-client relationship. Advisors would do well to introduce clients to the complexities involved with financial planning by presenting them with this book."
—NAPFA Advisor, The Journal of the National Association of Personal Financial Advisors

"If you're truly serious about developing an understandable and comprehensive financial vision for the future, The Quiet Millionaire *by Brett Wilder is the right book for you. The author literally guides you step-by-step through how to develop a million dollar financial future. When you finish, you'll have a powerful and workable plan for becoming and remaining The Quiet Millionaire."*
—Sharon Michaels, Author

"Wilder offers sage advice about loans, college funding and retirement income calculations; his retirement cash flow analysis is a dandy. This book is obviously a labor of love."
—Life Insurance Selling magazine

"If you could buy only one book that would comprehensively cover everything you need to know about managing your personal finances, get The Quiet Millionaire *by Brett Wilder. Take your time, read it slowly, make copious notes, in the margins, and discuss Brett's suggestions with family, colleagues, and friends."*
—**Bill Bailey, J.D., Ph.D.**

*"*The Quiet Millionaire *is loaded with valuable strategies for maintaining and growing weal throughout one's life."*
—**CPA Wealth Provider**

*"*The Quiet Millionaire *contains useful information for both the novice and experienced investor who are motivated to achieve their investment and comprehensive lifetime financial planning goals. I recommend this book to anyone who is in the process of searching for a financial advisor and as well to someone who wants to confirm the value of their existing advisory relationship."*
—**Sue Morrissey, Associate Professor Emeritus, Indiana School of Nursing**

*"*The Quiet Millionaire *dissects the complexity of wealth Management in easy to understand, layman terminology. What makes this financial advisory book unique is that the reader first learns how to define their true life values and goals before creating their financial plan. This ensures a successful navigation through the various stages of wealth management with conviction and commitment."*
—**Jan Kesselring, Retired School Superintendent**

The
Quiet
Millionaire

A Concise Guide for Accumulating and Keeping Your Wealth
to Eliminate Financial Stress and Enjoy a Lifetime
of Security and Independence

Brett Wilder
Certified Financial Planner™

QM GUIDANCE PRESS

The Quiet Millionaire---A Concise Guide for Accumulating and Keeping Your Wealth to Eliminate Financial Stress and Enjoy a Lifetime of Security and Independence
By Brett Wilder

ATTENTION CORPORATIONS, PROFESSIONAL ORGANIZATIONS, UNIVERSITIES, AND COLLEGES: Quantity discounts are available on bulk purchases of this book for educational, gift purposes, or as premiums for increasing magazine subscriptions or renewals. Special books or book excerpts can also be created to fit specific needs. For information, please contact Brett Wilder@QMGuidance.com.

ISBN (Print Edition): 978-1-09833-602-8
ISBN (eBook Edition): 978-1-09833-603-5

CONTENTS

INTRODUCTION

Meet *The Quiet Millionaire*

Achieving millionaire status used to be a noteworthy accomplishment. Today, it's more prevalent, and probably necessary for you to enjoy the financially independent lifestyle you dream of. You hear about the accumulated wealth of business stars such as Warren Buffett, Bill Gates, Jeff Bezos, and Elon Musk. However, you don't hear about the many people who have eliminated costly debt and accumulated wealth quietly and intelligently. I term these people *quiet millionaires®*.

Being a millionaire is a realistic aspiration if you're knowledgeable and diligent about becoming one. This book is about how to become a quiet millionaire® in the twenty-first century. It will guide you through the opportunities and pitfalls you face in managing today's fast-changing and challenging lifetime choices and financial issues. The successful journey outcome of the quiet millionaire® can be yours as well, if you choose your course wisely, and manage to overcome seven major obstacles.

Seven Major Obstacles to Achieving Financial Success and Living a Life You Dream Of

1. **Materialistic thinking:** Preoccupation with owning physical assets and things more than pursuing intellectual and spiritual endeavors to enrich your life.

2. **Undisciplined spending:** Spending impulsively, spending more than you make, and not tracking where your money is going.

3. **Burdensome costly debt:** Irrational, unintelligent, compulsive, wealth-robbing borrowing.

4. **Taxes:** A governmental levy that should be proactively reduced in magnitude, knowledgeably and legally.

5. **Inflation:** The silent erosion of wealth and purchasing power.

6. **Poorly structured investment portfolios:** Undiversified investments possessing an unjustifiable amount of risk relative to the potential for reward.

7. **Unforeseen life-changing, financially devastating events:** The major financial risks we all share in life: catastrophic medical expenses, divorce, job loss, disability, death, lawsuits, and long-term health care expenses.

Today, we encounter more opportunities than previous generations to accomplish our dreams, but more pitfalls as well. You're going to live longer, so you better get things right. The quiet millionaire® typified the profile of my clients while I was the founder and owner of a highly regarded, fee-only financial planning and investment advisory firm, which I sold for millions in 2016. My telling you this is not for bragging purposes. Rather, it's to convey that I know first-hand some proven practical ways for you to achieve a quiet millionaire® lifestyle where you can be free to do whatever you want, wherever and whenever you want, regardless of whether you choose to work.

Who is a quiet millionaire®? I describe a quiet millionaire® as someone who very often starts with modest beginnings, has specifically determined what's really important to them, planned accordingly, works smart (instead of just hard), quietly builds and sustains wealth, enjoys life unpretentiously, appreciates what they've accomplished, and often gives back to help others who are less fortunate. I attracted the quiet millionaire® type of person to my firm because that's what I advocate and advise professionally, and the profile matches my personal DNA as well. I succeeded because my clients succeeded. We grew and built our successes together utilizing the quiet millionaire® approach explained in this book.

What this book covers to help guide your journey. One of the reasons I wrote this book is because through my professional experience I realized how often people are misguided by either themselves or by far too many financial advisors who act with self-interest, incompetence, or both. Here are some of the topics I'll cover with you:

- How to determine where you're going, so you'll know how to get there.
- How to determine what's important about money to you and why you should know.
- How to have a positive cash flow to fuel your journey.
- How to be an intelligent borrower and eliminate costly burdensome debt.
- How to build your net worth by owning the right assets, and disowning the wrong liabilities.
- How to avoid paying too much tax.
- How to be an investment winner.
- How to prepare for financially surviving life's risks.
- How to manage and afford the college experience.
- How to maximize retirement assets and not run out of money regardless of whether you choose to work or not.

- How to evaluate and select a qualified and competent financial planner/investment advisor that's right for you.

Along the way, I'll share reliable resources that expand upon these topics and help guide you on your journey. While everyone's life is unique, there are common elements to successful financial management. In the twenty-first century, many of the old "tried and true" ways for accumulating wealth are worthwhile and still work. However, there are also new and previously unknown ways and opportunities for achieving financial success. But, they're accompanied by more hazards for failure and hardship as well. Planning and managing your course in today's fast-changing environment can be stressful. In this digital age, you're constantly bombarded with too much information from too many unreliable sources. You need to stay informed, but you also need to know when to tune out the daily noise that can be confusing and contradictory.

Use this book as a guide to discern and distinguish between what's beneficial for you and what's harmful noise. This book guides you in how to discern and distinguish between what information is beneficially useful and what's harmful to your financial well-being. As your needs and wants change along the way, you'll know how to best plan and adjust to manage these changes. You'll learn proven successful financial management strategies that might be contrary to advice being offered by financial advisors with hype and hidden agendas. You'll also know how to spot unregulated, misinformed, and often irresponsible media and marketing hype.

Realize that many financial advisors think more about what's best for themselves than what's best for you. You may decide that you need help from a professional financial advisor. Consider it with the same seriousness as seeing a doctor about maintaining your physical health or an attorney to solve complex legal matters. While there are some very good and dedicated professionals competently advising people, you must go through an intelligent and thorough due diligence process to find the right, trustworthy advisor for your particular situation. If you follow the advice in this book, you'll be properly prepared to select, and work with, a professional advisor *before* you hire one. You'll know what to look for in a good financial advisor, and you'll know whether your situation justifies paying for an advisor's help. Working with the right advisor can, and should, enhance your financial situation and provide you with more comfort about money matters.

Financial windfalls do happen, but don't depend upon one happening to you. Instead, take control with the right information to make well-thought-out, informed choices and actions. I'll guide you to determine where you're at currently, and how to plan and make priority decisions to close the gap between where you're at now and where you want to be.

Use the knowledge you learn from this book as the engine for becoming and staying a quiet millionaire®, and the money you gain as the fuel for implementing the recommended strategies. I guarantee you'll have a smoother journey getting to where you want to be. If for any reason you aren't convinced that the quiet millionaire® approach can benefit you, just let me know, and I'll refund your purchase price paid for the book. I'd be interested in having your feedback about the book, and I'm available to answer any questions you may have. You can contact me directly by email at BrettWilder@QMGuidance.com.

Best Wishes for Wealth, Health, and Happiness!
Brett Wilder

CHAPTER 1

Truly Know Thyself

D o you have a purposeful life that's pointed in a direction with a planned, charted course? The quiet millionaire® *does not* live just for today, drifting aimlessly, being consumed by life's daily activities, or mistakenly thinking that tomorrow will take care of itself. Rather, the quiet millionaire® *does* think about tomorrow as well as today. This way you can knowingly commit to funding your established goals and objectives and remain protected during stormy times.

Think carefully about this:

- If you had all the money you needed now and in the future, what would you be doing differently from what you are doing today?
- If you knew that you had only a few years to live, what specifically would you change about your life now?
- If you had complete freedom to decide, what unfulfilled dreams would you pursue, and which people would you choose to enrich your life?
- If you had to refocus your life to pursue your unfulfilled dreams, what meaningless activities that waste your time would you eliminate, and what people who you do not enjoy would you avoid?

By knowing the answers to these questions, you'll spend your time more wisely and meaningfully, and you'll more likely live life to the fullest, with less regrets.

QUIET MILLIONAIRE® WISDOM

*No goals, no plans, no strategies, no
perseverance, no financial success!*

Discover Who's the *Real* You and What You *Really* Want and Why

How you spend your time should reflect what you truly want from life and why. Mistakenly, people often are too busy with the daily activities *in* their lives to devote the necessary time and energy to working *on* their lives. You should discover who you are, what you want from life, and why, to establish your true identity. This means stepping back and taking time to contemplate and figure out what the "gut meaning" of life is for you, what your burning desires are, what your greatest fears are, and in what ways you want to be enriched and satisfied. You need to delve into your inner soulful self to figure out what enlightens you and what will sustain your commitment toward making happen what you want to happen. Furthermore, these questions need to be addressed repeatedly throughout your life to make sure that you are staying true to your course and that your ideals and core desires have not changed. Only by periodically taking time to think about and internalize honest responses to these questions can you chart a course and make adjustments along the way to achieve what it is that you *really* want.

Be aware that there are blockages that can sidetrack your thought process. Procrastination is a major roadblock, as is finding private uninterrupted time. Yet, in order to truly experience your feelings and listen to your inner voice as you evolve through the discovery process, you must find quiet space and time. You can also choose to become more mindful about how you're spending your time. Are you allowing distractions, disruptions, and commitments to interfere with what you need to be doing? Are television, movies, computer games, and other "easy" forms of escape robbing you of quality quiet time? If so, then focus on ways to get out of those ruts. Remember that the often-used definition of "crazy" is doing the same thing over and over while expecting a different result.

In this self-discovery process, you also need to manage expectations others have about you. This includes family, friends, and work associates, who may unknowingly rob you of time during this evaluation process. One way to manage this is to include family members into your thinking. Schedule meetings to discuss the family's intended direction, and to develop specific goals and objectives. Moreover, determine what are the overall dreams and expectations for each of the family members individually as well. Then, you can prioritize as a family unit what dreams and goals to pursue. Only by working together can the family as a whole see what conflicts of interest there might be and what goals need to be evaluated and changed, and then as a group determine and resolve any discrepancies that could hinder the success for achieving each other's goals. To have a better opportunity for attaining your own goals, you must derive harmonious consensus and support from those around you. With priorities set for desired goals and objectives, planning can be done accordingly and strategies can be implemented harmoniously without incurring unnecessary conflict and stress.

Friends and social commitments can consume your time. Most of us need to be social and participate in activities with others in life. However, often it gets out of hand and can consume a disproportionate amount of your time. Pay attention to the purpose and quality of outside friends and activities. Learn to say "no" sometimes. Also, be more selective about who you invite into your life. Don't become a "slurpee to the slurpers" who tend to pull you down instead of enrich your life. This doesn't mean you shouldn't be available to help others who might be struggling with a particularly difficult issue. However, there are those who choose to whine and gossip their way through life, and you're better off avoiding them.

With respect to your employment, when you go to work, work! Make the best use of your time and do so efficiently; get done what needs to be done within a normal workday. This way, you can structure a more balanced life and avoid a potential "burnout" situation. Work can always demand more of your time if you let it. However, in the end, you won't feel satisfied by having worked more hours than anybody else, resulting in an empty, unfulfilled life with only regrets for what never happened outside of the workplace. People will not come to your funeral and say, "I'll always remember him—he was a great guy, and he worked more hours than anybody." All of us are dispensable, as it should be, but our egos don't want us to believe that. Yet, it's amazing how things can in fact go on nicely when you aren't there, and if for some reason things don't, then it's most likely an ineffective work management issue.

QUIET MILLIONAIRE® WISDOM

*True personal self-discovery requires accessing
your subconscious thoughts.*

Two Methods for Personal Self-Discovery

Here are two methods for personal self-discovery that can help you learn more about your inner self. Both methods serve a different purpose and provide a different outcome.

1. **Listening to Yourself:** The first method is "listening to yourself." This process will help you to become more *honest* with yourself. I came upon this while I was trying to decide what to do about my financially rewarding but unsettling career in banking. I wanted to make a change but was anxious, uncertain, and immobilized about what to do. I had bought the book titled *What Color Is Your Parachute?* by Richard Bolles (updated annually), and it provided me with thought-provoking exercises to structure my career change thinking. However, I was struggling to commit with conviction about making the changes. I would sit and talk to myself out loud about the changes I wanted to make. By chance, I decided to record some of what I was thinking in order not to forget my thoughts. An interesting thing happened when I played my words back. I didn't recognize the ideas that I was hearing as mine. It was like someone else was saying the words, and some of it sounded like pipe dreams, while other ideas sounded wonderful. Listening to myself forced me to speak more truthfully about what I wanted and how I was going to get there. The recorder revealed the dishonesty in myself. At the time, I was seriously considering an offer from an investment advisory firm located in California. The firm wanted me to join, and I was excited about the offer. However, listening to myself discuss the opportunity revealed my honest feelings. I didn't really like the person in charge, and I didn't feel comfortable with the firm's investment approach or business culture. It was my ego that had been ruling my thinking. The result of my recorded self-conversation was that I turned down the offer much

to the firm's and my own surprise. Continuing with this "listening to yourself" approach, I came to realize without any doubt that I could never work for another employer in the financial services industry. I had to be the employer so that I could function entirely on my own inner convictions and "modus operandi." I became ready to commit to that course no matter what the sacrifice. That's when I began my own company. I was able to love what I do, help people, and get paid for it. What better combination can you ask for than that?

2. **Writing to Yourself:** The second self-discovery method is "writing to yourself." This process has helped me with enhancing my *creativity* and with deciding honestly who I am and what I want to do with my life. The idea here is to develop a free-flowing stream of consciousness, a "just let it rip" approach through writing or journaling. You will realize that this provides structure, consistency, and continuity to your thinking. Every day, in the early quiet morning with a fresh mind, sit down and write out in longhand anything that comes into your mind as quickly as you can without interruption until you have filled up three spiral-bound 8½ by 11 pages. Sometimes this activity is termed a "fast write" or "free write," with the writing limited to twenty or thirty minutes. I emphasize the importance of doing this in written longhand rather than using a computer in order to energize the most creative output. Writing long-hand stimulates the flow of creative juices from within that are closer to the heart, which will help you to find out what makes you feel happy and fulfilled. Write down anything that enters your mind, and don't worry about punctuation, correct spelling, or complete sentences. This is for your eyes only. It's personal. Here is where you do your whining, list personal to-dos, and let out your fears, your anger, your dreams, your ambitions. It doesn't matter what you write; just write whatever comes out as fast as you can without interruption or inhibition. Remember, these writings are your private thoughts and are not for anyone else

to read. Therefore, to not inhibit your written content, keep it private and well-hidden so that you can feel completely free to "let it all out." Although many times you may not feel like doing this spontaneous writing, and you can make tons of excuses for not following through (procrastination), I can't stress enough how important it is that you write every single day without fail. You'll be amazed at how much creative output and perspective will come forth to reveal your inner desires and excite you into taking action.

If you're truly motivated to learn about your inner self and not just drift through life aimlessly, you'll figure out your own most productive ways to overcome immobilization and blockages, and to make the necessary changes. Furthermore, you'll be surprised at your newfound energy and will become more committed over time as you think more and more about what's really important to you, your life, and about your money.

Money is the fuel for achieving your dreams and life goals and objectives. Money is emotional and reflects many of our inner needs and desires. Knowing your own money values helps to chart the directions you need to take in making life choices. Every choice made for using money, whether it's for capitalizing a career or structuring a happy home environment, a joyous family lifestyle, or a secure retirement, depends upon how you *personally* value money. You must make sure your values are harmonious with your goals and objectives. Otherwise, you won't have a burning desire to seriously commit to achieving those desired goals and objectives.

Why should you discover what's really important about money to you? Because everyone thinks differently about the importance of money, these differences can often cause financial conflict with others as well as within you. The importance of money goes beyond the goods and services it can provide. It plays a critical role in our ability to pursue goals, dreams, and desires.

Attitudes about money vary according to each individual's personality and ideals typically formulated and influenced by family background experiences involving the availability and usage of money. Knowing what's important about money helps make sure that your specified objectives and goals are in sync with your attitude toward money. If this is out of sync, then you'll have inner conflict, which decreases your likelihood for rewarding financial success. This will cause you to be insufficiently motivated to commit to the financial strategies required for accomplishing your goals and objectives. There are also psychological reasons, some healthy and some unhealthy, as to why you feel the way you do about money. Your financial decisions—good and bad—throughout life reflect your money personality. Starting during childhood, your family, your peers, and your society influence your attitude about money in general. Your success or failure with money depends upon how well you understand and assimilate and respond to these influences. You need to know your "true money self" to be financially comfortable with your money.

Reasons Why Money Is Important to People What's Yours?

Everyone's evaluation of money is unique. The following are some examples of what is important about money to people:

- **Security:** Having enough money to live without the fear of becoming impoverished is comforting, especially for anyone who has lived through or been preached to about tough financial times. Fear is a powerful emotion that can highly motivate some people to focus on saving as much money as possible but also possibly can cause them to be too risk adverse with their investments to keep up with inflation.

- **Freedom:** Being able to have enough money to live a meaningful life the way you choose, as well as occupationally work with enthusiasm and bliss, is healthy and exciting. Intelligent financial management allows you to be a money master, not a money slave.

- **Gaining love:** There's an old cliché that says, "Money can't buy you love." However, in a money-driven world, some people are, in fact, driven to have money in order to attract the opposite sex into their lives and find genuine love.

- **Respect:** Because money is respected, people often equate having money with a means for having the respect they strive to receive from others.

- **Power:** Money is a powerful force that can influence and control other people in either a positive or negative way.

- **Happiness:** While money may or may not bring happiness, it certainly can help to make life more enjoyable. However, spending money sometimes is merely a temporary mood elevator and can lead to financial trouble in the longer term. Living for the present moment can create short-term excitement at the expense of long-term peace of mind and financial security.

- **Self-worth:** Some people measure their self-worth by the amount of their net worth, while other people may have a high sense of self-worth that in no way correlates with the amount of money they have.

- **Accomplishment:** Money is often used as a scorecard for achievement and success.

- **Entitlement:** Some people feel that having money is an earned right because of past struggles, disappointments, or expectations in their life.

- **Helping Others:** Very often, money enables people to give back to help others because they themselves were given to and feel fortunate.

Your own self-discovery about what's important about money to you may include some facet of money importance that's beyond this list. The objective is to discover what you *really* feel and truly believe is important about money to you to understand the reasons behind your earning, saving, and spending activities, which can be financially healthy or unhealthy and may require adjustments. Once you've discovered the *most important* reason why money is important to you, then you can determine what lifetime events in your background may have influenced your current attitude and emotions about money. You'll learn whether your motivations for having and spending money are truly healthy, positive, and worthwhile or whether they're negative and troublesome. This knowledge can help reduce conflict about money within yourself as well as with significant others, and you can then properly prioritize and focus with motivation how you earn, accumulate, manage, and spend money.

QUIET MILLIONAIRE® WISDOM

Let money be your servant, not your master.

How to Be a Master Over Your Money

To be a master over your money and to control your own future rather than let money be the master over you, you must learn to manage your money and let it be the fuel for building a life of happiness and fulfillment. Only then will you know how to best balance living for the present moment while planning for the future. There are times when some people may seek help from professionals such as financial advisors and psychologists to understand their money self. However, many professionals probably don't take the time themselves to learn what's important about money to them, and don't understand the process. Furthermore, some financial advisors often base their financial review and recommendations for you in a manner that can be biased toward what's more in their best self-interest or beliefs than what's in line with yours. So, make sure that any professional guidance relates to your true inner self and why money is important to *you* to take the best direction in life.

Where Are You Going? How Are You Going to Get There?

Knowing where you are going and how you are going to get there requires more than vague statements such as, "I want to be rich" or "I want to own my own business." These are wishes, not specified goals and objectives.

> *"If one advances confidently in the direction of his dreams and endeavors to live life which he has imagined, he will meet with a success unexpected in common hours."*
> **—Henry David Thoreau**

While this is a wonderful famous quote and it's okay to dream and imagine, "unexpected success" requires that you take motivated action based upon honest and much more specific answers than mere dreamful wishes. *"You have to be specific to be terrific"* is an easy way to remember that you need to quantify specifically your direction and how you are going to get there. For example, if reducing your debt is important, then you need to know the amount of money required to make that goal happen, and you need to know how you're going to set aside enough money in the proper time frame. Knowing the specifics can make any necessary sacrifices more palatable. If you're highly motivated to accumulate what's necessary to achieve a specific goal, you'll more likely be committed to living more simply today to save like crazy for those future goals such as eliminating bad debt, buying your dream house, going into business for yourself, funding college for children, or retiring by a certain age. And, most important, you'll be well on your way to becoming and staying the quiet millionaire®.

QUIET MILLIONAIRE® SUMMARY

- **Discover who's the *real* you, what you *really* want out of life, and why.**
- **Know what's important about money to you.**
- **Make sure money is your servant, not your master, as you journey through life.**
- **Determine *specifically* the destination where you want to be.**
- **Plan how to fill the gap from where you are now to where you want to be.**

CHAPTER 2

Make Money Be Your Servant

T o be a master over your money and be in control of your future, you must learn to manage money to serve as the fuel for building a life of happiness and fulfillment. Only then will you know how to best balance living for the present moment while planning for the future. At times, do you feel overwhelmed by your daily financial commitments as well as the big-dollar obligations such as mortgage or rent, loans and credit cards, automobiles, groceries? If so, you may not be managing your personal finances and cash flow wisely. You're a servant to your money, not a master of your money.

"Money is a good servant but a bad master." **Francis Bacon**

Having an out-of-control financial situation can increase your debt and inhibit putting adequate amounts of money aside for achieving your dream lifestyle, and funding future needs, wants, and unexpected events. In turn, this often leads to money anxiety, stress, and conflicts. The quiet millionaire® refuses to live this way. Maintaining a positive cash flow is the core of intelligent personal finance. Just as a business needs to be profitable and maintain a healthy cash flow, so does the "business" of running a personal financial life. If successful companies have a financial business plan and cash management systems, then why shouldn't individuals develop a personal financial plan and management of their cash flow as well?

Know Where Your Money Goes

Staying on top of where you're spending money and making necessary adjustments is smart. Some people earning high incomes are notoriously lax about managing their cash flow because they don't feel as pressured financially. While they may not build up a lot of debt to fund their materialistic lifestyles, they often fail to pay enough attention to the fact that they are not saving sufficiently for the big financial commitments, like starting a business, funding college educations and retirements. Without being aware of it, they are creating a future cash flow problem because they do not evaluate, plan, and save accordingly for their future money requirements.

The increased number of two-income households has fueled consumer spending. Because of the combined higher income levels, there is a false sense of financial security. Expensive houses, multiple luxury cars, technological gadgets, eating out, expensive vacations, impulsive spending, and borrowing to the hilt have become the norm. Two-income families often depend upon both incomes to pay the bills, and this results in more vulnerability for potential financial trouble. In particular, when an economic recession hits, many dual-income households can experience a devastating loss of earnings and become financially overcommitted. *With two employed, there's twice as much chance that one of the earners will lose his or her job than in a single-income household.*

Reasons Why Good People Get into Bad Financial Trouble, Causing Stress and Anxiety

Impulsive and Compulsive Spending: With all the advertising and media enticements for goods and services, it's more difficult than ever to control impulsive and compulsive spending. "Keeping up with the Joneses" has become a hallmark way of life. We're out for more and bigger: homes, stuff for the homes, new cars, another new car, clothes, jewelry, gifts, electronic gadgets—you name it, we want it, we *need* it!

QUIET MILLIONAIRE® WISDOM

Don't fall prey to the financial disease that's spreading like crazy diagnosed as "Spendicitis."

Unfortunately, it's easier than ever to get what we want. We don't even have to leave the house to buy things, with the convenience of online shopping. Tempting deals abound, many are even interest free (for a while), and you often don't have to start paying for it until the next year. You get the picture: the easy dollars spent can add up fast to become potentially devastating cash flow problems for tomorrow. Here are some reasons why.

Poor Cash Management Practices: We know from statistics that most family arguments develop around money issues, sometimes creating irreconcilable differences because an inability to control spending increases emotional conflict and causes further financial damage. Poor cash management practices, leading to financial anxiety and stress, are a major contributor to divorce. Moreover, reckless spending can even force a bankruptcy, an action for high-income earners that is more times than not a result of unintelligent financial management practices. Keeping more money than you spend and monitoring spending habits reduce financial stress and struggles. Maintaining a positive cash flow is the way you can avoid financial trouble

Poor Communications: The quiet millionaire® recognizes that good communication and a sense of working together are the keys to harmonious and successful family financial management. In some families, one person may control how the family's money is spent. In other situations, family members may be spending money just as they please. For successful family financial management, planning meetings and cooperative discussions can be conducted for understanding and agreeing on the family's spending and savings plans. Just as successful companies schedule corporate board meetings, so should there be family planning meetings for financial peace and security.

Easy Credit Borrowing: Overspending often occurs because of today's easy credit borrowing. Even reputable banks behave as irresponsibly as loan sharks, tempting the most un-creditworthy of households to borrow foolishly. High-interest-rate consumer debt, especially credit cards, is flat out bad for your financial health. Not only are the interest rates high and not tax deductible, but also the impact upon cash flow is horrendous. For example, the interest cost for $12,000 of credit card debt charging a 21% interest rate represents a $210 per month or a $2,520 per year out-of-pocket cost, without reducing the debt. In a 25% income tax bracket, this means that $3,360 must be earned and $840 (25%) in taxes must be paid before the $2,520 in annual credit card interest can be paid. The result is that your hard-earned income is used to merely "rent" money from the credit card companies—valuable money that with controlled borrowing could be in your pocket for additional savings. Very often, high-income earners won't or can't track where they spend their money, and the biggest dollar expense category on their cash flow worksheet is termed "miscellaneous" or "other." They don't consider that the failure to track their uncontrolled discretionary spending can cause a serious cash flow problem. Most people are shocked when the totals for their spending categories are accurately accounted for. Especially surprising is how all the little daily routines can add up so quickly to represent big expenditures. Impulse spending often is a contributing reason for unhealthy credit card borrowing and cash flow crunches.

Automatic Teller Machines (ATMs): Using automatic teller machines (ATMs) allows ready access to cash that can be easily spent without any recording of the transactions. ATM usage is another reason why the biggest single expense category in a budget for many households is termed "miscellaneous" or "other."

Identity Theft: With respect to cash flow monitoring and spending, there's the rapidly growing problem of identity theft. Unfortunately, it may not be a matter of if, but more likely a high probability of when this will happen to you. Therefore, you should obtain at least annually a copy of your credit report. This will help to monitor whether someone else is spending your money. At times, you may not be aware of identity theft because the transactions are in small amounts relative to your spending patterns and therefore may not trigger red-flag alerts. By reviewing credit reports on a regular basis, you can wisely monitor your credit reporting information for inappropriate transactions. Another suggestion for partially protecting yourself from the threat of identity theft is to use a heavy-duty paper shredder to destroy all papers that contain *any* personal data. In addition, there is no reason to make your Social Security number and credit card information readily available to just any company or individual who requests it. You should be cautiously selective and suspicious about complying with such requests. Furthermore, you should be conscious about inadvertently displaying your Social Security number and credit card information. Your computer also makes you vulnerable and should have a firewall installed to block unauthorized access to your financial information. Check with a computer consultant or a local store for installing the most reliable computer protection, and remember that you must always update it to protect yourself from future threats.

Ways to Keep Cash Flow Positive, Avoid Costly Debt, Eliminate Financial Anxiety, and Save for Future Goals

Establish a Spending Plan: By knowledgeably establishing a financial budget, or spending plan, you are able to monitor actual expenditures versus budgeted amounts for each expense category. Importantly, this cash flow monitoring process will reveal the "big picture" of whether you're actually spending and saving money in accordance with what's important about money to you. This ongoing process can become a task that is surprisingly easy if you use a personal finance computer software program, which makes for a more controlled cash management plan that is convenient and accurate in monitoring your financial transactions.

Use a Personal Finance Software Program: Not only is using a personal finance software program a valuable tool for keeping track of how much and where you spend your money, but it also enables you to stay up to date regarding your assets, liabilities, investments, tax preparation issues, and bank accounts. With respect to managing your bank accounts, by using a personal finance software program, you can reconcile your checkbook in minutes as well as print out your checks to pay bills. Another advantage to using a personal finance software package is the ability to pay bills electronically through secure websites. By combining an electronic bill pay system with the use of a debit card, you can significantly reduce the number of checks you need to write manually. This saves a lot of time and lessens the chances for record entry mistakes. Three of the most useful software programs for you to choose from are Mint, Quicken, and YNAB.

Use Automatic Bill Paying: You can set up your automatic bill paying either on a predetermined scheduled basis, such as for mortgage, insurance premiums, and other regular monthly bills, or on the usual as-needed basis for the non-regular transactions. All transactions are automatically recorded according to the expense category for easy monitoring, and you don't have to be computer savvy to operate an electronic bill pay system. This will help your financial operating and planning system to become easier and more efficient. For bills that are the same amount every month, use your bank's auto pay to keep multiple accounts in one place. For accounts where your balance changes each month, such as a credit card, it's better to sign up for automatic payments directly through them, so they take the full amount owed.

QUIET MILLIONAIRE® WISDOM

If you spend before thinking, you'll probably spend more than you think.

Another advantage to establishing and managing an informed spending plan is that it controls unhealthy debt, especially credit card debt, caused by impulse buying. It's far better to "pay as you go" instead of impulsively buying something without accountability and feeling remorseful about it later. You can accomplish the "pay as you go" approach with easy record keeping by paying for all purchases over some stipulated small dollar amount such as $10 with a check, a debit card, or by using a single credit card that is *diligently* paid off every month (it must be paid off each month to work). Some people avoid purchases they have not planned for in advance by enforcing a "cooling off" period. If you see something that is tempting, force yourself to walk away and *think* about it for a day or more, to avoid impulse spending. You can also reduce tempting and recreational purchases simply by making it a little more difficult to do so by, for example, paying for purchases with cash only. However, remember that if you pay with cash, you need to be diligent about keeping good records for tracking how much money was spent and where. The following describes how Martha approached her impulsive spending:

Martha overcame her need to buy on the spot by writing down what it was she wanted at the time and waiting a week before buying the item. Then, every time she saw something else she wanted, she would add it to the list and do the same thing. However, the key was never to allow herself more than three items on the list at a time. To add the fourth, she had to remove one of the other items from the list. Martha found that she was constantly crossing off items to make room for the newest "must have" thing. She ended up making a lot of lists but fewer purchases. She also learned there is "always a deal and it's not a good deal if you really don't need it."

Determine How Much Cash Flow Is Required to Fund Future Goals and Objectives: The quiet millionaire® knows the amount of money that is required to fund desired future commitments. This is important because it establishes the proper balance between your spending for today and your saving for tomorrow. Remember, as a high-income earner, that while you may not be having a current cash flow problem paying your bills, you may have a future cash flow problem without even knowing it by not saving enough for future financial obligations. By having specific future goals to fund, knowing what is required to fund them, and putting aside enough, you'll be less likely to unwisely purchase things today that jeopardize accomplishing those goals of tomorrow.

> ## QUIET MILLIONAIRE® WISDOM
>
> *Wealth isn't accumulated by wanting many*
> *possessions, but by having fewer wants.*

As unbelievable as it may seem, outside of the poverty-stricken third-world countries, Americans are notoriously the worst savers in the world, being more committed to paying on their loans than to a savings plan. We like to spend and believe that tomorrow will take care of itself. Wrong! Sadly, the overall savings rate for most Americans is 0%, which is nothing more than a ticking financial time bomb that will seriously jeopardize being able to pay for challenging lifetime money commitments such as costly health care, educating children, and assuring a secure retirement. After eliminating unintelligent debt, the quiet millionaire® strives to save at least 25% of his or her gross income toward a variety of funding purposes, both near and long term. To accomplish savings goals, the quiet millionaire® skillfully sets up a cash management system in order to "pay himself/herself first," which is assured by having an automatic-deduction savings program. Multiple accounts can be established, with automatic savings in place for different purposes. Some accounts can be for funding major long-term goals such as college and retirement saving over and above your employer-sponsored retirement plan. Some accounts can be for some shorter-term purposes such as automobile replacement (instead of paying on an auto loan every month) and building a "kitty fund" for recreational and vacation spending.

Be an Accumulator Instead of a Spender: To become a quiet millionaire®, be an accumulator instead of a spender, a lender instead of a borrower. Affluent "showy" people earning well over $100,000 a year who spend every dollar they earn will never become financially independent enough to quit working. Many people earn much less money, yet they have become quiet millionaires® because they work at a patiently diligent accumulation program. Consider the story of Nancy, a quiet millionaire® extraordinaire.

Nancy is a single mother who has never made more than $68,000 a year. At age twenty she had two children and was struggling financially. Disgusted about her situation, it was then that Nancy vowed to take control of her life and her finances. So, she set a goal to become a millionaire. Today, at age fifty-five, Nancy has raised her two children entirely on her own and is a proud grandmother. She is also on the brink of reaching her planned goal to become a millionaire. How did she do it?

*One of the most significant things Nancy did was to diligently "pay herself first" and use the powerful benefit of compounding investment returns over time. When she planned her path to becoming a millionaire, she decided that **no matter what**, she was going to live her life so that she could save and invest 20% of every dollar she earned every single year, year after year. Now, Nancy is planning to retire soon and intends to devote her "retired" life to motivating and teaching as many of today's struggling young women as possible that financial success is achievable even when there are heavy-duty life obstacles to overcome. Nancy is leaving lasting footprints for others to follow. She is also a sterling role model for how a commitment to intelligent financial management can enable you to become the quiet millionaire® and to live a meaningful, rewarding life.*

It's important that you realize and use intelligent ways to control and monitor your spending and saving programs. You first need to know where your money is going and what amounts of your cash flow must be set aside to fund your future goals and objectives. Then, you must commit to follow through to become and stay the quiet millionaire®.

QUIET MILLIONAIRE® SUMMARY

- Make more money than you spend.
- Keep track of where and how you spend money.
- Control impulse spending.
- Establish healthy family communication about money issues.
- Just say "no" to easy credit.
- Walk on by ATMs.
- Establish a spending plan.
- Use personal finance software.
- Develop a "pay as you go" attitude to replace a credit card mentality.
- Purchase by check or debit card or by using a single credit card paid off monthly.
- Pay yourself first with automatic savings deductions.
- Plan your financial goals and objectives and save what is required to achieve them.
- Determine cash flow requirements to fund future goals and objectives.
- Prepare and monitor a cash flow plan.

CHAPTER 3

Pursue the Right Assets
to Enjoy and Invest

Assets are what you own. They can be either a blessing or a curse. Liabilities are what you owe. More times than not, they can be a curse. Your net worth is determined by calculating the difference between what you own (assets) and what you owe (liabilities). The bigger you build net worth, the wealthier you become. Many outwardly appearing affluent people earn high incomes, but they might have a negative net worth and are, in effect, bankrupt. Moreover, they may be living precariously close to unanticipated financial disaster, which can be caused by reduced or lost income. You've read about it in the newspapers and seen it on the nightly news: "unquiet" millionaires getting into financial trouble. With all that money, it seems unbelievable, and you might wonder, "How can that be?" Most likely, they didn't wisely manage their cash flow. They have a heavy load of costly debt from accumulating too many "things" that rapidly lose monetary value as well as usage value. The quiet millionaire® wisely knows that if you borrow heavily to live in a big showcase house, drive luxury cars, and own a bunch of showy possessions, while you might be "income" affluent, you are "asset" poor and merely a servant to the money changers.

QUIET MILLIONAIRE® WISDOM

Increase your net worth; you'll increase your self-worth.

Your goal should be to make the value of what you own go up and the amount of what you owe go down. Prudent debt management is discussed in the next chapter. This discussion about intelligent asset management isn't intended to tell you what to and what not to buy. That's for you to decide. Rather, the intent is to help you make more informed and wiser decisions about your purchases and management of assets and thereby increase your net worth. The quiet millionaire® incurs only manageable, intelligent debt to accumulate possessions and therefore is asset affluent, with a high net worth, and isn't just income affluent. The quiet millionaire® saves for emergencies and for funding pre-established goals and objectives. With today's readily available credit, many assets are made misleadingly affordable. This enables purchase decisions that are often impulsive and foolish. Thousands of precious dollars are wasted that could have been wisely invested to grow for meeting future desired lifetime goals and objectives such as funding college educations and retirement. The quiet millionaire® realizes that the actual possession of assets is often not as pleasurable as the expectation when *pursuing* them, and therefore pays attention to the difference between what is foolish and intelligent spending.

Two Kinds of Assets Pursued

Personal Use Assets: *Assets acquired with the intention of providing for necessity and/or enjoyment.*
Investment Assets: *Assets acquired with the intention of increasing wealth.*

Both are important and necessary provided you have an intelligent and knowledgeable approach of when to or when not to purchase.

Personal Use Assets: Types and How to Manage Them

Personal use assets include your residence, automobiles, home furnishings, clothing, computers, boats, electronic gadgets, and other personal "items"—those that are purchased for some combination of necessity and enjoyment. With the exception of your residence, most of these assets rapidly lose their dollar value and their usefulness.

Residence: Although your residence is primarily a personal use asset, it can also be considered an investment asset. Many homeowners have experienced financial bonanzas due to increases in the value of their homes. Buying a house can provide the combined financial benefits of owning an appreciating asset, financing it by using tax-advantaged mortgage debt, and paying no taxes on the gain when you sell it.

Owning a home can be your most expensive personal use asset as well as one of your best investment assets. This being said, it may also be the most costly personal use asset you'll ever purchase. The house purchaser must not overlook the fact that it costs a lot of money to own a home beyond the initial purchase price. There are the costs of mortgage interest and property taxes (even though tax deductible), homeowner insurance, and personal liability insurance. In addition, there can be sizable amounts of money required to be spent on maintenance, improvements, decorating, and home furnishings. The result is that homeowners can find themselves stressfully "house poor" because they bought their dream home with emotional influence and didn't thoroughly think through all of the financial ramifications of their purchase.

They didn't factor in all of the combined expenses associated with owning a house that can consume a disproportionate amount of their income. Their house then becomes not a home to enjoy but a burdensome financial drain. What was deemed affordable is actually severely affecting the accumulation requirements for handling the unexpected and is harming the funding of future financial commitments.

In most instances, it's preferable to own your home rather than to rent because of the benefits gained through market value appreciation, favorable tax advantages, and basic pride of ownership. However, there are circumstances when renting makes more sense, such as if you plan to move within three or four years, and you have to overcome the costs incurred when buying and selling a house. When you rent, you are paying for a place to live with more flexibility to move someplace new whenever you want. Furthermore, if the time is not right to purchase, by removing all of the responsibilities for maintaining a house, you will have more time for doing other prioritized things that you might value and enjoy more. When you buy a house, you're paying for more than just a place to live. You are also paying for the responsibility that comes with home ownership: fixing problems, and improving and maintaining the home and property to enjoy and increase the value of your investment. Then, when it comes time to sell, you will reap the financial rewards of any built-up equity (tax free) or, regrettably, experience any loss in value (yes, this can happen). Also, keep in mind the reality that the actual rate of return (the difference between the purchase price and the sale price) on the investment in your home is the net of all the costs associated with buying, owning, and selling the home, which include:

- Real estate agent commissions
- Mortgage interest
- Property taxes
- Title company settlement costs

- Maintenance and improvement costs

The decision to purchase a house involves making many choices, and if you allow your emotions to rule, they can override your actual living requirements and what truly makes sense within the context of your long-term comprehensive financial planning scheme. Very often the mental picture of your "dream home" costs more than what is appropriately affordable. What might be affordable in terms of your current cash flow may not actually be affordable in the long term because it's jeopardizing your ability to accumulate enough money for other financial goals and objectives. Again, this is why you need a solid base of knowing what is important about money to you. Even high-income earners do not have the luxury of living a "having it all" approach to life. Priorities still have to be set and comprehensive planning needs to be done accordingly.

Research reveals ways the quiet millionaire® buys a residence. The quiet millionaire® has figured all of this out and is an astute and savvy home buyer. While millionaires can choose to live pretty much anywhere, research by Thomas J. Stanley, Ph.D., reveals that they have a common, distinctive approach to house selection and purchase. The quiet millionaire® typically buys homes that are:

- **Older:** Between thirty and fifty years old, with a proven track record of having appreciated significantly. The houses are located in established neighborhoods with top-flight school systems. They avoid buying modern homes in new developments loaded with showy amenities. Their older, established homes don't have the same downside risk associated with owning a brand-new home in a subdivision filled with similarly priced houses that have not produced any history of price trend data.
- **Solidly constructed:** Well-constructed, more commonly brick or stone, some with slate roofs, usually with hardwood floors, and

they have predictable cash flow requirements for maintenance and upkeep expenses.

- **Smaller:** Four or fewer bedrooms and without much surrounding property to maintain, as opposed to newer homes with between five to eight bedrooms and a lot of grounds-keeping maintenance.
- **Bargains:** Resulting from a foreclosure, a divorce settlement, or an estate sale. The home buying process is part of an overall comprehensive financial plan. In negotiating for the purchase of a house, he or she is not hesitant to say no to the seller and is willing to walk away from any house of interest at any time. Emotions or ego does not come into play with the purchase decision. He or she hardly ever pays the initial asking price for a house unless research indicates it is a true bargain. This patient and disciplined approach allows for a smart business decision as well as for meeting living requirements and is why the quiet millionaire® never rushes to purchase a residence within a short span of time.

Automobiles: The quiet millionaire® considers automobiles as being necessary for transportation only. Owning them for pleasure is a discretionary added benefit usually too costly to justify. A super luxury automobile today can cost almost as much as some houses did in prior years. In fact, the quiet millionaire® purchases automobiles similar to the way he or she buys a house. Because automobiles are a very poor investment with diminishing monetary value, the quiet millionaire's purchase decision is not influenced by costly emotion. Instead, it's a practical decision based more upon actual transportation needs. Automobiles have a high ticket price, are expensive to operate and maintain, and rapidly lose their value. Most families today require having at least two cars as a minimum, with the added possibility of one or two additional cars for teenage drivers. As a result, if not careful, they can become automobile and car insurance poor. Today, it's commonplace for families to purchase three to four cars costing a total of $150,000 and more. On top of the initial purchase costs are the ongoing expenses for fuel, maintenance, and insurance, which can amount to as much as another $25,000 and more annually. In addition, if the automobiles are acquired with a loan or a lease, the cost of using the lender's money also has to be factored in, which can be an additional $5,000 a year. When all factors are considered for a multi-car family, it is possible that the combined costs of acquiring and operating automobiles could easily total as much as $50,000 a year or even more. These are staggering numbers, ones that hopefully motivate you to take a closer look at your own automobile situation.

Whether you purchase or lease an automobile, there are some general rules and guidelines to follow. Yet, as is often the case in the financial world, there can be exceptions. First, given the fact that new cars lose sizable value the minute they are driven off the dealer's lot, it's more economical to buy a recent model year used car with low mileage to avoid the immediate off-the-lot "discount." If the quiet millionaire® does purchase a new car, he or she often looks for the attractively priced deals that can result from overstocked cars at the end of each model year. Overstocked cars represent leftover car inventory, which the dealers are anxious to move with discounts.

Do as the quiet millionaire® does. Plan in advance, do your research, shop around at dealerships that sell the makes of cars you are considering, visit and make yourself and your specific car interest known to a salesperson with whom you feel comfortable, and have the salesperson keep an eye out for your interest. Choose vehicles with a track record of low fuel and maintenance costs. Become familiar with book values so you can intelligently negotiate from strength and knowledge, and most importantly so you can be prepared to walk away if you're not getting the deal you want.

Personal Property: Personal property as a category consists of the many possessions you use, sometimes use, or never use and includes such things as furnishings, clothes, jewelry, electronic gadgets, exercise equipment, etc. Depending upon how the items are paid for, you may or may not actually "own" them. Personal property items have different values, which include the purchase price, actual current market value, usage value, replacement value, sentimental value, and ego value. Personal property can be useful and worthwhile or useless and worthless. The real worth of most of our personal property is in the usage, yet the usage value can be questionable. Frequently, after the excitement of the initial use is gone, our impulsive purchases just sit around unused, often hidden from sight in drawers, closets, attics, basements, or garages so full that the automobiles have to sit outside in driveways. Fundamentally, if you don't use "it," then your personal property has no value. Monetarily, unless it is a collectible or antique, your extra "stuff" is usually not worth much compared to the price you paid for it. This fact is proven at every garage, rummage, or yard sale and every delivery made to a local charity or the worst fate of all, a trip to the trash pile and dump.

QUIET MILLIONAIRE® WISDOM

Control spending for today's wants to save and invest for tomorrow's wants and needs.

Because our wants for personal items often exceed our requirements for necessities, we can consume a lot of *wanted*, but not necessarily *needed*, things. Uncontrolled and unmonitored spending for personal property, or all the extra *stuff*, can excessively consume cash flow and insidiously affect your *monetary* net worth. Birthday and Christmas gifts can be particularly notorious for limited usefulness and fading enjoyment. We need to remember that we can love our family and friends, but it should be done without incurring burdensome debt. We can also help teach our children the true value of caring and love without indulging their every want and raising their expectations for getting more and more things as the only way to show affection. Furthermore, parents must learn how to manage peer pressure, their own as well as their children's. This means thinking independently from other parents who may be foolish about their spending, and not giving in to your children's demands of "needing" this or that unnecessary item to "fit in."

Do as the quiet millionaire® does. Avoid the tempting allure of purchases fueled by the entertainment and advertising media. Don't have a "buy now, pay later" mentality, and don't be enticed by easy credit. Instead, intelligent cash flow management should be always in the forefront, thus keeping your cash flow positive, avoiding costly debt, eliminating financial anxiety, and saving for future goals. As much as possible, plan in advance your purchases of personal property. Make the purchases a good financial management decision, as well as being a purchase that'll be used and enjoyed for a long time. When deciding to buy personal property, the quiet millionaire® compares whether the real usage value is worth the monetary price of the contemplated purchase. Make sure that the purchase price is worthwhile, remembering that it's not a good deal if the usage does not endure.

While you're entitled to enjoy your daily life activities, you need to also understand and prioritize the purchase of items as to how they relate to and affect your overall goals and objectives in life. The quiet millionaire® strives to save at least 25% of gross income to fund short-term and long-term financial requirements and avoid excessive debt. By being aware of what savings amounts are required to fund your determined lifetime goals and objectives, you're more likely to control current spending and bad debt.

Vacation or Second Homes: Most of us at one time or another dream of owning a home at the beach, on a lake, or in the mountains, most likely at a place we love being. The decision to purchase a second home is often an emotional one, with a rationalization that a home is a good investment rather than a good financial decision. Buying a vacation or second home can be a good investment, but require making a commitment of time and money. Remember the real estate rule: *location, location, location.* This means that you should choose a location where further development is limited or at least maturely established—the same basic concept as when buying a primary residence. As a result, the venture may be pretty pricey relative to less desirable alternatives.

Be wary about places where the increase in value is hyped to be a sure thing or where they have already become speculatively high. They could fall just as quickly to turn your dream house into a losing proposition, and it can take years to recover while your money is tied up and unavailable for more productive uses. Most certainly, the infrastructure for a second home location must be considered. While you may want to be tucked away from your neighbors, too much isolation can limit the investment value. The location's infrastructure has to be accessible, attractive, and appealing recreationally and culturally. For it to be a good investment decision, the second house's locale should ideally be in a compelling place for people to enjoy beyond just that of satisfying your desire for an idealized hideaway.

Even more risky and uneconomical is buying raw land for future building of a home. Be prepared for it to be a disappointing investment that will not return what you paid for it. Is it possible for raw land to give you a bonanza-sized investment return? Yes, but it is not likely to. More likely, it will play out to be an ill-fated investment that provides no appreciation, no income, no enjoyment, and it will cost you financially with loan payments, property taxes, and other assessments. Furthermore, if you are buying with the intention of later building a home on the land, you're also speculating on your own future. Your desired lifestyle objectives, geographic preferences, or the then-located residences of your loved ones may cause you to change your mind. Or, it could be that your financial circumstances at the time won't allow building a desired home for you that's affordable because you didn't plan properly. Or, maybe because the building costs for the required house relative to the land's value may make it an option that's not economically viable.

Financing, maintaining, improving, and furnishing a second home all cost you in the same ways that your primary residence does, and the value of your actual usage versus the costs to own needs to be realistically assessed. In addition, you need to consider the expenses associated with your time and money spent getting to and from the second home location. With some good planning, you may find that you're actually better off renting as needed to enjoy the area and not having an ongoing commitment associated with ownership. If you own a vacation home with the idea of renting it out for income to assist in the ownership commitment and make it a good investment, you need to understand all of the tricky tax rules, as well as the disadvantages of owning a rental property. Also, realize that it's very likely that the most opportune time for you to generate rental income is just about the same time you yourself would most want to enjoy the use of it. Importantly, when considering a second home purchase, you must address how the commitment affects your other financial commitments and objectives such as caring for an ailing family member, paying for college, and saving enough to actually retire. In the end, you need to ask yourself, is it really worth it?

Timeshares: The true value of buying a timeshare is that it gives you the ability to purchase in advance future vacations at today's prices. A timeshare is a personal future use asset, which has worthwhile value only if it is, in fact, used. Therefore, timeshares are poor investments and have value only if you use them. Timeshares certainly shouldn't be considered an attractive investment asset because they are difficult to sell and are typically sold at a loss in dollar value. If you do decide to buy a timeshare, you're most likely better off taking advantage of the purchase discounts available in the secondary timeshare market, which is loaded with owners trying to shed their purchase mistake. Here again, this purchase decision is typically an emotional one and probably not a good business decision.

Investment Assets: Types and How to Manage Them

Investment assets are acquired to create wealth, increase your net worth, fund your future goals and objectives, and gain your financial independence and security. However, a socioeconomic time bomb is ticking because most Americans are insufficiently accumulating money and investing it for future usage and financial security. Intelligent investing can make you wealthy; foolish investing can disappoint you and cause financial hardship. **Many investments go bad because of investor greediness whereby *"Greed turns to grief."***

This section is intended to give you an *overview* about the more common types of investment assets such as individual stocks and bonds, mutual funds, employee stock options, self-employment business ownership, and rental properties. Other chapters go into more depth as to the advantages and disadvantages as well as the risks and rewards of the various forms of investment assets. Some investments are situated in a taxable environment such as those within a bank or brokerage account. Unless these investments are designed to be tax-free, as is the case with tax-free municipal bonds, you pay taxes on the earnings and gains each year as they occur. Other investments are inside a tax-deferred environment, whereby no taxes are paid until the investments are withdrawn. The most commonly used tax-deferred accumulation vehicles for investments are 401(k) and 403(b) retirement plans, IRAs, annuities, and 529 college savings plans.

QUIET MILLIONAIRE® WISDOM

Deferring taxes in retirement accounts until you make withdrawals may not always be in your best financial interest if you expect to maintain your accustomed standard of living.

Many people believe that they will pay a lesser amount of taxes during retirement because they will no longer be earning an income. This can be a serious and harmful retirement planning mistake. It's very possible that future legislated tax laws will increase the income tax rates to higher levels, resulting in your paying a greater amount of taxes with less money available to spend. Moreover, even if the income tax rates aren't increased, it's very probable that you'll still pay more in taxes, especially if most of your retirement savings have been invested in tax-deferred retirement accounts. This is because to keep up with increases in the cost of living (inflation) and maintain your accustomed standard of living, you'll need to withdraw more money each year from the tax-deferred retirement accounts. And, the more you take out of the tax-deferred retirement accounts, the more taxes you'll have to pay on the money that has never been taxed. You're experiencing the very costly double-whammy of inflation and higher taxes, which can financially devastate your retirement portfolio and how long it will last. This is one of the reasons why, if you're eligible, contributing to a totally tax-free Roth IRA or Roth 401(k) or Roth 403(b) is such a good deal because not only do investments inside of those accounts grow tax-deferred but also the withdrawals are tax free if you abide by IRS rules.

Liquid Assets: Liquid investment assets consist mainly of cash located in checking and savings accounts, certificates of deposit, and money market accounts. Money in these accounts should be there only to meet emergency and current cash requirements and shouldn't be intended to fund long-term goals and objectives that require growth to protect against inflation and taxes.

Although the money in these accounts may be "guaranteed" against loss for the amount deposited, and earn interest, the interest rates paid don't keep up with inflation, causing a sure loss of purchasing power. In addition, the interest income earned is usually subject to current or future income taxes as well. This harmful combination of losing purchasing power as a result of inflation and paying taxes on the interest means that, in reality, you have guaranteed yourself an investment loss. Consider this example: You are in a 25% income tax bracket and purchase a $100,000 certificate of deposit (CD) that pays a 4% interest rate. Further assume that the inflation rate is 5% (this is a more actual and realistic inflation percentage increase than the government's published Consumer Price Index [CPI], which states that inflation has historically increased an average of only 3% to 4%). Here's how you end up having a guaranteed 2% ($2,000) annual loss on your "*riskless*" investment:

4%	$100,000 annual CD interest	$4,000
−1%	Annual taxes (25% tax rate)	−1,000
3%	Net after-tax annual interest rate	3,000
−5%	Annual inflation	−5,000
−2%	Guaranteed annual loss	−$2,000

The net result is that annually your $100,000 CD produces a minus 2% (−$2,000) negative real return, which means that you lose that dollar amount in purchasing power each year. This isn't an intelligent way to invest your money. The quiet millionaire® realizes that with this investment approach, you're actually lending your money to the bank at a loss so it can lend your money to someone else at a much higher interest rate, such as at 21% on credit cards, for big gains. This is an appealing financial transaction for the banks in which you lose and they win! Today, there are innovative working capital tools such as home equity lines of credit and brokerage margin loan accounts as alternatives for providing immediate liquidity and replacing the traditional need to maintain high cash balances. Therefore, you should limit the amount of unwarranted sums of cash being maintained for liquidity purposes, and definitely you shouldn't use liquid-type assets for long-term investing if you want to make more certain that you can overcome the ravages of inflation and taxes.

Stock (*Equity*) Investments: When you buy a stock, you are a partial *owner* of equity in a company. When you buy a bond, you are a *lender* to either a company or a government body that pays you a fixed income (interest) for the use of your money. You can purchase stocks and bonds either individually on your own or mutually with other investors through a mutual fund. Stock investments are purchased with the intention of making your money accumulations grow and keep up with inflation. The whole idea behind investing in stocks is to "buy low and sell high" for a profit. Many investors in stocks actually do just the opposite, and often their "greed turns to grief."

Bond (*Fixed Income*) Investments: Bond investments are considered less risky than stocks and are intended to provide more income than growth. Bonds can also serve as an anchor for reducing volatility in your overall investment portfolio. By combining the use of both stocks and bonds, you can diversify your investments to achieve growth while reducing the magnitude of the fluctuations in value affecting your total portfolio.

Stocks and bonds must be smartly managed to reduce risk and achieve growth. Investing is a loser's game for most do-it-yourself investors. They tend to invest more with their emotions than with a proven systematic, intelligent approach. In fact, it can be a loser's game even for the so-called "pros." Investment research shows that even most of the professional stock pickers and the market timers (those who profess knowing when to time getting in and out of the stock market) underperform a well-structured, diversified investment portfolio that stays fully invested at all times. You'll learn in a subsequent chapter about Nobel Prize–winning economic research that produces an investment approach that provides more highly predictable performance results, both short and long term and in accordance with your individually determined tolerance for risk. This academically sound research, which has been proven by real-life investment management experience, reveals overwhelmingly that a well-structured, diversified portfolio can win the loser's game of investing.

Employee Stock Options: Many companies offer their top executives and key employees stock options as part of their compensation package. Very simplistically, the company provides certain selected employees the option to purchase, or exercise the right to purchase, their company's stock for a very low price relative to the price at which the shares are expected to be trading in the marketplace. The whole idea is to have the employees with stock options work really hard to make profits for the company so that the market value of the share prices goes up. When that happens, they exercise their option to buy shares at the low option price relative to the higher-priced shares being purchased by outside investors. The employee then sells the exercised shares at the higher publicly traded price. *Employee stock options can make or break you.* Although it seems like a simple enough way to make some big bucks, the whole stock option exercise process is actually complex and can be very risky. If managed intelligently, stock options can make quiet millionaires®; if managed improperly, they can cause financial disappointment and even personal bankruptcy.

Business Ownership: Quiet millionaires® are often successful business owners. While not ALL are, statistically, most of them used this path to become one. Moreover, most quiet millionaires® seem to have some things in common: the willingness to risk it all; the possession of a strong, self-motivating inner drive; a burning desire to do "it," whatever "it" is, and to do "it" in their own way and on their own terms. This often isn't an easy journey, but it can be one that's the most fulfilling. They know that the road to building a successful, richly rewarding business involves stages that can be risky and rough. They're willing to make a steadfast commitment to whatever amounts of energy, time, and money are required to succeed.

Rental Properties: Owning rental properties can be very lucrative, provided you know what you're doing and you're willing to put up with a lot of potential aggravation. Television infomercials hyping how easy it is to make money in rental real estate are a lot of hooey for most real estate investors. In fact, most owners of rental properties don't know the real rate of return on their investment. They mistakenly believe that they're making a reasonable return on their investment and are benefiting from tax advantages. More times than not, the fact is that they're deriving an investment return that is less than what they would gain by having their money invested in a diversified portfolio consisting of stock and bond mutual funds and with a lot less hassle and risk. Rental properties can be a headache to manage and can provide you with a surprisingly poor investment rate of return.

The real rate of investment return for rental properties is determined by calculating the property's net operating profit, the appreciation in market value, and the tax benefits derived. You should earn a rate of return on rental property that, after all expenses to operate and maintain, is worthwhile relative to the risk and responsibility assumed. Managing a rental property is riskier and is more of a hassle than managing an investment portfolio of marketable securities. The *least* acceptable rate of return for your out-of-pocket investment money that's tied up in the rental property should be at least 1.5% per month, or 18% per year on your equity investment. For example, if you buy a rental property for $200,000 by investing $60,000 out of pocket as a 30% down payment and finance the balance with a $140,000 mortgage, you should realize a total dollar investment rate of return of $10,800 annually ($60,000 x 18%) *after* paying all expenses incurred for maintenance and improvement, mortgage loan interest, and taxes. Otherwise, owning a rental property is probably not acceptable as an investment asset to retain.

How Well You Manage Your Assets and Liabilities Determines Your Net Worth

Smartly managing your assets as well as your debt is the catalyst for living a lifestyle you want, and for achieving financial freedom and security. In the next chapter, you'll learn about the savvy and prudent ways for using debt to leverage your assets in order to maximize increasing your net worth.

QUIET MILLIONAIRE® SUMMARY

- Understand the distinction between *personal use assets* and *investment assets*, and be intelligent and knowledgeable about when to or when not to purchase them.
- Make purchasing assets a good business decision rather than an emotional or impulse decision.
- Realize that the quantity of what you own does not necessarily enhance the quality of your life.
- Understand how spending foolishly today negatively affects your life tomorrow.

CHAPTER 4

Borrow Intelligently to Avoid Troublesome Debt

U nfortunately, we learn more about how to accumulate debt before we learn how to accumulate money for building wealth. Some debt is happenstance dictated by the natural progression of our financial stages in life. However, increasingly, debt is the result of our cultural progression toward an attitude of having instant gratification, living for today, and letting tomorrow take care of itself. The quiet millionaire® lives an enjoyable lifestyle without being flashy, and can't relate to people whose financial philosophy is "Live for today, even if you have to borrow money to do it."

QUIET MILLIONAIRE® WISDOM

*If you're borrowed to the hilt, then you really
don't own anything—the lenders do.*

Two Cardinal Rules for Intelligent Debt Management

Intelligent debt management can be an important part of increasing your net worth. Debt managed intelligently can help create wealth; managed foolishly, debt drains the financial energy from any wealth accumulation program. Before getting into the specifics about what constitutes intelligent debt management, the following are a couple of cardinal rules that serve as the foundation for the entire discussion.

First Cardinal Rule: Always spend less than you make, not the opposite, to maintain a positive cash flow, and avoid troublesome high-interest-rate, non-tax-deductible borrowing such as credit card debt. Commit to not being a slave to the lenders.

Second Cardinal Rule: Always match the term of your debt to the purpose. It's not intelligent to borrow long-term to purchase items having a relatively short-term useful life. For example, you should not become so overloaded with credit card debt from purchases made for such items as clothing, electronics, vacations, etc., that you need to refinance your home mortgage in order to pay off the credit debt. Be aware that the *lending establishments* can cause you to be irresponsible about your financial well-being because they offer borrowing enticements that cause violations of this rule.

Types of Debt and How to Manage Them

Credit Card Debt

Enough *bad* can't be said about the worst debt of all—*high-interest-rate credit cards!* They should have no role in your financial life unless they are used intelligently and paid off every month without incurring any inter-est charges.

Two Reasons Why Credit Cards Are So Troublesome

Reason One: The repayment schedule for credit card borrowing often does not appropriately match the expected life of the item purchased. This is a violation of the second cardinal rule for borrowing, whereby you should always match the term of your debt to the purpose, as discussed at the beginning of this chapter. In fact, the only thing more foolish than investing in things that lose value is paying interest on money invested in things that no longer have any value. The following scenario illustrates this. Let's assume that you buy a computer costing $2,000 and finance it with a credit card. From the minute you take the new computer out of the store, it loses value very fast because of the rapidly changing technology. What will be the monetary value of the computer at the end of, say, three years? At best, it is probably worth a minuscule charitable income tax deduction even before the end of three years. Therefore, when the monetary value of the computer becomes less than the outstanding balance on the credit card resulting from the computer purchase, the borrowing is foolish. However, the foolishness may not end there. Let's say that after two or three years, you decide to upgrade to a new computer while you are still paying the balance on the now functionally useless computer. Now, you have a forever revolving credit balance not recognized for what it really is: a very costly debt for purchases that are either no longer around or hidden away and no longer used.

Reason Two: The interest rates charged on credit cards are usually the highest of any type of debt. Typically, the rates are extremely high and rob wealth. Let's suppose you use a credit card with a 17.8% interest rate to buy the above illustrated $2,000 computer, and you pay the minimum required monthly payment on the outstanding balance. The result is that it will take you almost fourteen years to repay a total of $3,759 ($2,000 for the computer purchase plus $1,759 in interest paid). In actuality, you pay nearly two times the original purchase price for an asset that is long gone. Let's take the above foolish computer purchase scenario one step further by assuming that you start using your credit cards to pay for groceries, entertainment, gasoline, vacations, gifts, utilities, etc., and you pay only the minimum required monthly payments. As the above illustration shows, borrowing at high interest rates can effectively double the original costs for everything put on credit cards, which is an ugly scenario and the reason why credit card debt is such bad news!

QUIET MILLIONAIRE® WISDOM

The quiet millionaire lives within his or her means and does not borrow money to do it.

In recent years, a significant amount of credit card debt and other high-interest loans was paid off by borrowers refinancing their home mortgages that fell to record low interest rates. This enabled homeowners to extract home equity dollars to pay off choking high-interest credit card debt and to alleviate a lot of the cash flow pressure. However, refinancing credit card debt can be financially dangerous if you once again continue to run up new credit card debt that is added on top of that which was paid off by the mortgage refinancing. With the added credit card debt, as interest rates head back up, more bankruptcies will occur as positive cash flows turn negative. Only this time, there might not be any home equity built up, and because of the recent changes in the bankruptcy laws, and going forward, it'll be much more difficult for overextended borrowers to get off the hook from paying back money owed. Remember, if you decide to refinance your house to pay off credit cards and start the credit card borrowing process all over again, you'll never become the quiet millionaire®, and for sure the credit card companies are the ones getting rich and depriving you of your wealth.

Student Debt

College costs are outrageously expensive. Most parents aren't sufficiently prepared to pay for college. As a result, students today have to borrow larger amounts of money to attend college than ever before. However, if intelligently managed, student loans do have favorable interest rates and repayment terms. Unfortunately, research by the *Consumer Financial Protection Bureau* has found that too many student borrowers aren't getting satisfactory customer service or clear information from student loan servicers on the best ways to manage that debt. While the student loan system appears confusing, navigating repayment is less complex than you might think.

Five Steps to Manage Student Debt

Step One: Know what you owe. You can find all your Federal loans by logging into StudentAid.gov. If you also have private loans, download a free credit report at *annualcreditreport.com* for a full picture of all of your debt. Once you have information on all your loans, set up an online account for each of them. Almost all student loan servicers have online systems where you can check your balance and make electronic payments. Make sure to keep your contact information up to date so you don't miss any important notices.

Step Two: Reduce your minimum monthly payments. If student loan payments will take too much of your income, sign up for an ***income-driven repayment plan*** like Pay As You Earn (or PAYE), which caps your minimum payment at just 10% of your discretionary income. Another repayment plan is Revised Pay As You Earn, or REPAYE. If you're in one of these plans and work as a teacher or in another public service job, after you've made 10 years' worth of on-time payments, any remaining debt may be forgiven. Everybody else can get their remaining debts forgiven after 20 to 25 years of payments, depending on their plan and whether they had any debts for graduate school. Private lenders, such as Sallie Mae and the big banks, generally don't offer as much repayment flexibility. If you can't afford your private loan payments, log into your account with the lender and send an electronic message asking for help. The *Consumer Financial Protection Bureau* has published a sample letter you can use.

Step Three: Do the long-term math. Reducing monthly payments now can be a critical way to stay afloat and avoid stains on your credit report, but remember: You'll have to pay these loans back eventually. The less you pay now, the more you'll have to pay later. But don't pay off your loans so quickly that you miss out on saving for retirement. If your employer offers a retirement plan match, be sure to contribute enough so you get the full match. You don't want to pass up that free money. Then, pay off your debts with the highest interest rates as quickly as possible. That means directing as much as you can toward high-interest debt such as credit cards or *private* student loans. Once those are clear, put any extra money toward your federal student loans. There is no prepayment penalty for student loans, but some servicers haven't made it easy for people who want to accelerate repayment. So instruct your servicer to apply your payments to loans with the highest interest rate by using a sample letter from the *Consumer Financial Protection Bureau.*

Step Four: Put your student loans on auto-pilot. Most student loan servicers encourage you to pay automatically through your bank account. You'll generally need to log into your account and sign up for "auto-debit" or "EFT" through each of your servicers. This will ensure you pay on time, avoiding late fees. And there's a bonus: Lenders usually reward you with a small reduction in your interest rate. The Federal government, for example, will reduce your rate by ¼ of a percent. For the typical borrower, this will cut your bill by a few dollars each month and save you hundreds of dollars over the life of the loan. But monitor your bank balance. If you don't have enough money in your account when the monthly withdrawal is made automatically, your bank may charge an expensive overdraft fee. Just one of those a year will eliminate all that year's interest rate savings.

Step Five: Try to refi your loans, but be careful. Private student lenders like Sallie Mae and many of the big banks typically won't tell you that you can try to refinance your private student loans, since they earn more if you're locked into a high interest rate. But refinancing can often lead to big savings. Borrowers who have steady jobs and good credit scores have a chance for getting low-rate refinance deals from lenders listed on sites such as ***Credible.com***. But be careful about refinancing federal student loans. While reducing a high rate can be tempting, you'll be signing away many benefits, including access to income-driven repayment plans and possible forgiveness.

Consumer Credit Debt

Prior to the advent of credit cards, unsecured consumer credit loans were the prevalent means to finance the purchases of appliances, furniture, vacations, etc. Consumer credit loans are not as convenient as credit cards because for every purchase, you must apply for a loan and be approved. The lender can turn down the borrower if there is too much other debt already outstanding or if the purpose is deemed unworthy. However, the use of credit cards has made consumer credit loans nearly obsolete.

Automobile Loan Debt

The purchase price for an automobile is expensive, with some luxury cars today costing what an entire house did not that long ago. Many families require two or more automobiles and therefore have to borrow to buy them. As a result, the loan amounts, interest costs, and monthly payments can be financially draining. The good news about automobiles is that they're built today with better quality to last a long time if properly serviced and maintained. The bad news is that they depreciate in value, some much more rapidly than others. You need to know how fast your particular car loses value in order to make sure that the outstanding loan amount never exceeds the value of the car. Carefully consider the structure of the size and the term of the loan to ensure that you do not get yourself into an "underwater" or "upside down" situation. This occurs when the automobile loan balance outstanding is larger than the value of the car upon selling it or in the event of an accident in which it is considered a total loss.

As a general rule, it's intelligent to make at least a 25% down payment and to limit the length of time for the borrowing to thirty-six months. Exceptions to this may be appropriate if the auto financing involves a zero or very low percentage interest rate that is offered as an incentive to purchase. However, you must still make certain that the value of the automobile always exceeds the loan amount outstanding at any given time, unless you have other resources to pay off the loan balance if required. This same loan-to-value thinking applies if you decide to use a tax-deductible, low-interest-rate home equity line to finance the automobile purchase. You need to make sure that the reduction of the amount under the credit line matches the decrease in the car's value.

Instead of borrowing to purchase a car, some people get caught in the leasing treadmill, which can be a very expensive proposition. Leasing enables you to drive a more expensive car with a negligible down payment and lower monthly payments than those made when purchasing with a loan.

However, unless the true cost and terms of lease are carefully reviewed and understood, you could be in for a very unpleasant financial surprise when the lease term is up. In effect, leasing is never-ending borrowing, and the true cost for a lease can be complicated and difficult to understand. With exceptions, general rules for leasing are to lease only a new car, never lease used, and be sure not to exceed the annual mile limits specified in the lease. The financial penalties for excess mileage and wear and tear are too costly.

First Mortgage Debt

Understand that a mortgage is not the actual debt instrument itself. Rather, it is the legal document that transfers full ownership of the property to you, the mortgagor (the buyer), by the mortgagee (the lender), upon payment of the debt and cancellation of the mortgage note. In the meantime, the lender essentially owns the property, and if you don't pay, the lender will take your house. So, you need to be serious and intelligent about taking on a mortgage borrowing arrangement that is for certain affordable and has the best borrowing terms available for meeting your needs.

QUIET MILLIONAIRE® WISDOM

*Seductively attractive mortgage loans can lure
you into a harmful financial situation.*

Not all mortgage options are beneficial, and any decision about which mortgage loan is the right choice needs to be carefully evaluated. You have to be especially cautious about mortgage loan offers that lure you with enticing, but potentially harmful, options. Examples of these types of mortgage loans include interest-only loans and low-interest-rate loans that change to less favorable terms after a certain time period has passed, usually three, five, seven, or ten years. At the end of the stipulated period, the interest-only or low-interest-rate "honeymoon" is over, and the interest rate and mortgage payment amounts can increase drastically. There are too many variations of these seductive loans to cover, but the main message to convey here is that they are financially dangerous because of all of the uncertainties that can arise regarding your personal situation and because of the relative unattractiveness of your loan options that occur at the end of the term. Unless you plan to be out of the house by the end of the stipulated term, it is usually safer to lock in the interest rate with a fixed-rate mortgage in to avoid having a cash flow surprise at the end of the initial favorable loan period.

In terms of what is affordable and intelligent first mortgage debt, the quiet millionaire® has a different viewpoint than that of the lenders. The lender wants to lend as much money as you can afford, at the highest interest rate possible. On the other hand, the quiet millionaire® prefers to intelligently borrow at the lowest interest rate possible and have enough additional money available to accumulate for funding other important goals and objectives. While the mortgage lenders may afford you a bigger house and mortgage loan, it may not be in your best interest if you want to accumulate money for your financial freedom and security. Accordingly, you should allocate no more than 25% of your monthly gross income to pay the combined total monthly amount of your mortgage, property taxes, and homeowner insurance. Committing an even lesser percentage of your monthly gross income is more beneficial.

Another important financial management consideration is whether to prepay your mortgage to pay it off early. Paying off a mortgage loan as soon as possible is often an emotional decision by some homeowners, especially older ones closing in on retirement. However, this emotional decision may not be an intelligent financial management decision if the mortgage interest rate is low or if the mortgage loan maturity is relatively close, with most of the interest costs having been previously paid.

Second Mortgage Debt

As implied, a second mortgage lender assumes a secured second position behind a first mortgage lender's home equity security. Because the second mortgage lender is taking a greater risk for getting repaid, the interest rate is typically higher than that charged by the first mortgage lender. Some mortgage lenders lend you as much as 125% of your house equity. It's financially dangerous to leverage your residence so heavily unless it's necessary because of unfortunate reasons beyond your control. Second mortgage debt is especially dangerous if it's used to pay off credit card debt and then additional credit card debt is subsequently built up on top of it. This financial burden and stress is one of the major reasons that homes are foreclosed upon, so manage your home equity debt responsibly and be cautious.

Home Equity Line of Credit Debt

This form of debt is prearranged prior to the need for a certain dollar amount that is available to borrow immediately at any time for any reason. It's a stated dollar credit line collateralized by your home equity. The interest rate charged is tied to a particular index such as the bank's prime lending rate or a government Treasury bill index. Therefore, the cost to borrow changes up and down as the index moves; however, the interest rate charged is usually the lowest that lenders offer and is tax deductible with limitations. A checkbook is provided to borrow for any purpose, worthwhile or not. Repayment options are flexible according to cash flow, and the line availability can be used over and over again. The credit line can be used as intelligent borrowing for short-term cash needs and even to finance a car purchase in lieu of using a non-tax-deductible, higher-rate automobile loan. It becomes troublesome borrowing if the line is used to pay off ongoing credit card debt created by frivolous spending, especially if you run the credit card debt back up again.

Timeshare Debt

The purchase of a timeshare is difficult to justify economically unless it is used extensively over the years for vacationing. Furthermore, it usually makes more financial sense to purchase your timeshare at a substantial discount from someone who is trying to sell the timeshare on the secondary market. You should also be careful about borrowing to own a timeshare and thereby making the purchase even more costly and uneconomical. In fact, if you have to borrow to make the purchase, you really can't afford the timeshare and should probably avoid the transaction. Some timeshare buyers use their home equity credit line to make their purchase. This can be a huge mistake unless the line usage is for a relatively short amount of time until other sources of cash become readily available. Otherwise, the line usage could turn into inappropriate long-term borrowing. Any borrowings under a home equity line of credit should be limited to financing short-term needs and should not tie up the credit line's availability on a long-term basis.

Retirement Plan Loan Debt

Be aware that there are no allowable loan provisions for borrowing against a traditional IRA, Roth IRA, SEP-IRA, or SIMPLE IRA. What is being discussed here are *allowable* retirement plan loans made against a qualified 401(k) plan, 403(b) plan, or defined benefit pension plan, when permitted by the employer. Depending upon the plan's summary description, which specifies the availability and eligibility for retirement loans, you may be permitted to borrow as much as 50% of your vested interest in the plan, up to $50,000. The loans typically must be repaid within five years.

Retirement Plan Loans Have
Two Potentially Devastating Pitfalls

Pitfall One: When you borrow against the plan, the amount borrowed is set aside separately from the investment funds to secure the loan. Instead of growth, you earn an interest rate of return that is equivalent to what your borrowing rate is on the loan. Basically, you're paying yourself interest, which is *not* tax deductible except in very limited instances involving a defined benefit pension plan as permitted by tax laws.

Pitfall Two: If you leave your employer for any reason, including termination, any outstanding loan balance against your retirement plan must be repaid in full. Otherwise, the loan is considered in default and deemed by the IRS to be a "retirement distribution" for the entire amount of the unpaid loan balance. Accordingly, the distribution is considered additional taxable income in the year that the loan defaulted, and the IRS expects you to pay income taxes on the remaining loan balance. Furthermore, it gets even worse if you are under age 59½ because the "deemed distribution" is also considered an "early distribution," which is subject to a 10% penalty. This penalty, combined with federal and state income taxes, could make your total liability as high as 50% of the outstanding loan balance. This is a heavy price to pay, so make sure that you keep all of this in mind before you decide to borrow against your retirement plan.

Borrow and Buy Smartly to Reduce Stress and Build Wealth

Intelligent management of debt is just as important as, if not more than, the intelligent buying of assets. Unintelligent, unnecessary borrowing incurs debt that increases stressful financial problems and diminishes net worth.

"Getting into troublesome debt is getting into a tanglesome net." **Ben Franklin**

The quiet millionaire® lives an enjoyable lifestyle without being materialistically flashy, and can't relate to people with the financial philosophy to "Live for today!" even if it means borrowing money foolishly to do it.

QUIET MILLIONAIRE® SUMMARY

- **Remember the two cardinal rules for debt management: Spend less than you make to avoid a troublesome debt situation and always match the repayment term of your debt to the expected usage life of the item purchased.**
- **Understand the different types of debt and how to manage them.**
- **Only borrow intelligently to leverage the purchase of your assets.**
- **Realize why credit cards are troublesome and why you should not pay a single penny in credit card interest.**
- **Intelligently leverage low interest rates with higher investment returns.**
- **Research your options for intelligent borrowing before incurring debt.**
- **Know the true cost of your debt and how it affects your wealth accumulation.**
- **Be an intelligent borrower to become and stay a Quiet Millionaire®.**

CHAPTER 5

Legally Avoid Paying
Too Much Taxes

C onsistent tax planning throughout the entire calendar year reduces
taxes more than waiting to take advantage of all the allowable
tax deductions when preparing your tax return. Even the most
competent CPAs are too busy to do meaningful tax reduction planning for
you during the height of the tax-filing season, so you need to constantly
manage your tax situation as part of an ongoing comprehensive financial
management program.

QUIET MILLIONAIRE® WISDOM

*Understand the difference between taking tax
deductions versus planning tax reductions*

The quiet millionaire® knows the difference between taking tax *de*ductions and planning tax *re*ductions. While intelligent tax *preparation* can
maximize your deductions, it's intelligent tax *planning* that provides the most
tax reduction. Gaining the highest possible tax reduction requires ongoing
planning and research about how to apply the changing tax laws as they relate

specifically to your situation. This chapter's information about taxes is *not* intended to educate you about all of the tax deductions you can take on your tax return; any competent tax preparer should do that. Instead, the focus is on beneficial tax *reduction* techniques and how they can be applied to your financial situation. Keep in mind that the tax laws are always changing, and this requires that tax reduction strategies be constantly reviewed and adjusted in response to these changes. Also, applying "rules of thumb" strategies to your situation can be inappropriate and very harmful. Strategies that might benefit one taxpayer could be worthless, even costly, to another, and they need to be individually implemented throughout the year.

> *"Anyone may so arrange his affairs so that his taxes shall be as low as possible. He is not bound to choose that pattern which best pays the treasury. There is not a patriotic duty to increase one's taxes."* **U.S. Federal Court Judge Learned Hand**

Taxes have to be paid, and they should be. However, it is not your patriotic duty to pay more than your fair share, and this should be legitimately *avoided*, but not illegally *evaded*, to the maximum extent possible. But, avoiding taxes should not be done at the expense of jeopardizing intelligent financial decision making. For example, not selling an investment because it has a large capital gain may not be in your best interest if the expected future appreciation of the retained investment is not as opportunistic as a substitute alternative.

Federal tax policy robs a few *Peters* to pay a lot of *Pauls*. Contrary to common belief, higher income earners *do* bear the brunt of the tax burden, and the next time you hear the outcry that "tax cuts benefit only the rich," consider this. According to the most recent IRS statistics available, if your annual gross income is $145,135 or more, you're considered to be in the top 10% of all income earners. You might be surprised to know that the top

10% of all income earners pays 70% of all federal personal income taxes paid. The top 50% pays 97% of income taxes paid, while the bottom 50% of all income earners pays only 3% of the total federal personal income taxes paid. Hopefully this will motivate you to do serious tax reduction planning beyond the ritualistic last-minute rigmarole at tax time.

Income Category	AGI	Percent of All Income	Percent of Income Taxes Paid
Top 1%	Over $515,371	21.0%	38.5%
Top 5%	Over $208,053	36.5%	59.1%
Top 10%	Over $145,135	47.7%	70.1%
Top 25%	Over $83,682	69.1%	86.1%
Top 50%	Over $41,740	88.8%	96.9%
Bottom 50%	Below $41,740	11.3%	3.1%

Source: _Internal Revenue Service data_

Taxes affect every financial decision. Most "normal" people think that the subject of taxes is an absolute bore and would much rather spend their free time thinking about more interesting, stimulating, and happier aspects of life. However, paying taxes is something that everyone wants to avoid, and like it or not, the subject of taxes is something that influences almost every financial decision. Often, people can be so concerned about paying taxes that they make personal and business financial decisions to avoid payment, which in turn costs them more than the amount of taxes they sought to avoid in the first place. For example, an investor decides not to sell an investment because of the taxes to be incurred on the gains, and then the investment declines in value far greater than the tax bite required to "lock in" the previous gain. While you need to plan to minimize tax consequences of a transaction, be careful about allowing taxes to drive your financial decision making.

The basic federal income tax structure is relatively simple, but the legislated tax laws make it complex. Underneath all of the complicated tax laws is a relatively simple income tax structure. Taxpayers add up their *income* from all taxable sources, subtract certain allowable *deductions* and *exemptions*, then apply the appropriate *tax rates* to the remainder, and finally reduce their calculated tax liability dollar for dollar with any eligible tax *credits*. Pretty simple until the government made the application complex and loaded the structure with costly pitfalls for the taxpayer.

The content of this chapter is intended to provide you an overview, as simply as possible, of the federal income tax structure, without including all the details, to give you a basic understanding of how your net taxable income is determined and why instituting tax reduction strategies is so beneficial. *(It would help your understanding by having a copy of your most recent Form 1040—the first two pages of your U.S. Individual Tax Return—to refer to while reading this chapter.)*

Basic Federal Income Tax Structure and How to Manage It

Gross Income: Gross income is the total amount of taxable earned and investment income from all sources. However, there are certain tax adjustments and deductions from your gross income that are allowable and that you should legally maximize to reduce your taxable income and resulting tax liability.

Tax Adjustments: Deductible from the gross income are certain allowable *adjustments* pertaining to education, self-employment, individual retirement account (IRA) contributions, and alimony, which result in your adjusted gross income (AGI).

Adjusted Gross Income (AGI): Adjusted gross income (AGI) is the resulting taxable income after deducting the allowable adjustments. Deductible from the AGI are certain *deductions* for personal *expenses* (standard or itemized) and *exemptions* ($0 for 2020).

Tax Deductions: The first type of deduction is for certain personal *expenses*, which can be taken either as a standard deduction or as an itemized deduction if the total itemized deductions exceed the standard deduction amount, which is adjusted upward annually for inflation. For the tax year 2020, the standard deduction amounts are as follows:

- Single individuals and married individuals filing separately: **$12,400** plus $1,300 for individuals age sixty-five or older.
- Married individuals filing jointly and surviving spouses: **$24,800** plus $1,300 for each spouse age sixty-five or older.
- Heads of household (single individuals with dependents): **$18,650** plus $1,300 if over age sixty-five.

If you have more personal expenses to deduct than the allowed standard deduction amount, you can itemize the expenses and total them for maximum benefit. The primary expenses allowable for deduction, *within certain limitations*, are mortgage interest, property taxes, state and local taxes, medical and dental expenses, property casualty or theft losses, un-reimbursed employee business expenses, charitable contributions, professional fees, and investment-related expenses.

QUIET MILLIONAIRE® WISDOM

*Tax avoidance is legal; tax evasion is
illegal and a criminal offense.*

Caution: Be honest when itemizing personal expenses for the purpose of taking tax deductions in order to reduce your tax liability. Plan your tax reduction strategies to legitimately maximize tax deductions rather than to imaginatively inflate them. It is not worth the risk of attracting IRS scrutiny, especially when good planning can produce worthwhile tax reduction results. Be aware that the tax laws phase-out the allowance of the personal expense deductions for high-income earners. As a result, high-income taxpayers may experience an increased income tax liability, and intelligent advance tax planning is required to avoid being penalized by the income limitations for these deductions.

Taxable Income: Taxable income is the resulting income used to calculate your federal income tax liability after taking all allowable adjustments and deductions. The tax rate system is divided into increasing tax rate brackets. This means that as your taxable income increases, you move up higher in the tax brackets, which results in an increasingly higher tax rate percentage being applied to your income. How much of your income falls into each bracket depends upon your taxpayer status, which can be one of the following five income tax filing categories:

- Married filing jointly
- Qualified widow(er)
- Single
- Head of household
- Married filing separately

The income amounts within the individual tax rate brackets are annually adjusted upward for inflation, and as of tax year 2020 the IRS tax rate brackets are as follows:

Tax Rate Bracket Schedules for Tax Year 2020

Tax Rate Bracket	Married	Unmarried	Head of Household
10%	$0 - $19,750	$0 - $9,875	$0 – $14,100
12%	$19,751- $80,250	$9,876- $40,125	$14,101- $53,700
22%	$80,251- $171,050	$40,126- $85,525	$53,701- $85,500
24%	$171,051- $326,600	$85,526- $163,300	$85,501- $163,300
32%	$326,601- $414,700	$163,301- $207,350	$163,301- $207,350
35%	$414,701- $622,050	$207,351- $518,400	$207,351- $518,400
37%	Over $622,051	Over $518,401	Over $518,400

The highest tax rate bracket to which your taxable income level increases to is your *marginal* tax rate.. For example, referring to the shaded box above, if you are married filing jointly and your **taxable** income is $180,000, every taxable dollar from $171,051 to $180,000 is taxed at 24%, and that is considered your marginal tax rate. By knowing the income breakpoints for the tax rate brackets, you can intelligently plan strategies to reduce your taxable income and thereby lower your graduated exposure to the tax rate brackets and lower your marginal tax rate. Using the same example above, if you are married filing jointly with a **gross** income of $225,000 and after taking advantage of all your tax deductions, exemptions, and credits, your **taxable** income is $180,000, your planning goal throughout the year should be to find ways to reduce as much as possible the amount of your taxable income being taxed in the 24% tax bracket.

So, if you could reduce your $180,000 taxable income to less than $171,051, your marginal income tax rate would be reduced from 24% to 22%, and none of your income would be taxed at the 24% rate. By reducing your marginal tax rate, you're also reducing your *effective* tax rate. Again, using the same example as above, if you're married filing jointly with a **gross** income of $225,000 and after taking advantage of all your tax deductions, exemptions, and credits, your **taxable** income is $180,000, and you learned that your marginal tax rate is 24%. However, your *effective* tax rate, which is the blended average of all the tax rate brackets that apply to your taxable income, is 14%, and referring to the above tax bracket schedules, the effective rate is calculated as follows:

Taxable Income	x	Tax Rate Bracket	=	Income Tax
$19,750	x	10%	=	$1,975
60,500	x	12%	=	7,260
90,800	x	22%	=	19,976
8,950	x	24%	=	2,148
Total $180,000				$31,359

The result is that you effectively paid $31,359 in income taxes on $225,000 of gross income, which makes your effective (blended) tax rate 14% ($31,359 divided by $225,000). As you can see, by reducing the amount of income in your *marginal* tax rate, you are also reducing your *effective* tax rate, which should be your tax reduction planning objective throughout the *entire* tax year.

Inflation causes your tax rate bracket dollar exposure to creep upward and causes you to pay more taxes. The upward creeping of the tax rate bracket dollar amounts subjects you to paying higher taxes. Creeping occurs when your personal income increases each year and the various tax bracket dollar amounts are inflation-adjusted each year as well. As this continues to occur during each tax year, you're automatically creeping toward a higher tax rate bracket, and you're exposed to paying more taxes. Although having an increasing income level is desirable, each year you need to project and monitor your taxable income to plan throughout the year on how to keep your taxable income from creeping into a higher tax bracket.

Tax Liability: The calculated tax liability on your taxable income is the amount you are obligated to pay the IRS unless you are eligible for certain tax credits, which provide dollar-for-dollar reductions from the tax liability.

Tax Credits: Tax credits are allowed for the elderly and disabled, education expenses, child and dependent care expenses, adoption costs, foreign taxes paid, certain retirement saving contributions, and affordable housing investments. For tax planning purposes, you should understand that a tax *credit* is a dollar-for-dollar tax *reduction* in taxes paid and is much more beneficial to you than a tax *deduction*, which reduces only the amount of income upon which your taxes are calculated.

Net Tax Liability (After Credits): Your net tax liability is the final destination for the federal income tax system unless you are determined to be subject to the alternative minimum tax (AMT).

Alternative Minimum Tax (AMT): Ironically, if you earn a relatively high income and do too good of a job of reducing your tax liability, the IRS can force you to pay a higher alternative minimum tax, or AMT. This complex and unfair tax is affecting more and more taxpayers as their incomes increase. In essence, the IRS is saying, "Your computed tax bill is too low, and we have an alternative minimum amount of taxes that you should pay." The computation for AMT is *very* complicated and is triggered by a number of combined variables beyond the scope of this discussion. Just be aware that as your income increases, there are certain triggers that may automatically cause you to become subjected to AMT. The following are the AMT triggers that, while fully tax deductible to reduce your regular tax liability as a high-income earner, do not fully reduce your AMT tax liability if, as an income tax deduction, they become disproportionately too high:

- State and local taxes
- Real estate taxes
- Home equity debt not used to buy, build, or improve your home
- Miscellaneous itemized deductions, such as accounting and legal fees as well as unreimbursed employee business expenses
- Personal exemptions
- Medical expense deductions
- Incentive stock options

AMT is costly for high income earners with a high dollar amount of deductions. So, it warrants doing a tax projection for your situation each year to determine whether you are wandering into AMT territory and to plan accordingly to avoid it. However, if you look at the above listed AMT triggers, there is a very limited ability to maneuver the dollar amounts for those tax deduction items, and each year more taxpayers, as their incomes increase, are being caught in the AMT web and can't escape it. In essence, as a high-income taxpayer, you're automatically experiencing a tax increase without the government having to legislate it.

Two Cardinal Rules for Reducing Taxes and Managing Your Available *After-Tax* Cash Flow

The existing tax laws are always subject to change at the whim of the politicians through tax laws. This means that what works effectively today may become obsolete tomorrow. However, there are two cardinal rules that never change, regardless of the political environment or what changes occur in the tax laws.

- **Cardinal Rule One: Proactively, throughout the *entire* year, perform intelligent tax reduction management to maximize your *after-tax* dollars for wealth accumulation and financial security.**
- **Cardinal Rule Two: In managing your cash flow, think in terms of what you must earn in *pretax* dollars to pay expenses and make your purchases with *after-tax* dollars.**

You pay way more federal taxes than corporations. Taxes at the federal level are collected primarily from the five sources shown below comparatively for the tax year 2016 (before Trump Tax Cuts and Job Acts of 2017) and the tax year 2019 (after Trump tax cuts). The overall percentage breakdowns might surprise you, as well as where the tax cut benefits occurred.

	2016	2019
• Corporation Income Taxes	9%	7%
• Personal Income Taxes	48%	50%
• Social Insurance (Payroll) Taxes	33%	36%
• Estate and Gift Taxes	7%	5%
• Excise (Consumption) Taxes	3%	2%
	100%	100%

(*Source: Office of Management & Budget-Historical Tables*)

The individual taxpayer, particularly the higher-income taxpayers, bear the brunt of all of the taxes collected in the above five areas of federal taxation. So, it merits paying diligent attention on how you can reduce your tax liabilities, and knowing how your tax money is being spent (too often wastefully) by the government. Because taxes permeate every aspect of your personal, employment, and business finances, you should be aware of certain tax myths while you plan tax reduction strategies.

Two Tax Myths That Can Hurt You

Tax Myth One: Deferring taxes is always good. There are two basic types of taxes you can incur when you file your income tax return each year:

- **Ordinary income taxes** (earned income and deferred income distributed from retirement plans).
- **Capital gains taxes** (gains on investments held in a taxable investment account). Short-term capital gains (held less than twelve months) are taxed at the higher ordinary income tax rates, which can go as high as 37%. However, long-term capital gains (held for at least twelve months or longer) get favorable tax treatment. They are taxed at lower rates 0%, 15%, or 20%, depending on the investor's taxable income. The three long-term capital gains rates are applied to taxable income levels, as follows:

Long-Term Capital Gains Rate	Single Taxpayers	Married Filing Jointly	Head of Household	Married Filing Separately
0%	Income up to $40,000	Income up to $80,000	Income up to $53,600	Income up to $40,000
15%	Income $40,000 - $441,450	Income $80,000- $496,600	Income $53,600- $469,050	Income $40,000- $248,300
20%	Income over $441,450	Income over $496,600	Income over $469,050	Income over $248,300

Data Source: Tax Cuts And Jobs Act

There was a time when the capital gains rate was 28% and relatively closer to the ordinary income tax rates. It made financial sense to defer taxes. However, with capital gains rates for now being relatively low compared to ordinary income tax rates, it's not as compelling to defer taxes by placing investments within retirement plans, regular IRAs, or annuities because the withdrawals from these investment plans are taxed at higher ordinary income tax rates. Alternatively, intelligently managed taxable investments can be structured to benefit from the lower capital gains tax rates. They can be made even lower by proactively offsetting taxable capital gains with capital losses throughout the tax year.

In fact, intelligent investment management combined with intelligent tax management can at times effectively reduce the tax on capital gains to zero. Therefore, with the lower capital gains tax rates in effect, deferring taxes is no longer a "given" best strategy even if you're able to contribute pretax dollars to a retirement plan. Of course, if your employer provides a matching contribution, you always want to contribute enough to receive the matched amount. Otherwise, with active investment management of a well-diversified portfolio combined with proactive tax-reduction management, it may be to your advantage to forego the immediate pretax contribution benefit of a retirement plan. In other words, you may be better off not taking the tax reduction opportunity on the smaller amount being invested—the *seed*—instead of looking toward the gain of a bigger tax break on the larger amount coming out—the *harvest*.

Another tax reduction planning opportunity that taxable investments offer involves making gifts. When gifting, it is always more beneficial to gift an appreciated asset than a depreciated asset or one that has had no increase in value. For example, you have a taxable mutual fund or stock that cost $5,000, and it is now worth $15,000, representing a $10,000 capital gain. You could liquidate the investment, pay a 15% capital gains tax liability of $1,500, and gift the net proceeds of $13,500 to your place of worship or favorite charity. Better yet, you could donate the un-liquidated full $15,000 taxable investment, which would result in no capital gains tax being incurred for either you or the recipient. The result is that you lowered your tax liability and made a larger contribution, which makes the recipient even happier. A legal win-win all around, except for the IRS.

Still another strategic tax reduction opportunity is to establish a uniform minor's account, which can be used as a gifting vehicle for highly appreciated assets owned by an adult who is subject to a higher tax liability than a minor child. Using the same example from above, if the appreciated asset is gifted to the minor child's account and then liquidated at the child's lower 0% capital gains rate, the tax liability on the gain would be reduced from $1,500 to $0, saving $1,500 in taxes.

Tax Myth Two: Taxes paid go down during retirement. Start by answering this question. Are you intending to reduce your accustomed standard of living when you quit working? I don't think so! Also think about this. If you're going to live essentially the same way as you live now during your retirement in the future, you have to account for inflation. To keep up with cost of living increases, you're going to need to access larger amounts of dollars in the future. Further, assume that all your accumulated retirement money is in a tax-deferred 401(k), 403(b), IRA, or annuity. As you need to take out more and more never-taxed money just to maintain your purchasing power, your taxes will steadily *increase*. The more you withdraw to live on, the more you are taxed and at the higher ordinary income tax rates. This double-barreled blast of inflation and higher taxes can devastate your retirement program and is another reason to also be alert about tax myth number one, deferring taxes.

Always be aware of your tax situation. By now, you have gotten a glimpse into how taxes impact your entire financial life and your ability to accumulate and preserve wealth, both now and in the future. Accordingly, you need to be diligent and knowledgeable about managing your taxes. You can start the process by using the below Tax Awareness Worksheet to determine how much *actual* spendable income you have available to meet current living expenses as well as investable income for putting money aside towards debt reduction, college savings, retirement, and other investment objectives. Using your most recent income tax return, pay stubs, W-2 forms, and property tax assessments as information sources, fill in the numbers below.

Tax Awareness Worksheet

Gross Income:	$ _____
Federal Income Tax:	$ (_____)
State Income Tax:	$ (_____)
Local Income Tax:	$ (_____)
SS/Medicare Tax:	$ (_____)
LESS: Total Income Taxes and SS/Medicare:	$ (_____)
LESS: Property Taxes:	$ (_____)
Net After-Tax Spendable/ Investable Income:	$ _____

Once you've completed the tax awareness worksheet and are aware of your actual net after-tax income that is available for you to spend, then you can establish a realistic spending and savings plan. Resolve to follow the previously described two cardinal rules for reducing taxes and managing your cash flow. If you're a high-income taxpayer, you have the most to lose by running your tax program on cruise control. Therefore, you should proactively plan how to reduce your taxes throughout the entire tax year and program your spending mentality to be in terms of after-tax dollars.

You may want to seek help from a *fee-only* professional advisor with no hidden agenda to sell you financial products offering supposed tax benefits. While certain financial products may be warranted, they shouldn't be the motivating force and certainly shouldn't be costly commission driven. Rather, an intelligent comprehensive tax reduction planning process, as well as an after-tax cash management program, should be put into effect.

If you decide that professional help is necessary, the fee you pay to receive competent guidance should prove to be worthwhile.

QUIET MILLIONAIRE® SUMMARY

- Understand the difference between taking tax *deductions* vs. planning tax *reductions*.
- Understand the basic structure of the federal income tax system in order to reduce your taxable income.
- Abide by the quiet millionaire's two cardinal rules for reducing your taxes and managing cash flow.
- Understand how the two tax myths can hurt you; plan and invest accordingly.
- Complete the Tax Awareness Worksheet to know the actual amount of after-tax money you have available to spend and save.
- If necessary, seek expert *fee-only* professional assistance for tax reduction and after-tax cash flow management.

CHAPTER 6

Be an Investment Winner

C onsider investing as only one of the numerous wealth building tools needed to meet your comprehensive financial planning goals and objectives. Building a well-structured investment portfolio is in many ways similar to building a solid home that's just right for you, one that won't fall down when the first bad storm arrives. If you believe you're skilled and handy with tools, you might attempt to build it yourself. Doing so requires using the best set of tools available and having the knowledge and experience to do the job right. However, if you intend to build only one house, many of the required construction tools are too costly, and require a certain skilled proficiency to operate properly. Instead you might decide it's wise to hire a skilled professional to build the financial house you want constructed.

There are many proclaimed sure-fire approaches to investing money. Few are consistently reliable. This chapter discusses an investment approach that's founded upon Nobel Prize–winning economic research, and has been proven practically to be the most successful approach during both good and bad times. It's important you understand how this winning investment approach is accomplished to be certain that it's being practiced correctly. Investing requires making ongoing decisions that are knowledgeable, businesslike, and not overridden by emotions. Managing your emotions can be your biggest challenge and obstacle to being an investment winner. For example, if you make investment decisions based upon greed during the good times or fear during the bad times, you are well on the way to losing at the investment game.

How to Build and Maintain a Less Risky Investment Portfolio That's More Certain to Grow

Plan and coordinate your investment portfolio as part of a comprehensive financial planning program. Your investment program must include answering such questions as:

- How much money will you need for achieving each financial objective and goal?
- Will you have enough saved?
- When will you need the money?
- How can you keep more by paying less in taxes?
- How will inflation and taxes impact the portfolio's purchasing power?
- What can you realistically expect for investment performance relative to making assumptions in your financial planning?

Always structure an investment program within the context of a comprehensive financial plan.

Knowledgeably structure and manage your investment portfolio in a disciplined, emotionally controlled manner. There are no secret shortcuts or black-box formulas for successful investing. You need to tune out all the hoopla from the media, the investment gurus, and the stock pickers. Instead, structure and manage unemotionally an investment portfolio built upon a solid foundation that's going to hold up your "financial" house through both the sunny and the stormy times.

Realize that everyone is an investment genius in a raging bull market. During times when investment values keep going nowhere but up, cocktail parties and other similar gatherings often sport lively and boastful investment conversations. However, this is also the time for unrealistic investment expectations to occur and can be a reliable indicator for the foolish investor on the horizon. You'll also notice that when investments start to perform poorly, no one seems to be openly discussing their investment prowess. Investment management is paradoxical because when investments keep going up in value, it seems straightforward and easy to make money. On the other hand, when investments start to turn sour, successfully managing money on your own becomes difficult and complicated.

Successfully managing your money can be equated with successfully driving a golf ball long and straight up the fairway. It seems easy while you are in the middle of an open fairway, but it becomes difficult when you are faced with sand traps and water hazards. It takes knowledge, experience, and steady emotions to win at golf, and the same ingredients apply to being an investment winner. While investing may seem exciting when the investment environment is productive, it's when the going gets tough that uncertainty and fear set in, and it becomes more difficult to make smart decisions.

Know your tolerance for risk before investing. Before you invest in anything, you need to understand and measure your tolerance for risk with respect to your investment program. This means going beyond non-measurable risk terminologies such as "conservative," "moderate," or "aggressive" that are often used to define an investor's risk tolerance profile. Instead, you must get more specific by asking yourself questions such as:

- What is a reasonable average rate of return (reward) to expect?
- What volatility (risk) can be expected and is acceptable in order for you to achieve the expected rate of return?
- What is a proper time horizon for achieving the expected results?
- How should the portfolio be structured to assure that your planning requirements and performance expectations are accomplished in a way that provides you comfort?
- **And the most important question is:**
  What is the most amount of money you can stand or afford to lose in the single worst year of your entire investment time horizon? For some people, an investment loss of 5% in any single year is too much risk, while for others, a 25% decline in any given year would be acceptable. Having a negative result occur that's greater than expected for the performance parameters is what unnerves investors. However, if you know your risk tolerance level, you then can intelligently structure your investment portfolio based upon a personal risk tolerance assessment and thereby avoid disconcerting negative surprises. Meeting performance expectations that are realistic and established in accordance with your particular tolerance for risk is more important than whether the performance beats some arbitrary, unrelated news-reported index such as the Dow Jones Industrial Average (the Dow) or the Standard and Poor's 500 Composite (the S&P). If the portfolio is intelligently structured in a way that meets your reward and risk expectations, then you should be happy during the good times and not be anxious during the tough times.

Prepare a written investment policy statement. A investment policy statement provides specific investment guidelines for your investment portfolio. It provides a clear understanding about how the investment program is to be managed and diligently followed by you and any investment advisor you might work with. Any investment advisor who doesn't help prepare and abide by one should be considered suspect. The policy statement should specify how the portfolio is to be structured, the targeted average rate of return, the time horizon for expected results, the risk tolerance level parameters, the amount and timing for anticipated contributions and withdrawals, and the emergency liquidity needs. Having a written policy statement provides a constant reminder about the expectations for the portfolio, and helps to monitor the performance accordingly. By being organized and prepared, you're less likely to fall into the "emotional investor" category and more likely to be able to stay focused on monitoring the portfolio's performance relative to meeting your particular financial planning goals and objectives.

Seven Investment Mistakes You Must Avoid Making

Mistake One: Focusing on the least important investment decision first. When investing, many investors think that the first and most important decision is which stock, bond, or mutual fund to buy. While this is important, it's actually the least important investment decision to make. Sometimes the decision is based upon a hot tip from a friend or family member. Or it might be based upon the recommendation of a financial magazine, investment newsletter, or a money talk radio or TV program. Keep in mind that these media outlets are unregulated as to what they print or say and are unaccountable as to the advice they give. Therefore, it's often best to regard media noise with suspicion. These financial mumblings may seem professional, informed, and convincing, but they can be actually misleading and harmful. Most often, the true agenda isn't to educate, but mainly to make money for the noisemaker by creating excitement or alarm to attract your attention.

Even relying upon reputable investment rating systems and financial analyst recommendations can be harmful if not properly used.

Mistake Two: Failing to understand the investment risks and true costs you incur when buying and selling (trading) individual stocks. Many investors believe that they can successfully trade (buy low and sell high) a mishmash of high-expectation individual stocks. When stock prices are running up in value, making money seems easy and can be fun. While this may happen in the short run during an up market, it can't be done consistently over the long run. Ultimately it's a losing investment approach, which lacks the diversification required for you to be an investment winner. The stock trading game can be almost as risky as gambling at the casino. Too often there's a time of having to reckon with more overall losses than gains. In fact, the odds are even more heavily stacked against you because when trading individual stocks, there are significant "hidden" transaction and tax costs involved. When brokers advertise "discounted" or "no" fees for buying and selling stocks, they don't mention the impact of underlying "hidden" costs involving the technical aspects of stock trading. Specifically, it's important that you be aware and understand the costliness of you not having received the "best execution" transaction and the narrowest "spread" between the "bid" and "ask" price when trading stocks. Furthermore, you have another piper to pay when you trade stocks with short-term gains—the IRS. There are tax consequences on investment gains in a taxable portfolio, which are especially onerous when the gains are short-term (less than one year). They are taxed at higher ordinary income tax rates instead of lower capital gains rates.

Mistake Three: Attempting market timing. Sometimes investors foolishly try market timing by deciding when's the best time to buy and sell an investment. The problem is that negative and positive emotions and susceptibility to outside hype can rule many investment decisions. This means that many investors buy enthusiastically when things appear great (but usually it's too late), and they tend to sell fearfully when things appear gloomy (yet again it's too late). Repeatedly, investors react to decreases in the value of their investment portfolio by liquidating to safer cash positions at the wrong time. The result is that they lock in their losses and miss opportunistic gains, which cause serious harm to their financial well-being. Ironically, typical reactionary investor behavior is often a predictable market timing indicator of exactly what not to do. **Caution:** Don't be foolish enough to believe that professed in and out market timing strategies are successful over the longer term when compared to that of maintaining a fully invested, diversified portfolio approach. Investment research confirms that even the so-called "market timing gurus" can't correctly time the movements in the investment markets on a prolonged, sustained basis. This is because when market shifts occur, they often do so very quickly and dramatically in brief spurts. Just one incorrect market timing decision can be very costly for a long-term investment program.

Mistake Four: Making emotional investment decisions. Investing your own money can be very emotional and can interfere with intelligent decision making. When an investment keeps going up and up in value, the experience can be exhilarating and make you greedy for more; when it keeps going down and down in value, the experience can be frightening and cause you to panic. Investment *greed* often turns to *grief*! These are powerful emotions that can distort your thinking. The decision to sell a soured investment is too often made out of panic during disconcerting times rather than being based upon sound fundamental analysis of the investment and as part of a strategic plan for comprehensively managing the portfolio. Some investors hold on to a poor investment too long, hoping that its value will recover, but do so at the cost of missing out on better investment alternatives for increasing value.

QUIET MILLIONARE® WISDOM

If you would not buy the same investment you own today, then you probably should sell it.

Make proactive business decisions, not reactive emotional decisions. This doesn't mean that you never makes an unprofitable investment decision. But, when you do, the decision to sell should be treated as a lesson learned. Consider it an opportunity to make a more profitable investment decision next time. A savvy professional investment advisor can help you take the emotions out of your investment decision-making process and, therefore, help you to attain the performance goals for your portfolio.

Mistake Five: Not taking advantage of tax loss harvesting. Tax loss harvesting is not some special tax break for farmers. Rather, it's a very valuable tax reduction strategy. Many investors don't realize that by holding onto a soured investment in a *taxable* portfolio, they may be missing out on tax reduction opportunities enabled by selling the investment for a capital loss to offset future capital gains. This strategy is termed *tax loss harvesting,* which can save you thousands of dollars in taxes being paid on earned income and the sale of profitable investments.

Here's how tax loss harvesting works. Let's say that you invest $10,000 in an international mutual fund in January, and by January of the following year, it's worth only $5,000. That represents a $5,000 loss. But, now the international markets look very promising. You've two choices: either hold the fund and wait for it to go back up or sell the existing international fund, *harvest* a tax loss, buy a different, but similar, international fund for $5,000. Then, wait for it to go up instead. Now, let's say that at that same time you harvested the above $5,000 tax loss, you now have a health care mutual fund that has a $5,000 gain and that, after owning it for a couple of years, you decide to sell. Upon the sale, there'd be no tax on the $5,000 gain because you harvested the $5,000 tax loss from the sale of the international fund. And, because you still have an international investment presence with the replacement fund, you don't miss out on the opportunity to participate in the growth expected to occur in the international markets. This valuable tax planning strategy replaces an investment loss with a tax loss that lessens the tax bite when you go to file your income tax return, without sacrificing an investment gain.

What many investors can experience without tax loss harvesting is the really painful circumstance of having to pay a big tax bill on an investment that has decreased in value. This often occurs with taxable, actively managed mutual funds in a declining investment environment. When things get rough, mutual fund investors start to bail out. This forces the mutual fund manager to liquidate profitable long-term holdings for meeting cash redemption requirements, causing sizable taxable gains. The tax consequences are passed on directly to the fund's remaining investors, even if their investment in the fund has suffered a loss. It isn't pleasant having to pay taxes on a losing mutual investment, but it can occur especially when the markets get shaky and investors are nervously withdrawing their downtrodden investment money. Looking for opportunities to harvest tax losses should be monitored throughout the year by offsetting investment gains with losses. This makes taxable growth portfolios tax efficient and productive, and may be able to save you thousands of tax dollars.

Mistake Six: Not realizing that a negative investment environment can be positive. Ideally, while saving and investing money, you want to buy low and then sell high when you withdraw and use the money. However, this perfect market timing doesn't happen in the real investment world. Therefore, the surest way to capture the lows when they occur is by establishing an automatic savings deduction program whereby you "save first and live on the rest." During the accumulation stage of any type of savings program, whether it's for college, retirement, or any other purpose, it's an advantage to be saving when the investment markets are down in value. By adding to your portfolio during that down time, you're able to accumulate more investment units because the unit purchase prices are relatively low and undervalued. You benefit from a lower average investment cost. Then when the holdings increase in value, you benefit from owning more accumulated units. The result is that there is more money available for you to take out when you need it.

Mistake Seven: Losing too much investment value during down-market periods. If your investment portfolio loses 50% in value, it requires a 100% gain just to get back to even, which can easily take years. Consider the following performance comparison of a $100,000 losing investment portfolio, consisting of some individual "hot" stock selections, with that of a $100,000 winning investment portfolio that's well-structured with more diversification to lessen its volatility:

$100,000 Original Investment

	Losing Investment Portfolio		Winning Investment Portfolio	
	Gain(Loss)	Balance	Gain(Loss)	Balance
Year 1	+50% +$50,000	$150,000	+33% +$33,000	$133,000
Year 2	+24% +36,000	186,000	+18% +24,000	157,000
Year 3	(-50%) (-93,000)	93,000	-13% (-20,000)	137,000
Year 4	+12% +11,000	104,000	+ 8% +11,000	148,000
Year 5	+15% +16,000	120,000	+12% +17,000	165,000
Average Annual				
Rate of Return:	**+10.2%**		**+11.6%**	

The most significant thing to notice in the above illustration is that although the losing investment portfolio started out much stronger for the first two years (+$86,000 vs. +$57,000 gain) and outperformed the winning investment portfolio in every year except for year three (-$93,000 vs. -$20,000 loss), the end result was much less rewarding ($120,000 vs. $165,000 ending value) because it lost too much investment value during the down-market period. The winning investment portfolio *"won by not losing."*

QUIET MILLIONAIRE® WISDOM

The investment psychology of a losing portfolio investor can be self-destructive.

The **losing portfolio investor** in the above illustration might panic sell "the hot investments turned cold" and bail out during year three. However, because so much dollar value had been lost, the investor in that situation typically holds on reluctantly and hopes for a recovery to occur before selling. The investment environment during a severe down-market period can be very unnerving when the mood is gloomy and clouded with pessimistic talk about corporate scandals, job layoffs, terrorism, recession, etc. As the portfolio continues to sink still further underwater, the losing investor becomes fearful and anxiously hopes for it all to end. Finally, not able to take it anymore, the losing investor often sells the downtrodden investments and heads for safer ground to cash before everything is lost. Earning a safe 1% becomes more tolerable than losing any more money, and the new risk tolerance comfort level for the losing portfolio investor has shifted away from being aggressive to being overly conservative, just when things are beginning to brighten again. The losing portfolio investor's bad experience often causes immobilization on the sidelines and missing opportunistic growth spurts that occur sporadically and very quickly.

The **winning portfolio investor** constructs and maintains a diversified investment portfolio that is comfortably protected against large losses of value during down-market periods. Therefore, he or she is willing and able to remain calm, patient, and fully invested during jittery, negative-performing investment times and to be ready to participate in future portfolio growth when it does occur.

Use a Nobel Prize Winning Investment Approach to Construct and Maintain an Investment Portfolio That Funds Your Dreams and Financial Independence

In 1974, economists Harry Markowitz and William Sharpe were awarded the Nobel Prize in Economics for their investment research, which produced the **Modern Portfolio Theory** approach for constructing a winning investment portfolio. This is the investment approach that has most proven to produce winning results. Specifically, the Modern Portfolio research revealed that the individual investment selections (what stock, bond, or mutual fund to purchase) and market timing decisions (when to buy or sell an investment) play only minor roles in an investment portfolio's growth. **Strategic asset allocation is the most important investment decision.** The Nobel Prize–winning research determined that more than 90% of a portfolio's total investment return is attributed to the asset allocation decision—how the portfolio is strategically allocated to various asset classes on a diversified worldwide basis. The following is a description of the major asset classes:

Description of Major Asset Classes

- **Money Market Funds:** *U.S. money market funds used to provide cash for ready liquidity and reinvestment.*

- **Domestic Bonds:** *U.S. corporate and government bonds having short-, intermediate-, and long-term maturities to serve as an anchoring stability element for the portfolio.*

- **International Bonds:** *Foreign government and corporate bonds that include either hedged or unhedged positions for managing currency fluctuations.*

- **Domestic Large-Cap Growth:** *Large U.S. companies possessing high-growth characteristics selected according to certain target criteria for sales growth, return on equity, i.e., fast growth and low or no dividends.*

- **Domestic Equities Large-Cap Value:** *Large U.S. companies possessing undervalued characteristics selected according to certain target criteria for per share market price relative to company earnings, i.e., low price earnings, low price to book, and possible relatively high dividends.*

- **Domestic Equities Mid-Cap Growth:** *Medium-size U.S. companies possessing high-growth characteristics selected according to certain target criteria for sales growth, return on equity, i.e., fast growth and low or no dividends.*

- **Domestic Equities Mid-Cap Value:** *Medium-size U.S. companies possessing undervalued characteristics selected to meet certain target criteria for per share market price relative to company earnings, i.e., low price earnings, low price-to-book value, and possible relatively high dividends.*

- **Domestic Equities Small-Cap Growth:** *Small-size U.S. companies possessing high growth characteristics selected according to certain target criteria for sales growth, return on equity, i.e., fast growth and low or no dividends.*

- **Domestic Equities Small-Cap Value:** *Small-size U.S. companies possessing undervalued characteristics selected to meet certain target criteria for per share market price relative to company earnings, i.e.,* *low price earnings, low price-to-book value, and possible relatively high dividend payout.*

- **Specialized Sectors Equities:** *Specialized investment sectors such as health sciences, financial services, energy, leisure, natural resources, technology, utilities, real estate, and certain geographically focused international equities such as the Far East and emerging markets.*

- **International Equities:** *Companies located outside the United States.*

Each Asset Class Has Its Own Time in the Sun to Flourish. The investment climate isn't sunny all the time for any given asset class. Therefore, you must create a portfolio asset mix where something is shining brightly at any given time. You can't expect all asset classes to shine brightly at the same time. Another way of saying that the assets classes all have their individual time in the sun is to say that their performance correlates differently with each other. These different asset class correlations are historically measured and kept updated so that the results can be used as tools to structure an investment portfolio.

The timing as to when good and poor performances will actually occur for each asset class is not predictable. However, by statistically combining the historical performances and correlations of the asset classes, it's possible to reasonably predict how the overall structured portfolio will perform in the future. Accordingly, if investors know their own particular tolerance for risk, then their investment portfolio can be structured to perform within certain specified best- and worst-case ranges for risk and growth. This is comforting to investors because the portfolio performs in accordance with their expectations.

Your individual tolerance for risk and expectations for investment growth determine how your portfolio should be strategically allocated to each of the individual asset classes. Accordingly, the most important part of the investment structuring process with allocating is the periodic rebalancing of the specified target percentages for each asset class comprising your portfolio. Be aware that it requires specialized professional knowledge, experience, and investment software tools to skillfully assemble and manage investing according to the Modern Portfolio Theory approach. Therefore, it's important that you find an investment advisor who is a trustworthy advocate, competent to either guide you with, or manage this investment approach for you.

Five Steps to Build and Maintain a Profitable and Less Risky Investment Portfolio

Step One: Determine your tolerance for investment risk. Knowing your investment risk tolerance is important to structure a portfolio that will perform in accordance with your expectations and comfort level. Competent investment advisors have ways to help you measure your risk tolerance. The result should establish realistic expectations for your portfolio's performance, and not subject to disturbing surprises.

Step Two: Structure an investment portfolio with target weighted asset class allocations that will perform according to your tolerance for risk and expectations for reward. In structuring an investment portfolio that's comfortable for you, it's important that you set target percentage weightings for the various asset classes within. With the target asset class weightings designated specifically for your portfolio, you'll become aware with a high degree of probability what ranges of investment performance and dollar outcomes to expect. The expected results are only a guideline, not a guarantee. Once the asset class allocations for the target portfolio have been established, the most important decision has been made for structuring the investment program. As already mentioned, most investors think that the first and most important decision is what stock, bond, or mutual fund to buy. However, with the Modern Portfolio Theory Approach, that's the last and least important decision to be made. Instead, it's the weighted presence in each of the various asset classes that's paramount.

QUIET MILLIONARE® WISDOM

Piecing together the asset classes in a well-structured investment portfolio is much like piecing together the pieces of a mosaic to produce a beautiful result.

Many investment portfolios are an unstructured mishmash of security holdings that don't fit together properly. As a result, there's uncertainty about what downside risk and performance results to really expect. The Modern Portfolio Theory Approach to investing ensures that more predictable performance results will occur during both the good and not so good investment environments. This is because a *well-structured* portfolio includes multiple global economies for more investment diversification than can be accomplished with an *unstructured* portfolio, consisting of too few asset classes and a limited number of individual holdings. The individual holdings within an undiversified portfolio typically have too high a degree of investment correlation, which means that all of the holdings go up or down in value at the same time. It's more beneficial to *structure* a diversified investment portfolio by allocating a targeted array of low-correlation asset classes across the world's most attractive markets. This way, the various components of the portfolio that are performing well at any given time can offset some of the parts that are experiencing challenges. The result is that you get a smoother ride on the path to successfully reaching your reward expectations because the component parts do not rise and fall at the same time, i.e., their values do not correlate with each other. Use the Modern Portfolio Theory Approach to assemble a diversity of target asset classes that produces a well-structured portfolio most suitable and reliable for meeting your lifetime goals and

objectives. Then, the next decision is to determine what individual investment pieces should be used to fill the target asset classes.

Step Three: Fill the individual asset classes with no-load, low-cost
mutual funds and exchange traded funds (ETFs). Once the asset class
structure for the portfolio has been determined, the next decision is which
investment holdings will be used to carry out the investment performance
objective for each asset class. For diversification purposes, this filling of the
asset classes is most successfully accomplished by using high-quality, low-ex-
pense mutual funds and exchange traded funds (ETFs). There are literally
thousands of mutual funds and ETFs traded globally, that are available to
choose from. Reliable research is required to screen for the most appropriate
ones to select. Mutual funds provide a way for investors to *mutually* pool
their money together to invest as a group in buying shares or units of the
fund. They can be either actively managed or passive index funds. ETFs are
marketable securities that track an index, a commodity, bonds, or a basket
of assets, much like an index mutual fund. However, unlike mutual funds,
ETFs trade like a common stock on a stock exchange. ETFs experience
price changes throughout the day as they are being bought and sold. The
investment objective for each mutual fund or ETF placed within an asset
class must match exactly the investment objective for the specified asset class.
For example, an international fund consisting entirely of foreign holdings
outside of the United States should be used to fill the international equity
asset class, and so forth for all the individual asset classes.

Unfortunately, many providers of financial services and products, including fund providers, often try to finesse their way around fully disclosing
information about their true performance and internal costs. Furthermore,
the disclosure materials (primarily a document termed a *prospectus*) that the
regulatory agencies require to be given to investors for enlightenment are too
overwhelming and not read by most investors. Instead, naïve investors more

often rely upon investment newsletters and the financial media's magazine and TV hype, all of which are totally unregulated and unaccountable. Don't be fooled by hype spewed by the financial "biggies" (mutual fund companies, banks, brokerage firms, insurance companies, etc.). They have huge advertising budgets and sales commission payouts—which are paid for by, guess who, you! Be highly selective and savvy about the potential costliness of funds used to fill the asset classes.

4 Ways Costs Can Be Imposed Upon Investors That Decrease the Net Return of Invested Money

1. Sales Charges: Some mutual fund shares of ownership can be purchased directly from a mutual fund company without a sales charge (no-load). Some shares can be purchased *only* through an intermediary salesperson who is paid a commission. The mutual fund company deducts a sales charge (termed a load) directly from the amount of money that you invest. The following are descriptions of the three main categories of mutual fund shares that deduct a costly sales charge (load) directly from your investment, which you should avoid purchasing:

> *A-Shares (charge one-time, front-end load):* When an investor purchases mutual fund A-Shares, a one-time, front-end sales charge (load) is assessed, which can be as high as 7% of the amount invested. The sales charge is immediately deducted from the investment amount, and then the remaining net balance is invested.
>
> *B-Shares (charge one-time, rear-end load):* When an investor purchases mutual fund B-Shares, the full amount is invested but with the stipulation that a one-time, rear-end sales charge (load), which can be as high as 7% of the amount invested, will be deducted

if the investor withdraws the money within a certain number of years, typically during the first seven years.

C-Shares (charge ongoing, annual load): When an investor purchases mutual fund C-Shares, the full amount is invested, but an ongoing annual sales charge (load), which can be as high as 3%, is deducted yearly from the amount invested and reduces the rate of return. Some C-Shares impose in addition a one-time, front-end sales charge (load), which can be as high as 1% of the amount invested. Because the annual load is imposed continually, this can cause a bigger negative impact upon the investment rate of return than the other two load categories.

2. Marketing and Advertising Fees: In addition to imposing sales charges (loads), mutual funds (whether no-load or load) often charge ongoing annual marketing and advertising fees (termed 12b1 fees), which can be as high as an additional 1% annually on the investment amount.

3. Operating and Administrative Fees: Besides imposing sales charges (loads) and 12b1 marketing fees, mutual funds (whether no-load or load) charge ongoing annual operating and administrative expenses, which can be as much as an additional 2% or more annually on the investment amount.

4. Redemption Fees: A redemption fee is a market timing fee, or short-term trading fee, usually 1% to 2% of the transaction amount, to discourage investors from making a short-term round trip (i.e., a purchase followed by a sale within a short period of time, usually 30 days).

Both Active and Passive Investing Have a Role to Play in Filling the Asset Classes of a Diversified Investment Portfolio

As part of deciding what's most appropriate for your portfolio, you need to choose among investments that are either actively or passively managed. An actively managed investment attempts to *outperform* or beat the performance of a specific market index benchmark for each asset class. This is difficult to do, and mostly doesn't happen.

QUIET MILLIONAIRE® WISDOM

Accentuate the passive; be highly selective with the active.

The alternatives to actively managed funds are *passive index funds* and *exchange traded funds (ETFs),* which avoid sales charges (loads), and reduce the amount of marketing, advertising, operating, and administrative fees that you pay. *Passive index funds* are structured to passively *match* (as opposed to attempting to *beat*) the performance of a particular market index benchmark for each asset class. The most familiar indexes are the Dow and the S&P 500, but you should be aware that there are numerous other domestic, international, and specialty indexes, which are established and available for passive investing in each asset class. *Exchange traded funds (ETFs)* are passive index funds that are available to buy and sell at various prices constantly throughout the day on the various stock exchanges, just as stocks do.

Why should you consider passive investing to match index performances as opposed to active investing striving to outperform an index? The primary reason is that greater than *80%* of all active investment funds actually "under-perform" their targeted index. This is because active investments have higher internal costs, as discussed above. Moreover, they incur higher transaction costs and potentially more taxation when actively buying and selling holdings. So, why would any investor select active funds if passive funds have more advantages? The answer is that through diligent and intelligent research, the best of the approximate **20%** of active managers that do outperform their target indexes can be discovered and included in your investment portfolio. This is especially true for actively managed international and specialty funds. Therefore, the framework of a well-constructed, winning investment portfolio can consist of a core group of passively managed index funds and ETFs that are then surrounded with a very select group of actively managed no-load, low-cost funds, which might outperform the comparable indexes.

Step Four: **Measure and monitor your investment performance in a way that is meaningful and accurate.** Daily checking of investment performances is meaningless, and can drive you crazy. People often ask, "What's the market doing today?" For most people, they are referring specifically to the Dow and S&P 500 indexes. The more appropriate reply is, "Which one? There are hundreds of them." By participating broadly in the diversified global investment markets, you can more importantly focus your attention on what's happening during longer term full investment cycles, and observe that every asset class has its "day in the sun."

QUIET MILLIONAIRE® WISDOM

The gains in percentage performance can be deceiving relative to the actual gains in dollar value performance.

Investors evaluating their investment portfolio often simply want to know whether they had a gain or a loss during a certain period. They typically measure and judge the performance success of investments by percentage rates of return, which can be misleading and might not necessarily reflect the real return on the amount of money that they invested. Let's look closely at the performances for two $100,000 portfolios, which demonstrate how the percentage rates of return can mislead you about the actual dollar gain for your investment portfolio.

$100,000 Initial Investment

Year	Portfolio #1		Portfolio #2	
1	+35%	$135,000	+22%	$122,000
2	+30%	175,500	+14%	139,080
3	-14%	150,930	-1%	137,689
4	-16%	126,781	-4%	132,182
5	-22%	98,889	-5%	125,573
6	+29%	127,567	+16%	145,664
Average Annual Rate of Return:	**+ 7%**		**+7%**	

Notice that both portfolios show the same 7% average annual rate of return, which is calculated by totaling the percentages shown for each year and dividing by the number of years (6). However, also notice that the resulting portfolio dollar amounts are quite different at the end of year six, with Portfolio #2 being $18,097 further ahead. This is because the magnitude of ups and downs for Portfolio #2 was much less than for Portfolio #1. The smoother performance produced by Portfolio #2 demonstrates how important it is to "win by not losing" when you invest. Moreover, there are different ways to measure investment performance that result in different reported outcomes. Don't be fooled by percentage return numbers when evaluating investment performance.

QUIET MILLIONAIRE® WISDOM

Be aware that there are different methods for measuring investment performance, which can produce different average annual rates of return and dollar growth results for the same portfolio.

Most investors are completely unaware of their portfolio's actual performance. Those investors who attempt to understand their rate of return are often confused about what the true results are. Investment performance measurement requires having special technological tools and professional skills.

When measuring and monitoring your investment performance, you should understand that there are three different methods that can be used to measure your portfolio's performance, which will result in different average rates of return and dollar outcomes.

1. Holding Period Return (HPR). HPR is the method used by most investors to intuitively measure their portfolio's average annual rate of return. It is the only one of the three performance measurement methods that can be calculated manually without using computer technology. You simply calculate the *total* rate of return for the number of years involved, and divide it by the number of years. Although the HPR method is a somewhat valid way to measure a portfolio's performance, it's too simplistic to be accurate. It doesn't account for how the performance is affected by the timing of multiple transactions (dividend and interest reinvestments, cash inflows and outflows), which can occur during the measured time period. Therefore, more sophisticated performance measurement tools are required to make daily inputs and calculations for improved accuracy.

2. Time Weighted Return (TWR). TWR is the preferred method by investment advisors to measure their rate of return performances because it removes how both the positive and the negative effects of cash inflows and outflows made by the client influences the investment performance. Investment advisors can't control the amounts and timing of cash deposits and withdrawals made by their clients. These factors are what can make the performance result seem *better* or *worse*, depending upon the following cash flow circumstances:

Better performance results if:

*Investments go up in value after cash **inflows**, more dollars going up.*

*Investments go down in value after cash **outflows**, less dollars going down.*

Worse performance results if:

*Investments go up in value after cash **outflows**, less dollars going up.*

*Investments go down in value after cash **inflows**, more dollars going down.*

By stripping away the effects of all deposits and withdrawals made by the investor, TWR is the purest method for performance measurement when the investor wants to accurately compare how the portfolio has done as a direct comparison with other money managers for the same period without the influence of any deposits or withdrawals to the portfolio. Be aware that when you see the published performance of a mutual fund or individual stock, it does not necessarily reflect the true performance of your particular investment in that mutual fund or stock. The difference in the reported performance can be worlds apart from your portfolio's actual performance because your performance depends upon when you buy and sell the fund or stock and how long you hold onto it. For your portfolio's performance to accurately match the reported result of a particular mutual fund or stock, you must have held the investment for the exact same holding period that is being reported, and you must not have made any deposits or withdrawals. To calculate the TWR, the performance data *must* be gathered and updated on a daily basis without fail. Therefore, the TWR calculation requires a computerized performance measurement program that can measure on a daily basis your particular portfolio without the effects of any and all cash flow transactions. Accordingly, the TWR performance result may not be the actual dollar result for your portfolio. There is a third method to do that.

3. Internal Rate of Return (IRR). Investors do in fact want to know how their own portfolio has done in terms of dollar growth and with respect to their desired or target rate of return for financial planning purposes. Therefore, the internal rate of return (IRR) measures the TWR and takes into account a DWR performance as well. As discussed, the TWR measurement doesn't take into account inflows and outflows of cash; however, the DWR does. Therefore, the DWR calculates more heavily the periods when the portfolio is larger. This is because if a large amount of money is invested at the time the portfolio starts to perform well, the added money has more of a positive impact on the portfolio's measured performance. The opposite negative effect can happen with a surge of new money when the portfolio's performance is struggling. Therefore, if you want to determine whether your particular investments are growing adequately for achieving your financial planning objectives, then combining both the TWR and DWR performance measurements to calculate the IRR is the most meaningful and accurate. Be aware that if there are no cash inflows or outflows for the time period being measured, then there is no difference in the average annual rate of return for the TWR and IRR because the DWR is not an influential factor. As with the TWR, be aware that you can't manually calculate the above IRR performance result. It also requires using a sophisticated computer performance measurement program that accounts for every transaction on a daily basis without fail for the period being measured.

Step Five: Strategically rebalance (adjust) the portfolio's asset class exposure as required to ensure that the results meet your tolerance for risk and expectations for reward. Periodically rebalancing (adjusting) your portfolio's asset class exposure is a vital part of managing a diversified asset allocation program. By strategically rebalancing the out-of-balance differences in your portfolio's target versus actual asset allocations, you maintain the portfolio's basic structure for it to more reliably perform according to your expectations for risk and reward. The rebalancing process strategically takes profits from the asset classes that have become over-weighted because of relatively strong performance (sell high) and reinvests in the asset classes that have become underweighted because of relatively weak performance (buy low). Portfolio rebalancing is not an attempt to *time* the investment markets but rather a process to *tune* the portfolio. In essence, the strategy is to sell high investments within asset classes that have increased in value and to buy low investments within asset classes that have not had their time in the sun.

Rebalancing should not be considered an automatic activity when the out-of-balance situation occurs because, strategically, it may be advantageous or prudent to delay or accelerate making shifts in certain asset classes. For example, if a particular over-weighted asset class is expected to continue its strong performance, it may be a good investment decision to let the asset class remain somewhat over-weighted in order to have more dollars contributing added growth for the portfolio. Alternatively, if a particular over-weighted asset appears to be overvalued and is expected to tumble, then the over-weighted asset exposure might be prudently reduced to an underweighted status in order to assume a more defensive position for the portfolio. With a well-diversified portfolio, you don't have to be right 100% all of the time, but instead you have to make correct investment decisions only most of the time. However, at some determined point, rebalancing of the asset classes to be closer to the target allocation must be done to maintain the integrity of the portfolio's structure for achieving expected downside risks and upside rewards. Furthermore, when rebalancing, there may be tax consequences that have to be monitored and considered as part of the decision-making process.

Use the Modern Portfolio Theory Approach to Be an Investment Winner

Be aware that there can be certain times when a hyped hot stock or mutual fund within a particular asset class may be outperforming your overall diversified portfolio. But, be assured that the plodding, steady tortoise approach to investing always beats the rapid rabbit approach to the finish line of a long-distance run. It is only a matter of time before the rabbit wears out and investment *greed turns to grief.* You will be more successful if you *win by not losing.*

Find Investment and Financial Planning Advice That's Reliable and Right for You

If you're uncertain, overwhelmed, or too busy to invest intelligently without emotion and in accordance with a coordinated comprehensive financial plan, then maybe you should consider finding a competent financial planning/investment professional to help. Subsequently you'll be told *how* to find the right advisory assistance best suited for you, but for now here's what type of advisor to look for:

Registered Investment Advisor (RIA) who is regulated by either the federal Securities and Exchange Commission or the individual state securities commission. Be sure to obtain a copy of the advisor's registration, which is required to be filed with the appropriate regulatory authorities.

Fee-Only Advisor who provides comprehensive financial planning as well as investment advisory services (total wealth management). Advisors who are paid commissions may recommend more frequent transactions for your portfolio than warranted or investments with unnecessary sales charges and high expenses, causing negative impacts upon your wealth accumulation outcome. Understand and be comfortable with the advisor's comprehensive financial planning guidance along with his or her investment philosophy and approach. Determine whether the investment approach relates closely to the Modern Portfolio Theory approach discussed in this chapter.

QUIET MILLIONAIRE® SUMMARY

- **Know the requirements for a well-structured investment portfolio and then wisely plan, coordinate, and know your investment program.**
- **Know your tolerance for risk.**

- Become knowledgeable on how to construct and maintain a winning investment portfolio.
- Be aware of the seven biggest investment mistakes you must avoid.
- Use the Five-Step Modern Portfolio Theory approach to construct and maintain a winning investment portfolio to fund your dreams.
- Seek out the right professional for you to provide reliable, fee-only comprehensive financial planning and investment advisory guidance.

CHAPTER 7

Prevent Devastating Health Care

P aying for health care is expensive and can be financially devastating. Receiving affordable and high-quality health care is a number one concern for most people. In 2010, the Affordable Care Act (ACA), more commonly termed Obamacare, was enacted as a political effort to resolve deficiencies embedded in our health care system. However, the ACA is continuously embroiled with political controversy. The social challenge for affordable health care is yet to be met. The future structure of the U.S. health care system is uncertain. What's certain is that the structure will change out of necessity. For your own certainty, the best advice is to proactively take charge of your particular situation, whether you're young and raising a family or elderly and living on a fixed income derived from your accumulated investment portfolio.

QUIET MILLIONAIRE® WISDOM

Research thoroughly and monitor continuously what type of health insurance plan is best for paying your medical needs.

By becoming informed about your health care insurance options, you can plan how to manage and adequately fund your own specific needs for health care. This chapter will prepare you to understand and intelligently manage the many challenging decisions and changes on the horizon in how affordable health care is delivered, received, and paid for. Informed planning is the only sure way to make the most intelligent choices for you and to implement affordable strategies that will prevent the costs of health care from financially wiping you out. The federal government's health care website HealthCare.gov is a useful resource for your planning as well.

Most people who have medical, dental, and vision insurance participate on a group basis through their employer, which helps make the protective coverage more available, especially if you have adverse health issues. This is because there's usually no individual health underwriting requirement to participate in a group plan. Also, group health insurance is usually more affordable because some employers contribute money to subsidize some of the out-of-pocket premium costs for their employees.

Another way that employers help employees pay premium costs is by offering a Section 125 "cafeteria plan." The name of the plan came about because the cafeteria plan offers a menu of expense options that the employee can pay for using pretax dollars. These expense options include insurance premiums for group medical, dental, and vision as well as group life and disability insurance. Some cafeteria plans also permit paying out-of-pocket expenses for medical and dependent day care with contributed pretax dollars. Contributions to the plan are tax deductible by employee participants, and the withdrawals are tax free. The only catch is that previously the pretax contributed money must have been entirely used before the end of the tax year or it was forfeited under the "use it or lose it" rule. This rule has been liberalized, with a now allowable extended two-and-a-half-month grace period beyond the end of the tax year for using the money before losing it.

Despite all the benefits associated with group health insurance, there are some downsides to the plans, and there are no easy solutions to these problems. Take Bernie and Carolyn's story, for example:

Bernie and Carolyn are in their mid-fifties. They have raised two children, Heather, age twenty-six, and John, age twenty-four, both graduated from college and now out on their own. Because the kids are no longer a financial responsibility, Bernie, an engineer with a Fortune 500 company, would like to quit his stressful, unrewarding job. In fact, the only reason he became an engineer was because his parents insisted that he needed to become a responsible professional who earned a steady paycheck rather than a rock musician with an uncertain future. He has been a fish out of water for all of his adult working years. Both Bernie and Carolyn love music and are talented musicians. Carolyn has taught piano lessons for years. Now they both long to open a music academy, Bernie to teach guitar and Carolyn to teach piano. There is only one problem—health insurance. In the past three years, Bernie has had two heart attacks, and Carolyn developed diabetes. The result is that Bernie can't afford to leave his employer and pursue his dream because he needs to keep his group health insurance coverage until Medicare kicks in at age sixty-five, nine years from now. Bernie is also worried that he won't even make it til then because his peers have been getting forced into early-retirement severance packages. He fears it's only a matter of time before he is next on the list.

Bernie's health insurance dilemma could have been avoided if he and Carolyn had done some planning in advance while they were both healthy. In their case, they knew, prior to their health issues developing, that once their financial responsibility for the children was over, they wanted to open the music academy. It would have been an intelligent strategy to have taken out a high-deductible and, therefore relatively inexpensive, individual policy earlier even though they had Bernie's group coverage. While he remained with his employer, they could have continued using the group health benefits and would not have submitted any claims against the individual policy. Then, when he quit his employer, the previously underwritten individual policy would have been there for them regardless of the health problems that materialized subsequently. Retaining affordable health insurance coverage is a huge problem affecting a larger number of people who leave their employment because of career change, termination, or retirement. Many workers like Bernie are being forced to remain in jobs that they dislike because they would otherwise be without affordable health insurance.

QUIET MILLIONAIRE® WISDOM

Always advance plan to make certain you're never financially vulnerable without affordable, catastrophic health insurance.

Losing affordable health insurance is a particular hardship for others who are being involuntarily "let go" from their employer and now must face a life without affordable health insurance until they are eligible for Medicare at age sixty-five. Those people without group health coverage always have the option to buy an individual policy; however, if you have a preexisting adverse health issue, an individual policy can be prohibitively expensive and can lack the full coverage if it excludes the preexisting condition. The likelihood of needing health care is a matter of when, not if. This is why the premiums to insure against medical risks are high. In addition to the premium, there are often other out-of-pocket costs associated with medical insurance coverage. The *deductible* is a predetermined dollar amount that you must satisfy every year before the health insurance company begins to contribute any money toward your medical costs. In addition to the deductible, there may be *co-payments*, where you are required to pay a certain dollar figure for each medical service provided, and/or *coinsurance*, where you are required to pay a certain percentage of your health care costs. Medical insurance companies are protected by a "lifetime payout provision" that limits the total amount they will pay out over the lifetime of the insured. The amounts usually range between one to five million, and the higher maximum lifetime payout ensures that the coverage won't be prematurely depleted.

Types of *Private* Health Insurance Plans and How to Manage

Deciding which type of medical plan is best to purchase, whether as a group participant or individually, is a confusing process. The following is a review of the features and benefits of the various types of plans available:

- Fee-For-Service Indemnity
- Health Maintenance Organization (HMO)
- Exclusive Provider Organization (EPO)
- Preferred Provider Organization (PPO)
- Point of Service (POS)
- Health Savings Account (HSA)

Fee-For-Service Indemnity Insurance Plans: Fee-for-service indemnity health insurance plans are the *original* type of health plans, where the emphasis is on the treatment of unexpected illnesses as opposed to preventive medicine. The insured is allowed total control over the choice of physicians and hospitals to be used. After an annual deductible and co-pay or coinsurance is paid, the insurance company indemnifies in full for *any* medical service provided. While the indemnity type plan is the most flexible and provides payment benefits regardless of which physician and medical facility are used, it's the patient's responsibility for keeping medical receipts and bills and for completing the claim forms for payment. The fee-for-service indemnity health plan doesn't usually cover preventive medicine services; fees for checkups, office visits, and shots are your responsibility. This can make indemnity insurance impractical for a large family that requires a lot of routine visits and preventative care. Because of skyrocketing health care costs and an emphasis on preventive medicine, managed health care has become the more prevalent medical service approach. While the managed health care form of insurance is a more affordable insurance alternative to the pure indemnity type plans, the offset is that there are restrictions in your choices for getting medical treatment.

A fee-for-service indemnity plan may be an acceptable option if you:

- Want greater flexibility and choices for doctor and hospital selections.
- Are fine with paying higher premium rates in exchange for more control over where services are provided.
- Can accept the burden of increased administrative claims paperwork.

Health Maintenance Organizations (HMO): HMOs paved the way for the development of managed-care medical insurance plans. Unlike the consumer-driven, higher-cost fee-for-service indemnity plans, HMOs are medical provider driven and, with controlled costs, are a lower-premium health insurance alternative. The basic concept is to manage care and control costs by limiting medical care access to an assembled preapproved network of physicians and hospitals. From the network, you choose a primary care physician (PCP), who, acting as a *gatekeeper*, is responsible for your overall health care as well as for making referrals to specialists and approving further medical treatment. Usually, your choice of doctors and hospitals is limited to those that have contract agreements with the HMO to provide for your health care. Because the HMO managed-care emphasis is on preventive medicine and treatment, most doctor visits, checkups, and shots are typically fully covered, with the possibility of a co-pay or coinsurance requirement for each service activity being the only out-of-pocket cost. Generally, there is a standard co-payment amount per doctor visit and a pre-approved payment amount to cover prescriptions. No claim forms are required to be filed for services provided. Instead, as an HMO member, you merely present an ID card at the doctor's office or hospital, which then submits the service claim directly to the HMO for payment. The drawback of any HMO policy is that no care can be received outside of the network without a highly restrictive prior approval by the PCP being obtained. Therefore, except for emergency treatment, any medical service sought outside of the network is limited, and the expenses incurred are usually not fully covered, if at all. This restricted network referral process makes it difficult to access specialized care outside the HMO network, which can be a detriment to you receiving the best required medical treatment available without incurring a huge out-of-pocket financial cost.

An HMO may be an acceptable option if you:

- Seek lower premiums.
- Accept that PCP authorizations are required for out-of-network health care services.
- Desire coverage for preventive services such as checkups and immunizations.

Exclusive Provider Organization (EPO) Health Insurance Plans: An EPO is an Exclusive Provider Organization. EPO plans are similar to HMO plans because they have a network of physicians and hospitals that are required to be used, except for emergency situations. A primary care physician (PCP) provides referrals to only in-network doctors, hospitals, and specialists.

An EPO may be an acceptable option if you:

- Seek lower premiums.
- Accept that no coverage is provided for out-of-network doctors and hospitals.
- Desire coverage for preventive services such as checkups and immunizations.

Participating Provider Organizations (PPO): The PPO is an evolved type of managed-care plan that is growing in popularity. It was developed to combine the lower cost of a managed-care plan with the greater degree of choice found in a traditional indemnity health insurance plan. Although your health care is managed with restrictions, you're granted a more lenient degree of choice in providers. A PPO health insurance plan operates in a similar manner as an HMO in that you pay a fixed monthly premium, and in return you receive medical services from the health care provider network. However, a PPO does differ from the original HMO blueprint in that under a PPO insurance plan, a primary care physician (PCP) or "gatekeeper" physician isn't required. As a result, seeing a specialist does not require a referral. If you need or want health care provided from *outside* the network, you're required to pay a higher co-payment than if the provider were from within the PPO network. Each time you need medical attention, you can decide between a higher-costing fee-for-service indemnity plan format with freedom of choice for provider care or a lower-costing managed-care option that restricts your care to within the provider network. PPO insurance is typically more expensive than an HMO managed-care plan. Even if the premium is comparable to an HMO, there are other out-of-pocket costs associated with a PPO. For receiving non-network care, you must satisfy a deductible before the health insurance company begins payment benefits. After the deductible is met, you must pay coinsurance, which is higher than network provider coinsurance amounts. Furthermore, you might also be required to pay the difference between what the non-network health care provider charges and what the plan deems to be "reasonable and customary" for the service. However, these extra costs associated with a PPO may be worthwhile to you because overall the PPO is less costly than an indemnity plan and more flexible about accessing provider services than an HMO.

A PPO may be an acceptable option if you:

- Don't want a PCP requirement.
- Want flexibility for choosing doctors and hospitals in-network for lower cost and out-of-network for higher cost.

Point of Service Plans (POS): POSs are a lesser known type of managed health care plan operating similarly to a PPO, but they are slightly less expensive and more restrictive about provider choices than a PPO. When you enroll in a POS plan, unlike the PPO, you are required to select a network primary care physician (PCP) from the network who's primarily responsible for your health care and who's designated as your "point of service" physician. The primary POS physician is permitted to make referrals *outside* the network but with limited payments being made to the non-network provider by the health insurance company. For medical visits within the health care network, there's no claims paperwork to complete. For services provided outside the network, it is your responsibility to keep track of health care receipts, complete the claims forms, and submit bills for payment.

A POS may be an acceptable option if you:

- Are okay with the PCP, point-of-service requirement in exchange for lower premiums.
- Need some flexibility when choosing doctors and hospitals.

Health Savings Accounts (HSA): A health savings account (HSA) is not a health insurance plan unto itself. Instead, it is a tax-favored savings account that is used in combination with a PPO health insurance policy.

The HSA is used for paying out-of-pocket medical expenses with pretax, nontaxable dollars. Here is how the combination HSA–health insurance policy works. The managed health care policy has a high deductible, which allows a relatively low premium. With the premium savings, the extra money available can be regularly deposited into the completely tax-free HSA. The maximum amount that can be contributed annually to the HSA is the lesser of the amount of the health plan's high deductible or the maximum specified by law, which is adjusted annually for inflation. As of 2020, the maximum annual allowable contribution amounts to an HSA are $3,550 for individual coverage and $7,100 for family coverage, plus $1,000 if over age 55. The HSA includes a checkbook that may be used to pay for medical expenses using non-taxable, pretax dollars until the health insurance high deductible is met and the policy's benefits begin. Any HSA account funds not used during a given year remain in the account, invested to grow without taxation, and are available for future medical expenses or for retirement income purposes, similar to a traditional IRA. Note: This is unlike the employer sponsored group Section 125 "cafeteria plan," which requires that all pretax contributed money must be entirely used within a given tax year or the money is forfeited under the "use it or lose it" rule.

An HSA may be an acceptable option if you:

- Are okay to save tax-free to pay for medical expenses not covered by a lower premium, high deductible health plan.
- Want protection from catastrophic health care costs only, and are not concerned about paying day-to-day medical expenses from HSA.
- If you own a small business and want a lower cost health insurance alternative.

When evaluating whether to select an HMO, EPO, PPO, POS, or HSA health insurance plan, the following checklist of questions can be used as a guide:

Health Insurance Plan Evaluation Checklist

- How many doctors are in the network to select from?
- What hospitals are available through the plan?
- Where are the offices and hospitals in the network located?
- Are my preferred doctors and hospital choices in the network?
- How are referrals to specialists handled?
- What is the coverage policy for emergency care?
- What health care treatment services are covered?
- What preventive services are covered?
- Are there limits on medical treatments or other services?
- How much is the health insurance premium?
- Are there deductible, co-payment, or coinsurance requirements?
- What are the additional costs and restrictions for using non-network providers?
- Is there an annual out-of-pocket maximum?
- What is the lifetime maximum dollar benefit?

In addition, depending upon how much you want to pay or what your family health history is, you might want to include other less common coverage in your medical insurance policy. Some of these "extra" coverage areas might include:

- Dental insurance
- Vision care
- Care by specialists
- Care for mental health
- Services for drug/alcohol abuse
- Family planning services, OB-GYN
- Chronic disease care
- Physical therapy

- Nursing home and hospice care
- Chiropractic care
- Maternity care
- Well baby care (immunizations, etc.)

Specialized Disease Insurance: Specialized disease insurance policies are available for specified diseases such as cancer, heart attack, or stroke. These policies provide benefits only if you contract the specified disease. However, the policy will not cover the specified disease diagnosed in existence *before* you applied for coverage. Some policies will deny coverage if learned subsequently that you had the specified disease at the time of purchase, even if you did not know it existed. Importantly, be sure you understand what conditions must be met before the policy will start to pay your bills.

QUIET MILLIONAIRE® WISDOM

Say "no" to specialized disease insurance.

Purchasing specialized insurance is an emotional purchase decision, not an intelligent purchase decision. Although a comprehensive medical insurance policy has a higher premium than specialized insurance, it is a much better value because it covers all diseases and medical treatment needs. Buying specialized disease insurance is a waste of money. Agents who sell it play on the purchaser's emotions and often use misleading sales practices that are scrutinized by state insurance regulatory agencies.

Types of *Government* Health Insurance Plans and How to Manage

Affordable health care is a growing social problem as a result of rapidly increasing medical costs and an aging population requiring more frequent and more expensive treatments. The managed-care approach has held down costs somewhat but at the expense of limiting consumer choices for health care providers and services. Each year, health care costs are consuming a larger amount of the consumer's spendable income. More and more people are living without health insurance coverage, and by necessity, the government's allocation of resources to subsidize this health care crisis appears to be increasing. Currently, the main government programs for subsidizing health care are Medicare, which helps senior citizens pay for medical and prescription expenses, and Medicaid, which is a welfare program that provides custodial long-term care for patients who have no financial resources.

Medicare: Medicare is a federal health insurance plan that is the primary means for paying health care costs by most people age sixty-five or older and for some disabled individuals under the age of sixty-five. Medicare consists of two parts: Part A (hospital insurance) and Part B (medical insurance). Below is an overview summary of Medicare and supplemental forms of insurance coverages. See the Medicare.gov website for further in-depth details.

Medicare Part A (Hospital Insurance): Most people, if they qualify for Social Security benefits, are automatically enrolled for Medicare Part A when they turn age sixty-five, and no monthly premium is required. People who do not qualify for Social Security benefits may enroll for Part A but have to pay a monthly premium, which in 2020 is up to $458 per month. Part A does have in-patient, out-of-pocket deductibles but no coinsurance requirement. In 2020, the out-of-pocket deductibles are:

- $1,408 deductible *total* for a hospital stay of 1–60 days each benefit period.
- $0 deductible *per day* for days 1–60 of a hospital day each benefit period.
- $352 deductible *per day* for days 61–90 of a hospital stay each benefit period.
- $704 *per lifetime reserve day* for after day 90 of a hospital stay each benefit period (up to a maximum of 60 days over your lifetime). Beyond this, you're responsible for all hospital costs.

In addition to paying for a portion of in-patient hospital care, Medicare Part A pays a portion of skilled nursing care, hospice care, and limited rehabilitative care provided in home or in a skilled nursing home facility. Be aware that Medicare does not pay for long-term custodial care requiring assistance with daily activities such as dressing, bathing, and cooking. Such long-term custodial care provided by a skilled nursing home facility or in-home care must be paid for out of pocket or by a long-term-care policy. The last resort for paying custodial care costs is Medicaid, which is government "medical welfare."

Medicare Part B (Medical Insurance): Medicare Part B is medical insurance that helps pay for doctor services, outpatient hospital care, and other medical services that Part A does not cover, such as physical and occupational therapy and some short-duration home health care. There is a premium cost for Medicare Part B, which in 2020 is $144.60 per month or higher depending upon your income, and can increase annually. In addition, there is an annual deductible requirement, which is $198 for 2020. Once the annual $198 deductible requirement is met, you pay 20% of the Medicare-approved amount for the medical services provided. Furthermore, there may be additional out-of-pocket costs if your doctor charges and requires you to pay more than the approved Medicare amount. It's important to enroll in Part B when you are first eligible at age sixty-five. **The Social Security Administration recommends that you apply for Part B coverage three months before turning age sixty-five.** This is when the initial enrollment period begins, and it continues for seven months. If you delay enrollment, the Part B premium is permanently increased by 10% for each year of delay. The only exception is if you are still working or have group health coverage after age sixty-five.

Medicare Part C (Medicare Advantage): In many parts of the country, you have the option to select privately issued Medicare health insurance plans that are subsidized by Medicare, known as Medicare Advantage (formerly Medicare + Choice). The Medicare Advantage plans are available in various formats: indemnity fee for service, HMO, or PPO formats described previously. Most of these plans generally provide extra benefits and lower co-payments than required by Medicare. However, you usually must see doctors who belong to the plan and go to certain hospitals for medical care. To sign up for Medicare Advantage, you first must enroll in Medicare Part A and B and pay the required Medicare Part B monthly premium. Besides paying the Medicare Part B monthly premium, there is an additional monthly premium charged, which varies among the private insurance companies providing Medicare Advantage coverage. However, despite the additional monthly premium, your out-of-pocket costs could be less than for Medicare because of lower deductibles and expanded coverage. While Medicare Advantage plans provide Medicare Part A and B coverage, some might not include Medicare Part D prescription drug insurance coverage (discussed next), and therefore whether to purchase separate prescription drug coverage has to be decided upon. However, with Medicare Advantage coverage, there is no need to purchase a Medigap policy (discussed below). Be aware that if you ever become dissatisfied with the Medicare Advantage plan option, there is a safe harbor by being able to revert to Medicare.

Medicare Part D (Medicare Prescription Drug Insurance): Medicare recipients have the voluntary option to purchase Medicare Part D prescription coverage through a separate drug insurance policy for a monthly premium amount based upon your income. Monthly premiums vary according to which plan you enroll in. In addition, there might be deductibles and cost-sharing limits subject to future year upward adjustments. For those Medicare recipients who already have prescription drug coverage that is better than Medicare Part D's, the coverage is termed *creditable*, and they can sign up for Medicare D later if at any point the coverage is no longer creditable. However, for those recipients who do not have creditable coverage and do not voluntarily enroll for Medicare D coverage when first eligible, there is a penalty assessed in the form of higher monthly premiums if they enroll subsequently.

Medigap (Medicare Supplement) Insurance: Medigap policies (also termed Medicare Supplement Insurance) are health insurance policies sold by private insurance companies that generally cover the costs not covered (gaps) by Medicare such as deductibles, co-payments, and coinsurance that you must otherwise pay out of pocket. However, you must first enroll in Medicare Part A and B to purchase this insurance. **Anyone upon attaining age sixty-five should immediately apply for a Medigap policy before the initial, one-time-only, six-month open-enrollment period ends.** Waiting beyond the open-enrollment period may result in you being denied or charged more for this protective insurance coverage if there are health issues in existence. The insurance companies must structure the coverage in their Medigap policies to comply with federal and state laws. Therefore, there are twelve standardized policies (plans A–L) that are available in most states, and what your Medigap policy covers depends upon which plan (A–L) you buy. Although the plans are standardized, the premiums charged vary according to each insurance company provider and by state of residence. Generally, the more benefits the policy provides, the higher the premium, which is in addition to the Medicare B monthly premium. When you receive medical care, Medicare pays its share of the benefits, and then your Medigap policy pays its share. All new Medigap policy purchasers must also enroll in a separate Medicare D prescription drug plan that covers prescription drugs only. For more information about Medicare and the other insurance plans that supplement and complement Medicare, the following resources are available: www.medicare.gov (the official government website for Medicare information), and www.aarp.org.

Long-Term-Care (LTC) Insurance

The 2019 Genworth Cost of Long-Term Care Survey reported the median cost of a private room in a nursing home in the United States was $102,200 per year or $8,517 per month. The median cost for an in-home health care aide was $52,560 per year or $4,380 per month. The median cost for an Assisted Living Facility was $48,545 per year or $4,045 per month. Demographically, the need for long-term care is a growing social problem. As of 2020, it's estimated that more than 47% of men age 65 and older will need long-term care. For women, the estimated percentage is even higher at 58%. The following story about John and Christine shows the importance of LTC planning:

> *While John and Christine were still healthy and active and nearing retirement, they planned for their possible long-term-care needs. They had money, but they knew how expensive long-term care could be. The last thing they wanted to happen was to ever become a burden for their three grown children who had their own family responsibilities. They were also concerned that a long-term-care event could*

eliminate their retirement savings and cause them to run out of money and ruin their financial security and independence, so they bought LTC insurance. Because of their planning, there was no conflict or concern among their three children about how John and Christine spent their money during retirement. After twelve years of paying combined annual LTC premiums of $5,000 per year ($2,500 each), John died from a stroke after spending only one month in a nursing home. Until then, they had paid a total of $60,000 in LTC premiums, and their premium payments appeared wasted on John. But, looking at it from a positive perspective, thank goodness John did not suffer a prolonged illness in a nursing home. However, Christine's need for LTC became an entirely different story. She eventually did need LTC after having paid premiums for fifteen years then totaling $75,000. She started out with home health care when she was diagnosed with Parkinson's disease and her health was failing. Christine now lived alone in her own home in Cincinnati. Although her one daughter Lisa lived close by, she was busy with her banking career and raising two teenagers. Christine's other two children, Michael and Jean, lived away in Dallas and Atlanta. Eventually, Christine had to move from her home to an assisted-living facility, which took wonderful care of her. The assisted-living facility was ideal because it had a responsive, qualified staff and other seniors in similar situations for Christine to share living with. And, best of all, the living environment had a homey atmosphere, unlike a sterile nursing home, which was the type of facility that Medicaid would have paid for if Christine had run out of money. Her children visited as much as their busy lives and distance permitted. Just about every time they visited Christine, she said, "I'm so thankful that we have the long-term-care policy and that I'm here." Her children could not have agreed more. Christine died after spending five years in the assisted-living facility. The LTC policy *had paid out more than $375,000 in benefits. It took only one year of insurance-paid benefits at $205 per day before the entire $75,000 of out-of-pocket costs for paying the policy's premium were overcome. Christine would have never been able to pay that much on her own, and she would have outlived her money. In addition, Christine had LTC choices that she would not have had otherwise, and her children were relieved that she was being looked after with care and dignity. Planning had really paid off!*

Because they planned ahead, John and Christine's LTC experience was better than those families who just drift into the event.

In many cases, unpaid family members and friends provide much of the long-term care for the elderly. However, this is a challenging function, especially when undertaken by an elderly spouse. More often than not, the "free" caregiver gives out first. Paying for professional long-term care is often the better or only option. Contrary to common misconceptions, Medicare *does not* cover the costs for long-term care beyond one hundred days, or less when the care provided is custodial and no longer deemed rehabilitative. Furthermore, the care must be provided in a nursing home and subsequent to a hospitalization. Of all paid long-term care, Medicare benefits account for only 14%.

QUIET MILLIONAIRE® WISDOM

Know in advance how you'll pay for long-term care.

Three Choices Available to Pay for Long-Term Care: Self-Insure, Privately Insure, Government's Medicaid Welfare

Self-Insure: If you decide to self-insure the costs of long-term care, you will need to accumulate a substantial amount of money because the costs for long-term care are overwhelming and the premiums to insure against the potential out-of-pocket costs are high. The cost for this care, whether given in the home, an assisted living facility, or a nursing home, can cost $50,000 to $100,000 or more per year, and that's after first paying taxes on the money! The magnitude of this can destroy your retirement plans and financial resources if paid out of pocket. Any competent retirement cash flow analysis must contingently account for this potential financial event. The analysis should compare how the cost of paying a premium versus the cost of self-funding will affect your retirement cash flow and deplete investment assets. Otherwise, you may find out the hard way that the costs of long-term care can devastate your planned retirement cash flow and accumulated resources.

Private Long-Term-Care (LTC) Insurance: Purchasing private insurance to pay for long-term care should be considered if you can afford the premiums and are relatively healthy at the time the policy is being underwritten for approval. However, don't assume that you can't qualify for LTC insurance because you have been turned down for life, disability, or health insurance. The underwriting medical requirements for each of these types of insurance are different. The federal government provides tax deduction incentives on premiums for private long-term-care insurance. However, be aware that accessing the benefits for tax-qualified (TQ) policies are more restrictive than for non-tax-qualified (NTQ) policies. When deciding whether to purchase a TQ or NTQ long-term-care policy, make sure you understand how the tax deductibility of the premiums affects the accessibility of the policy benefits.

Purchasing LTC insurance is confusing for most people. According to the Health Insurance Association of America (HIAA), nearly 50% of all people who look into LTC insurance don't buy it because they're confused about which policy is right for them. Furthermore, of the 130 companies that sell LTC insurance, only a relative few of them are appropriate for consideration. A cheaper premium offered today by a company may cause heartache and hardship tomorrow when the premiums are subsequently increased dramatically or when small-print escape clauses enable a claim to be denied for your LTC need.

Another potentially harmful consequence with LTC is that while you might purchase a policy from one of the best LTC insurance companies, you could make a bad decision about the structure of the policy. Or, you could purchase a policy that is appropriately designed for your LTC need, but it is with an insurance company that will not be around in the future to pay the benefits as expected. It is not within the context of this book to educate you sufficiently about LTC planning or which insurance company and policy structure is best suited for you. There are too many variables to consider in the decision-making process. Rather, the intent is to inform you about what factors to consider and where to seek trustworthy and competent guidance for making an informed decision that will best meet your particular LTC insurance need.

Here are some basic guidelines regarding LTC planning:
- If you can afford to pay a premium for LTC insurance protection, then you can afford to hire a fee-only financial advisor to evaluate your particular situation on a comprehensive planning basis without bias or motivation to sell you a policy. Then, once a well-structured LTC insurance needs analysis is completed, locate an *independent* insurance

broker who specializes in selling LTC insurance and represents a number of different high-quality LTC companies in order for you to obtain a most suitable and affordable LTC policy. If necessary, ask the fee-only financial advisor to refer you to a qualified independent LTC insurance broker.

- The best time to consider purchasing LTC insurance is when you are in your mid-fifties because the premiums begin to accelerate after that. The difference in premium amounts for a 50 year to 60 year old is not nearly as great as the difference in premium amounts for a 60 year to 70 year old.

- Most LTC insurance consumers spend a lot of time deciding whether to buy a policy and which company to buy it from. However, once these decisions are made, they do not focus enough time on the most important decisions of how to properly design the policy to adequately cover their LTC risk in the most cost-effective manner.

- The benefits of an LTC policy are triggered by the inability to perform certain activities of daily living (ADLs), which in turn requires custodial care. There are six standard ADLs: bathing, dressing, eating, continence, transferring, and toileting. Not all LTC policies list and require the same ADL loss. Bathing is usually the first ADL that most people cannot perform. Therefore, make sure that bathing is listed along with all of the other ADLs because a policy that does not include bathing will most likely delay triggering benefit payments.

QUIET MILLIONAIRE® WISDOM

Know and understand the features and benefits of private long-term care insurance to make the best decision.

Basic Policy Benefits to Evaluate When Purchasing a Private Long-Term-Care Insurance Policy

Daily benefit: The daily benefit is the amount that an LTC policy pays for services per day. Typically, you can purchase a daily benefit that ranges from $50 to $350 per day in today's dollars. Determine the costs for daily LTC in your area, and deduct from this amount what you would be able to afford to pay out of pocket in the event of a need for LTC arises both before and during retirement. The difference is the minimum amount of daily benefit you should consider. However, remember to build into the calculation the effects of inflation. It is better to purchase a higher daily benefit than a longer benefit period because with most policies, whatever amount of daily benefit you do not use extends your benefit period. So, if your home health care costs $100 per day and you have a policy that pays $200 per day for two years, your benefit will actually last four years.

Inflation protection: Most LTC policies are sold without inflation protection because it significantly increases the premium. This is a very big mistake because without inflation protection, the compounding increases for the cost of LTC detrimentally erode the value of the policy. Inflation protection is available on a simple or compound benefit increase basis. The simple inflation benefit increases each year by 5% of the *original* daily benefit, while the compound inflation benefit increases 5% by each year's then-current benefit. The compound inflation benefit is recommended over the simple inflation benefit, and the following example explains why. If in today's dollars, the LTC daily rate is $200 and assuming an annual inflation factor of 5% (the typical assumption for LTC policies), then in twenty years, the daily rate will be $505. The following demonstrates the difference between a 0% inflation increase and a 5% simple and compound inflation increase for today's $200 per day daily benefit:

Policy Year	No Inflation	5% Simple	5% Compound
1	$200	$200	$200
5	200	240	243
10	200	290	310
15	200	340	396
20	200	380	505

Notice how the compound benefit really starts to make a difference beyond ten years to keep up with the ever-increasing costs for LTC. If premium affordability is a factor, it's better to reduce the benefit period than to reject the valuable compound inflation protection.

Elimination period: The elimination period is the waiting period before the benefit payments start and is the equivalent of a deductible with a health insurance policy. Most policies have elimination periods between twenty and one hundred days. In order to reduce the premium amount, you should choose the longest elimination period you can afford before the insurance benefit kicks in. Keep in mind that Medicare does provide limited rehabilitative nursing home benefits for up to one hundred days of care upon discharge from a hospital stay.

Benefit period: This is the length of time that the insurance company pays for long-term-care services once your claim starts. The benefit periods available for selection range from three years to a lifetime. If you have designed the policy according to the above steps, the proper benefit period is the one you can afford. Many people choose a three-year benefit because they are told that the average nursing home stay is two to three years. However, that average includes stays ranging from one month to ten or more years. Therefore, forget about the average statistics, and focus on purchasing what you can afford rather than the average. The total amount of dollar benefit available within a policy is determined by multiplying your daily benefit by the number of days in your benefit period. For example, a policy that pays

$200 per day with a three-year benefit has a value of $219,000 ($200 daily benefit x 365 days in a year x 3 years). In turn, a policy that pays $100 per day for a six-year period has essentially the same dollar benefit if you use it for the entire benefit period; if you do not, then the policy is less valuable. Again, this is why it is better to select a higher daily benefit for a shorter period if the premium cost to insure is a concern.

In the Event You Can Neither Afford to Pay Out of Pocket for LTC Nor Purchase an LTC Insurance Policy, Then Applying for Medicaid Welfare May Be Your Only Option

Medicaid (Government Welfare): Be careful not to confuse the government's Medicaid and Medicare programs. As discussed before, **Medicare** provides only very limited rehabilitative nursing home coverage for up to one hundred days after a hospitalization but usually is less once the care becomes custodial and is no longer deemed rehabilitative. **Medicaid** is a government medical welfare program that pays for more than 45% of all long-term nursing home care in the United States. Be aware that Medicaid pays only for custodial care provided within a nursing home, not for in-the-home care. Furthermore, not every nursing home facility accepts Medicaid patients, and you or a family member could be forced to go for long-term custodial care at a facility many miles away from home and family.

The funding for Medicaid comes from the federal government and from each state. The benefits vary by state, and are available only to those who are considered destitute. This means that you must own next to nothing in assets and have negligible income. If you have assets, you must "spend down" almost all your financial resources. With long-term care costing as much as $60,000 or more a year, this can happen quickly and deplete all your retirement money accumulations as well. Allowable retained asset limits (termed *countable* assets) vary by state. According to federal guidelines as of 2020, the limits (excluding home, personal belongings, and necessary automobile) are typically $2,000 for a single person and $128,640 for a married couple (higher so that the non-Medicaid spouse is not impoverished). Strict eligibility rules are applied as to how the applicant's assets were used for up to a period of five years prior to applying for Medicaid. This is termed the "look-back" period, and the penalties are severe for trying to hide assets, with heavy fines and jail time imposed for Medicaid fraud. Any Medicaid planning is complicated and should never be done without the guidance of a qualified elder law attorney. For more information about Medicaid, go to HealthCare.gov and ElderLawAnswers.com.

Can Affordable Health Care for Everyone Be Achieved?

Our society is challenged to provide affordable health care for everyone. Health care has become so expensive because people live longer and expect to receive the highest quality health care available. The costs for research, development, and delivery of modern medical technology are astronomical. The amount of money spent on health care per person and as a percentage of our gross domestic product (GDP) is spiraling out of control. There are conflicting interests that must be addressed and need to be overcome to stabilize our health care system. As medical service consumers, ideally we want affordable health care for any medical reason, large or small, on demand any time we want it and from the best physicians and medical facilities we choose to use. However, this ideal vision conflicts with that of the health care and insurance companies, which strive to control costs to be profitable. In addition, the government faces tough and politically unpopular budgetary decisions necessary to publicly subsidize this financially demanding social issue.

Unfortunately, as a society we tend to address difficult political and social issues such as health care in a crisis management manner as opposed to a proactive manner. We'll be forced to respond to and implement a comprehensive system of more responsible administrative and financial management by all parties: the health care system, the government, and all of us individually. In the meantime, plan diligently to manage and fund your own health care needs to avoid depending upon others. As a reminder, the federal government's website HealthCare.gov is a useful health care information and planning resource.

QUIET MILLIONAIRE® SUMMARY

- **Know and understand the features and benefits of all health insurance programs offered.**
- **Understand the variety of plan formats offered: Fee-For-Service Indemnity, HMO, EPO, PPO, POS, HSA.**
- **Don't purchase specialized disease health insurance.**
- **Understand and don't confuse the different benefits provided by Medicare and Medicaid.**
- **If affordable, consider purchasing long-term-care insurance to fund costs that can't be self-funded out of pocket.**
- **Diligently plan your own course for managing the costs of health care and the potential for financial hardship.**

CHAPTER 8

Be Prepared for Life's Unexpected Risks

Every day, we face the risk of something unexpected happening to us. When it's good, it's called a pleasant surprise, being lucky, or even a miracle. When it's bad, it's called an accident, a tragedy, or a catastrophic event. Life is full of different types of risks. Starting a new business or buying a hot stock is a risk taken for gain, but sometimes these risks end up being a loss. Some risks such as skydiving and horseback riding are taken willingly for pleasure and excitement. Other risks can be downright foolish such as smoking or drinking too much. Certain risks are taken as a part of our everyday life, such as driving an automobile with the risk of an accident, getting married with the risk of divorce, having children with the risk of childbirth, or eating certain foods with the risk of becoming ill. Some people worry about risks that may never happen and live a very uneasy and sheltered life, while others may defy risks that are almost certain to happen and live recklessly. Managing risk often involves purchasing insurance protection. This chapter discusses how to manage the different types of risk using the various forms of insurance available, as well as how to purchase the insurance you decide upon in a way that's most cost effective.

Five Ways to Manage and Protect Against Life's Risks

1. **Avoid:** You can try to avoid risk. If you never drive your car, you'll never have an accident. Some risks can't be avoided because they are certain to occur, such as the risk of needing health care. You can try to avoid investment risk by keeping your money in bank certificates of deposit, but then you take on the certain risk of inflation and lessening the amount of time before you run out of money while living off your investments. Avoidance of some risks isn't always in your best financial interest.

2. **Control:** You can try to control or limit risk. Having a fire extinguisher in your home can put out the fire if it happens and can prevent the entire house from burning down. If you take medicine to control your high blood pressure to prevent having a heart attack, this is controlling a risk. If there is a fast-sinking investment that's causing you to have anxious sleepless nights, then you can sell the investment and limit further loss to control the amount of risk.

3. **Reduce:** You can reduce risk by replacing hazardous electrical wiring, getting rid of combustible materials in your home, driving defensively, or having routine health checkups. But, most important, you can reduce financial risks by reviewing and updating your financial plans.

4. **Retain:** You can retain some of the risk of loss by having a high deductible on your health, homeowner, and auto insurance policies. This makes financial sense if you can afford the out-of-pocket costs of the deductible amount in exchange for paying a lower insurance premium. Having no life insurance is a retained risk that may or may not be prudent depending upon whether survivors can withstand the outcome of a death without your income.

5. **Transfer:** You can transfer risks by buying various types of insurance, which protect you against having to self-fund the financial consequences

of whatever risk the policy covers. However, people are often uniformed or misinformed about the most intelligent ways to transfer risk to an insurance company, and they end up paying too much for this form of risk management. This is because insurance products and their terminologies can be difficult to understand and because insurance agents are motivated to sell policies that pay them the highest commission. Intelligent insurance planning evaluates the actual need for transferring a risk, and determines how to do so in the most cost-effective manner possible.

How to Determine and Purchase the Most Appropriate, Affordable, and Right Amounts of Insurance Needed for Transferring Protection Against Everyday Risks

Throughout the overview in this chapter of the types of insurance products available for protecting against the various risks in life, it's *very important* to keep these basic premises in mind:

- *If the insurance premium or cost to insure is cheap, then either the chance of the risk occurring is low or the amount of the risk being transferred is limited.*
- *If the insurance premium is expensive, then the chance of the risk occurring is likely or the amount of the risk being transferred is high.*
- *If the insurance policy's deductible and co-pay provisions are high, this means that you have to pay more dollars out of pocket before the insurance company pays out dollars for its share of the risk incurred, and this lowers the premium amount charged.*

Life Loss Risk

When considering loss of life insurance, we want to believe that the likelihood of dying is a long way off, and don't pay enough attention to the fact that tomorrow isn't promised. Most likely, we won't die any time soon, but the risk is that we don't know for sure. Purchasing the proper type and amount of life insurance for the right price that's affordable is an important part of the comprehensive financial management process. However, life insurance is usually acquired piecemeal, and the result is a costly mish-mash. The purchase decision relies mainly upon the insurance agent, whose incentive is to sell as much as the buyer can afford, which sometimes means purchasing policies that pay the most commission. Don't be the person who says in jest, *"I don't need life insurance because when I die, I want it to be a real tragedy."* Unfortunately, this is too often the actual outcome because of an uninformed and unplanned insurance program. Here's a word of warning to women about life insurance. They need to pay serious attention during the insurance decision-making process to make sure that intelligent insurance planning is accomplished. This is because according to the mortality statistics, women usually outlive men and are typically the survivors in a family situation.

Let's look at some basic life insurance facts. There are four parties involved with a life insurance policy: the insurance company, the policy's owner, the policy's insured (which is usually also the owner but not necessarily), and the beneficiary (which can be multiple parties). While most people think of life insurance mainly as a means to replace lost income in the event of a breadwinner's death, there are many other purposes for having life insurance. For example, life insurance proceeds, which are *not* taxable to beneficiaries, can be a means to provide cash liquidity for paying estate taxes or for providing financial resources to keep a business operating in the event of an owner's or key person's death. Sometimes life insurance can make sure that a surviving spouse won't run out of money during retirement. It also can be a way to fund a legacy such as providing a college education to grandchildren or contributing to a valued charitable organization or an alma mater. Insurance companies use mortality statistics to figure out according to health, age, and gender when deaths usually occur, and they then price the insurance policy accordingly. The higher the risk of death, the higher the insurance premium or the likelihood of not being insurable. Because women usually live longer than men, the insurance premiums are typically less for women. The premiums for smokers are always higher, which reinforces the warnings that smoking is a killer. Furthermore, because of the added mortality risks associated with obesity, being overweight requires a higher premium to be paid.

Two Main Types of Life Insurance Products to Choose From: Term or Permanent

The basic difference between term and permanent insurance is this. Term life insurance provides a *limited-time* death benefit only. Permanent life insurance provides a *lifetime* death benefit combined with a cash value investment component. There are three forms of permanent insurance policies that you can choose from: whole life, universal life, and variable life.

Term Life Insurance: Term insurance is the most common type of life insurance offered on a group basis to employees by employers. It is also available for purchase on an individual basis outside of work. Term insurance is intended to cover a death risk for only a specified number of years, usually for terms of one year to thirty years, and it is anticipated that the need for the death benefit will be gone at the end of the specified term. The premiums for term insurance are cheap when you are young and increase as you age to where the insurance coverage becomes too expensive to keep. Therefore, most term policies are dropped and never pay a death benefit, except in the event of a premature death. Insurance agents are not thrilled about selling term insurance because the commissions paid to them stop when the term policies are dropped, and the commission amounts are meager while the policy is in force.

As mentioned, many people have group term insurance coverage offered to them through their employment. Because the insurance company underwrites the coverage as a group for all employees, people with health problems and smokers are included in the premium pricing. This causes the group term rates for each employee to be relatively higher than the rates for the employee who is individually insured as a healthy nonsmoker. Therefore, employees should always compare the differences in premium cost for their group coverage versus what it would be if they obtained their own individual policy outside of work. Another disadvantage with group insurance is that you lose the coverage upon leaving the employment for any reason, and you may not be able to replace it individually if a health problem develops. This is another reason why any employee who is a healthy nonsmoker should consider opting for individual coverage that continues upon leaving the employment. It's very important to remember that whenever you purchase individual term insurance, you should make sure that the policy is *convertible* to a permanent type of insurance without another underwriting being required, just in case a health problem should materialize in the future. Be aware that this convertibility feature is generally not available with group coverage. The website www.insure.com is a very informative place where you can obtain instant term insurance premium quotes from more than two hundred leading insurers, and you then have the freedom to buy your insurance directly from any of the companies that are most competitively priced for you.

Permanent Life Insurance: Permanent insurance is intended to remain in force for an entire lifetime and eventually pay out a death benefit amount upon the death of the insured. In addition to providing a lifetime death benefit, permanent insurance also has an investment component that builds up cash value inside the policy during the earlier years to keep the future premium amounts level and more affordable during the later years. However, to build up the cash value during the earlier years of the policy, the premium amounts for permanent insurance policies are much higher and less affordable than they are for term insurance policies with the same size death benefit. Insurance agents prefer to sell more costly permanent insurance policies instead of term insurance because the premiums are higher and continue for the insured's entire lifetime. This provides the agent a more lucrative upfront commission as well as a longer sustaining commission payout on a residual basis. Furthermore, you should also know that if you drop a permanent policy early, there are costly surrender charges that can remain in effect for as long as fifteen years, whereby the insurance company keeps a significant amount of your cash value accumulated inside the policy in order to make sure it recovers the high commission payouts to the agent. Unfortunately, the sales practices and disclosures by agents can be misleading, and this makes understanding the true cost for the complicated components of permanent insurance difficult. To make matters worse, the regulation of the insurance industry is not sufficiently protective to the consumer.

Three Different Forms of Permanent Life Insurance: Whole Life, Universal Life, Variable Life

1. Whole Life (WL): Whole life (WL) insurance is the original form of permanent life insurance, also known as ordinary or straight life insurance. With whole life insurance, you pay a level premium for your *whole life*. The size of the death benefit is a fixed amount agreed upon and approved by the insurance company when the policy is issued. A fixed rate, low interest investment account within the policy accumulates cash value on a tax-deferred basis. The insurance company (as opposed to the policy's owner) assumes the full risk to ensure that the cash account's performance is sufficient to keep the policy from lapsing, and that the owner is never required to pay more than the originally quoted premium amount. Significantly, the accumulated cash account is a legally owned asset of the insurance company, not the policy owner. This means that if the insurance company gets into financial trouble, the cash value can be confiscated by its creditors and lost to the policy owner. Therefore, it's important for you to know the financial strength and business practices of the insurance company that you do business with. The policy's accumulated cash value can be borrowed against by the owner. However, if a policy loan is still outstanding upon death, the death benefit is lowered by the amount owed. Alternatively, the cash value may be withdrawn, but the policy might be terminated and subject to possible surrender charges and income taxes. WL insurance is the least flexible form of permanent insurance and limits your abilities to adapt the policy as a tool for meeting changes in insurance planning needs in the future.

2. Universal Life (UL): Universal life (UL) insurance evolved from the above WL policy. It's also known as an adjustable or a flexible life insurance policy because both the death benefit and the premium amounts can be adjusted upward or downward. The death benefit can vary based upon the amount of premium paid and the interest rate earned on the policy's built-up internal cash value account. A portion of each premium is deposited into a tax-deferred, fixed-income cash accumulation fund, with an annually adjusted interest rate. The amount of the premium paid can vary depending upon the investment performance of the cash accumulation fund. Harmful insurance sales abuses can occur when the UL policy is sold with an unrealistically high-interest-rate assumption for the cash accumulation fund in order to make the policy appear more attractive. The result is that the policy's owner shockingly may need to increase the amount of the premium paid to prevent the policy from lapsing. This is because the policy's owner assumes the full risk for the fund's investment performance being adequate to prevent the policy from lapsing, which is unlike the WL policy, where the insurance company assumes the full risk. However, similar to the WL policy, the UL policy's cash value is considered an asset of the insurance company and, therefore, is subject to attachment by the creditors of the insurance company. As is the case with the WL policy, loans can be made against the cash value of a UL policy, but the death benefit is reduced by any loan amount outstanding if the loan is not repaid during the insured's lifetime. Alternatively, instead of borrowing against the policy's cash value, a portion or all of the cash value may be withdrawn at any time. But then, the policy may be subject to termination, surrender charges, and income tax consequences.

3. Variable Life (VL): Variable life (VL) and a variation known as variable universal life (VUL) evolved from the above discussed universal life (UL) policy. The insurance industry developed the VL- and VUL-type policies to provide policyholders with more competitive and attractive investment options for their cash accumulation accounts. The main difference between VL and VUL is that VUL allows for flexible premium payments and the ability to modify the death benefit (same as UL), and VL does not. For purposes of this discussion, the term VL is used to describe both VL and VUL. The descriptive word "variable" for these policies means that the investment results for the internal cash accumulation fund will *vary* for each policyholder. This is because each policyholder can specifically select where to invest premium contributions from a diversified array of stock and bond mutual fund options made available within the variable policy by the insurance company. As is the case with the UL policy, the VL policyholder assumes the full risk that the cash accumulation account will earn an investment return that will be adequate to prevent the policy from lapsing, and, if not, then increased premium payments may be required to make up for any shortfalls. However, unlike the cash accumulation account with both the WL and UL forms of permanent life insurance, the cash accumulation within the VL form is kept completely separate from the insurance company's invested assets. Therefore, in the event the insurance company experiences financial problems, the policyholder's accumulated cash value is not in jeopardy.

VL is the insurance industry's version of "buy term and invest the differ-ence." To sell VL, the insurance agent must have a securities license as well as an insurance license. This is not the licensing situation for every life insurance agent. Very importantly, the money invested inside the VL policy must be proactively monitored just like any other investment program. However, too often the investments are not diligently managed after the initial policy sale is made, and they drift on cruise control. This can result in the policy's investment performance being riskier than is appropriate and possibly being underachieving. The outcome is that the policyholder may be required to pay additional premium amounts than originally intended to keep the policy from lapsing and losing the death benefit. VL policies have relatively high internal operating costs because of the additional administrative and record-keeping requirements associated with maintaining the separate investment accounts. Therefore, to overcome these expenses combined with the life insurance mortality costs, VL policies require funding to the maximum allowable amount. The policyholder must commit to making sizable premium payments, an ongoing cash flow commitment that might be better directed elsewhere even though the accumulated cash value can be diversified to grow sheltered tax-free inside the policy. Nevertheless, if structured and managed properly, the VL policy can be considered a financial "Swiss army knife," meaning it can be useful for implementing comprehensive financial planning strategies. However, the appropriate implementation of VUL is complicated to structure and must include ongoing monitoring that requires maintaining up-to-date knowledge about the policyholder's personal circumstances and staying on top of the changing insurance, investment, and tax environments.

Too often, VL insurance policies are sold for inappropriate reasons, and then are neglected after the initial sale is made. The rationale used for VL is valid in that the policy does provide an income-tax-free death benefit and has internal investment options that can grow tax deferred, and the built-up investment accumulations are available for future use with favorable tax consequences. The problem is that these features and benefits are often misrepresented by VL salespeople and misunderstood by the policyholders, causing the planning concepts to be misused and poorly implemented without the required ongoing monitoring being diligently carried out. For example, frequently VL is presented as a beneficial way to save for college or retirement in a manner similar to that often proposed for using variable annuities (VA). However, keep in mind that both VL and VA are insurance products that have higher internal costs to overcome than do other financial tools available to save and invest your money. Therefore, you must be cautious about using insurance products for investment purposes and be certain that the rationale for using them as an investment substitute is legitimately compelling. To make certain that VL is the most appropriate tool for meeting your goals and objectives, you should work with a comprehensive **fee-only** registered investment advisor who is licensed for non-commission insurance products, and not an insurance agent with motivation to sell the VL product for a commission.

How Much Life Insurance is Enough?

Research reveals that most policyholders have the wrong types of insurance and the wrong amounts of death benefit. By instituting an informed, cost-effective, coordinated insurance planning program, you can control premium amounts. In turn, this can improve your cash flow for other beneficial financial planning and investment purposes. Using the rule-of-thumb approach and generalities to determine how much insurance you need is not appropriate. For example, people are often told that a multiple of anywhere between five to ten times their annual salary is a way of gauging how much insurance to buy. What if you are underpaid? Many stay-at-home parents are certainly more valuable than their annual salary and may need life insurance. To know how much life insurance is an appropriate amount, what really must be determined is how much investment capital survivors will need. To do an accurate capital needs analysis, you will most likely require the guidance of an insurance planning professional. Keep in mind that a commission-paid insurance salesperson is often motivated to sell you as much insurance as possible regardless of your actual investment capital needs. Once again, for purposes of objectivity it's usually best to seek the advice of a comprehensive *fee-only* financial planning advisor who is licensed for insurance, but not motivated to sell you insurance for a commission.

The following is a checklist of what determinations should be included in a capital needs analysis for you to make an informed decision about life insurance protection.

Life Insurance Analysis Checklist

- **What is the estimated amount required for paying final expenses?** Include all out-of-pocket medical costs, funeral expenses, taxes owed, and costs to settle your estate.
- **What is the total amount of outstanding debts?** Be aware that it may be better for survivors not to pay off a low-interest-rate mortgage balance and instead to invest and use the life insurance proceeds to continue making mortgage payments.
- **What is the estimated total for survivor education funding costs?** Adjust these expenses for inflation, which for college is averaging upward of about 8% annually.
- **What is the amount of investment capital required to cover the survivor's (or survivors') annual living expenses *before* retirement?** This calculation requires that adjustments be made for taxes and inflation. Offsetting this total capital need *before* retirement is the total amount of earned income and Social Security benefits expected for survivors *before* retirement.
- **What is the amount of investment capital required to cover the survivor's (or survivors') annual living expenses *during* retirement?** This calculation requires that adjustments be made for taxes and inflation. Offsetting this total capital need *during* retirement is the total amount of pension income and Social Security benefits expected for survivors *during* retirement.

- **What is the total amount of investment capital that you currently have?** Include all bank accounts, investment accounts, and retirement plans, but don't include any expected inheritances.

- **What is the total amount of current life insurance in force?** Is any of this amount term insurance that will become too costly and need to be dropped or replaced? Don't include group life insurance, which is not portable upon leaving employment, or accidental death insurance policies, which don't include a death benefit for natural causes.

- **Based upon the above calculations, what *net* amount of investment capital is required from life insurance proceeds? Are you over-insured or under-insured?** A capital needs analysis should be performed at least annually in conjunction with a thorough review and update of all beneficiary designations and estate planning documentation.

Disability Risk

Private Disability Insurance is expensive and difficult to understand. As much as people are uncertain and uninformed about their life insurance needs, they are even more uninformed about how to survive financially with reduced or no earned income as a result of a disability. Understanding disability insurance is a complicated undertaking because the insurance companies load the policy provisions with subtle pitfalls that avoid or reduce their exposure to potential claims. Simplistically, keep in mind that if the disability insurance premium is low, the policy's fine print is likely loaded with wording to escape from paying the benefits you expect. The loss of income as a result of a disability can destroy the lifestyle you are accustomed to living. Most people don't have any protection against lost income and live one paycheck away from suffering a financial disaster if they became disabled and unable to work.

The financial cost of a disability can be far more devastating than the death of an income earner. This is because the disabled income earner is still alive as an added burdensome expense, but he or she is no longer able to contribute income unless that income stream was insured against disability. Even then, if insured, usually only 60% of the income is replaced by an insurance benefit. In addition, the disability income can be taxable as well, thereby further reducing the net available for meeting daily living expenses.

The risk of a disability occurring is greater than the risk of a premature death, an auto accident, or your house being destroyed. This is why the premium cost to adequately insure against disability is so expensive and why qualifying for disability insurance on an individual basis is very difficult. Another reason is that the disability insurance industry has been shaken up by massive claim payouts because of its previous liberal underwriting and aggressive sales approach. Many of the biggest insurers have either involuntarily gone bust or voluntarily dropped out of the business. And the disability insurance companies that are still around have dramatically tightened up their approval underwriting procedures. Gone forever are the days of receiving a lifetime income payout due to stress, backaches, or chronic fatigue syndrome. Today, to be individually underwritten and approved for a disability policy, you MUST be in near-perfect physical and mental shape. In addition, if you do become disabled, then there are hoops you have to jump through to receive a benefit payout, which has limits for how much and how long.

Most people who have disability insurance protection usually obtain it through group coverage with their employer. However, here again the high cost restricts the number of employers that offer disability insurance as a benefit. Moreover, in most instances, the group coverage does not adequately replace lost income required for meeting current financial requirements and certainly is not sufficient to fund major financial commitments such as college and retirement. Group disability insurance typically covers only 50% to 60% of your base monthly pretax earned income, not including bonuses. Furthermore, there are dollar limits imposed as to the maximum monthly income benefit paid that severely impact high-income families, and the benefit payout period rarely extends beyond age sixty-five. The disability insurance company wants to make sure that the benefit received is not lucrative enough to deter you from returning to work. Another common restriction of benefits is that they may stop after a couple of years of receiving disability income because you cannot perform the duties of your own occupation, but you are deemed able enough to work at some other occupation. Depending upon how the policy is written, you might end up working at a chain discount store and not receive any more disability benefit payments. There are also income tax ramifications to consider with respect to disability income received. To the extent that the employer pays the premium for the employee, the benefit is taxed as ordinary income, thereby making the actual lost income protection even less worthwhile. Group coverage can be supplemented with a private policy that will increase overall disability protection up to 70% to 80% of lost earned income. However, obtaining disability insurance to replace that level of lost income is challenging because of today's tougher underwriting guidelines.

Social Security Disability Insurance is mainly regarded as a source of retirement income from the federal government, but it also has a disability income benefit as well. However, more than 80% of the applicants fail to derive any income because it is extremely difficult to qualify for Social Security's disability benefit. Accordingly, there are lawyers who earn a nice living fighting through the disability appeals process on behalf of denied applicants. Even if you do qualify, the income received is below the government's poverty level guidelines.

Workers Compensation Insurance is a form of disability insurance that the individual states require most employers to provide to their employees. Insurance premiums are paid to the state by employers to fund the program, but a benefit is paid to the employee only if the disability is caused by a job-related incident. The workers compensation programs vary by state law, but the disability benefits paid are typically very low and last for only a few years.

Suffering a Disability Can Be Devastating Financially and Emotionally

Unless you diligently feather your nest with a combination of savings and disability insurance protection, drastic and painful lifestyle adjustments will be required in the event of lost earned income. Understanding the intricacies of disability insurance and adequacy of coverage is complicated. Be alert to the fact that the protection is subject to tricky loopholes that can impact your expected coverage. Furthermore, a disability insurance review should be done as part of a comprehensive and coordinated financial management review. If you are confused and uncertain, seek guidance from a knowledgeable, independent, fee-only advisor who is not influenced by an insurance sales commission. The following is a short checklist of the basic policy provisions to be considered when evaluating disability insurance protection.

Disability Insurance Analysis Checklist

- What is the amount of the monthly income benefit? Are there provisions that allow for the income benefit to be increased as your earned income increases?
- What is the maximum monthly income benefit amount payable? In particular, group insurance programs can have very low dollar maximums that are not sufficient to protect high-income earners. Even if the program's dollar maximum is high, you'll be hard pressed to find a disability insurance company that pays a dollar amount greater than $15,000 per month. Furthermore, the maximum dollar amount is subject to the limitation that no more than 70% to 80% of the insured's earned income is being replaced.

- In the event of a disability, is the benefit income amount fixed, or will cost of living increases be provided? Most disability policies have a fixed monthly benefit that does not increase once the benefit is being paid out.

- What is the definition of a disability? Is it the inability to perform the duties of your specified occupation (own occ), or is it the inability to perform the duties of any occupation (any occ) for which your education and training make you qualified?

- What is the waiting period, or the amount of time you must be disabled, before benefits are paid? Waiting periods can range from one week to two years, and the longer you wait, the lower the premium cost.

- What is the benefit period, or how long will you receive monthly income once the policy benefit starts? The benefit period can range from six months to age 65 and in rare instances for life. The longer the benefit period, the higher the premium to insure.

- Does the policy have a rider that pays a benefit if you're able to return to work part time?

- Does the policy have a Social Security offset rider that guarantees that if you qualify for disability payments under your insurance policy but do not qualify for Social Security disability—a common occurrence—the disability policy will also pay the Social Security disability amount?

- Does the policy include an additional purchase option that guarantees you the right to purchase additional disability insurance in the future, regardless of your health at that time?

In summary, disability insurance is expensive, and the income benefit is usually inadequate to meet current expenses, causing financial hardship and painful adjustments in your accustomed standard of living. Therefore, any intelligent comprehensive financial management program must include a prioritized allocation of earned income to accumulate a financial reserve and insure against lost income.

Property and Casualty Loss Risk

Property and casualty (P&C) insurance protects you against the risk of property damage and loss and against liability in the event of a lawsuit. Having adequate P&C coverage for your residence, automobiles, and business ownership is required to protect and preserve your monetary assets and accumulated wealth. This review of P&C insurance will cover only the elements of *personal* P&C coverage, not information relating to commercial or business P&C coverage. However, you should be aware that because of terrorist attacks and the multiple catastrophic hurricane events that cause horrific losses of property and life, P&C insurers have adjusted their premium levels upward nationwide for personal and business coverage to take into account these higher insurance underwriting risks.

Your P&C cost and coverage should be evaluated and compared periodically to make certain that you are paying a competitive premium amount for the protection that you require. This why it's usually preferable to work with an *independent* P&C insurance agent who is reputable and experienced and who represents a number of different insurance companies for determining what specific coverage amounts are available and most appropriate for your particular situation. However, be careful to look beyond the price comparison alone. It's extremely important that the insurer be financially sound, have a good claims paying record, and will not be quick to drop you after a claim is filed. In all cases, it's wise to limit your P&C insurance claims to the catastrophic, big-dollar event. Small claims or too many claims can drive up your premiums or cause you to be dropped. There are many choices and decisions you must make, as well as many loopholes you must understand, with respect to P&C insurance. As you read the descriptions of the various P&C insurance policies and coverages, you will benefit by referring to the coverage declaration pages of your own existing auto, homeowner, and personal liability umbrella policies.

Automobile Accident and Liability Risk

Automobile insurance premiums have gone up with the increased sophistication and material costs associated with today's automobiles. In addition, most families own multiple cars, and in addition, the risk associated with teenage driving is high. Typically, there are three component coverages within an automobile insurance policy: liability, medical, and collision and comprehensive.

Auto Liability: Liability insurance coverage is required by most states to protect you against the cost of property damage and bodily injury involved in an accident in which you are deemed to be responsible and liable. Liability is even required in so-called "no-fault" insurance states. Auto insurance policy declaration pages reflect split liability coverage limits that are shown as split numbers. For example, the split numbers 50/100/25 mean your coverage limits for an accident are as follows:

- $50,000 for bodily injury caused to another person
- $100,000 for bodily injuries caused to everyone
- $25,000 for property damage

The cost for liability protection can amount to more than half of the total auto insurance premium. Each state has minimum liability coverage requirements; however, it is recommended that you insure to exceed these relatively low minimums for adequate protection. A major premium cost consideration with respect to liability coverage is whether to purchase *unin-sured* motorist protection, which covers you when the other driver has no liability insurance, and *under*insured motorist coverage, which covers you for costs that exceed the other driver's coverage maximum. In most states, this coverage is optional. However, although uninsured and underinsured coverage is optional and does increase the liability premium, if you can afford the premium, you cannot afford to exclude this added protection. There are many uninsured drivers on the road, and if you're involved in an accident with one, you won't be reimbursed. At the very minimum, you should carry the same limits as your own liability coverage.

Auto Medical: Medical payment insurance coverage provides for the immediate treatment of injuries caused by a car accident. You, your family members, and other passengers in your vehicle are covered, regardless of who is at fault for the accident. Auto medical payment coverage is required only in certain states, typically the so-called "no-fault" insurance states. Be cost conscious about purchasing the medical component of an auto insurance policy if you already own a comprehensive medical insurance policy because you may already be adequately covered.

Auto Collision and Comprehensive: Collision coverage pays for damage to your auto in an accident regardless of fault. Comprehensive coverage pays for damage to your auto caused by something other than an accident (i.e., weather, theft, vandalism, etc.), including the loss of personal property within the car. Collision and comprehensive coverage typically carries a deductible, the out-of-pocket amount for which you are responsible, usually between $250 and $1,000. The higher the deductible is, the less expensive the premium is. Keep in mind that making small claims may ultimately cost you more, with resulting increased premiums. Therefore, it is advisable to retain as high of a deductible amount as you can afford in the event of damage. Having collision and comprehensive coverage is not mandatory. Therefore, with an older-model car, you need to weigh the premium cost against the salvage value because the cost to repair may be more than what the auto is worth.

Homeowner Risk

Homeowner insurance covers the risks associated with damage to your home and its contents and provides liability and medical coverage as well. Homeowner insurance coverage is limited to owner-occupied dwellings of no more than two living units and does not include rental property that you may own. If you rent rather than own your residence, a tenant or renter's insurance version can be obtained to provide protective coverage for damage to the contents within the residence. There are different forms of homeowner insurance to select from depending upon which combination of risks, or perils, you are to be insured against. It's important that you carefully evaluate and understand what risks the policy covers and make sure that adequate coverage amounts are kept up to date. The following are the different homeowner (**HO**) forms of insurance available and the perils covered:

- **HO-1:** Fire, smoke, lightning, windstorms, hail, explosions, riots, civil commotion, vehicles, aircraft, vandalism, theft, and glass breakage.
- **HO-2:** Same as above, plus falling objects; the weight of ice, snow, and sleet; the collapse of buildings; accidental discharge or overflow of water or steam; the explosion of steam or hot water systems; frozen plumbing; heating units; air conditioning systems; domestic appliances; and power surges.
- **HO-3:** The most popular homeowner insurance package because it covers all perils, with the exception of earthquakes, floods, termites, landslides, war, tidal waves, and nuclear accidents.
- **HO-4:** Tenant insurance that is usually similar in coverage to HO-3.

- **HO-5:** Similar to HO-3, plus extended coverage to your personal belongings.
- **HO-6:** Condominium or cooperative insurance, similar to HO-4; make sure coverage fully supplements the condo's or co-op's insurance coverage.

Homeowner insurance replacement coverage can be either for the actual cash value or for the replacement cost of the asset. There is a significant difference in the premium amount and in the claim amount received. With the less expensive cash value replacement policy, the insurance company deducts a certain amount for depreciation from the cash value when it settles the claim in order to account for the fact that the asset was not new when damaged or destroyed. The actual amount determined may mean that you receive only $500 for property that costs $1,500 to replace, while with replacement coverage you would receive $1,500. While it is important to adequately insure personal belongings, it becomes especially important to monitor and maintain adequate *full replacement cost coverage* when insuring your house. You should record and maintain an inventory listing of your possessions and their values. The most expeditious way to do this is to videotape or take pictures of everything inside and outside of your home. In addition, it's wise to keep receipts for the very expensive items. This kind of documentation can be invaluable for recollecting the multitude of accumulated possessions owned and for establishing monetary amounts in an insurance settlement. Under the homeowner policy, you're able to purchase additional specific insurance coverage for precious valuables such as jewelry and artwork that can increase in value over time. The specified items are listed and valued on a separate schedule and should be kept updated with written appraisals that reflect current full replacement costs.

Personal Liability Risk

Personal liability umbrella insurance is an often overlooked form of P&C insurance even though it is relatively inexpensive. The premium is low because the likelihood of you actually using the insurance to protect against the personal liability risk isn't great. However, if you have wealth to preserve, get it. Today's lawsuits are frivolous and high dollar, and if you are perceived to have deep pockets as an affluent high-income earner, you have a greater chance of being sued. Though not likely, it takes only one serious accident occurring in your home or automobile with you faulted for injuries or death to value this protection. Most insurers require you to have both auto and homeowner insurance with them to coordinate and put an *umbrella* over the underlying liability coverage. To obtain umbrella protection, the underlying amount of liability coverage for auto and homeowner insurance usually has to be at a level of at least $500,000 per accident. However, for a reasonable cost, you can obtain a personal umbrella policy to increase your overall liability protection for an amount totaling $1 million and up.

Plan for Insurance Protection and Purchase Insurance Products Only As Part of a Comprehensive Financial Planning Process, Not Piecemeal

When it comes to the topic of insurance, most people are either uninformed or misinformed. Navigating the insurance marketplace can be confusing and the policies purchased often don't include the protections needed or expected. Doing intelligent research and comparing insurance products, policy coverages, and costs are important. However, it's even more important to do this due diligence as part of a comprehensive financial planning process. Use reliable online resources to research insurance product information. The Insurance Information Institute (iii.org) is a reliable insurance information resource that does not sell products. For direct advisory assistance, seek help from a trustworthy comprehensive financial advisor who is compensated by *fee-only*, and not by commissions. You can locate a *fee-only* advisor through the National Association of Personal Financial Advisors (NAPFA) or through the feeonlynetwork.com.

QUIET MILLIONAIRE® SUMMARY

- **Determine and then carefully balance the different ways to manage and protect yourself against risks in life.**
- **Transfer as much catastrophic risk to insurance companies as you can afford to insure.**
- **Understand the intricacies of term and permanent life insurance, and purchase the right kind and amount of protection.**
- **Know how much life insurance is enough.**
- **Don't overlook protecting against the risk of disability, which is more likely to occur than most other forms of risk.**
- **Acquire and maintain adequate automobile, homeowner, property, and casualty insurance protection.**
- **Plan for insurance protection and purchase insurance products only as part of a comprehensive financial planning process, not piecemeal.**

CHAPTER 9

Plan Smartly to Manage
the College Experience

P lanning and managing the college experience is probably the least understood and most underestimated, time-consuming, and expensive financial commitment outside of managing the retirement experience. Some of you may have no personal interest in the college experience, or may have no need to consider this area of financial management. However, keep in mind that others in your life might someday face this challenge, and it could be beneficial if you share this knowledge with them. In particular, if you're a grandparent, you should be aware of the information in order to make college more affordable for your children and grandchildren.

QUIET MILLIONAIRE® WIDSDOM

*If you have a college funding problem, then you'll
also have a retirement funding problem.*

If you have a college funding problem, then you'll also have a retirement funding problem because the two are closely intertwined. Trying to play the catch-up game to meet these financial challenges is playing high-risk financial roulette. The planning required for college and retirement is extensive and must be approached knowledgeably, proactively, and with a long-term perspective using a multitude of comprehensive and coordinated financial management strategies. The huge dollar-size commitment for funding college has a rippling effect upon all areas of your financial life from the day that your child is born to beyond the day that he or she graduates from college. College planning can be overwhelming, and unfortunately, most times it is done on a crisis planning basis.

The college planning information that is presented here will give you a big-picture overview so that you can grasp what challenges you are facing, what needs to be done when, and what the logical approach to the entire college planning process is. By having this knowledge, you can decide whether to undertake the entire college planning process on your own or to seek competent professional help. Unfortunately, sometimes even with professional advice, some of the best college management strategies often are not known or just not used. This is why it is important for you to do your homework and to heed the college planning strategies presented here. These strategies have been tested and proven successful through applied experience and are geared especially toward high-income families who must overcome challenges for receiving college financial aid.

So what are your options for planning and managing the college experience? Save or pay as you go? Borrow or rely on scholarships? Attend the cheapest school possible? Not go to college at all? The best choices will result only through comprehensive college planning, which involves a serious commitment of participation by both the student and the parents. Let's first take a look at some facts about today's college costs and some disturbing trends challenging the affordability of college.

Disturbing Trends Affecting the Affordability of College

College is costly, and costs differs widely. Depending upon the information source, there are differing and confusing figures provided about what the costs are to attend college. This is because some sources refer only to tuition costs, while others include *all* of the costs associated with college: tuition, fees, books, room and board, living expenses, travel expenses to and from college, and pizza money. During the 2019–2020 academic year, the *average* annual combined costs of tuition, fees, room and board was $30,500, totaling $122,000 for a four year degree. This can vary widely. For more detailed information about college costs, go to EducationData.org. Keep in mind that these costs don't include all the other forms of extra costs mentioned above. Most importantly, these dollar costs are *after-tax* numbers, and therefore it is the larger pretax dollar amount that you must accumulate.

College costs are increasing at an annual inflation rate of 8% to 12% depending upon the school. This increase rate is two to three times faster than the annual increases in earned income. Parents with college-bound students are overwhelmed by how much money it takes to pay for a college education. Although the cost for everything increases because of inflation, the costs for college are inflating two to three times faster and consuming a larger percentage of the household budget. Furthermore, state-supported schools are receiving reduced subsidies because of state government budgetary woes. As a result, tuition for state schools have been increasing even more rapidly than for private schools, while the financial aid assistance from the state schools has been decreasing as well.

College costs per year for educating just one student can consume between 15% to 30% of a household's net after-tax earned income. Let's put the percentages into a dollar perspective. If you earn $150,000 gross annual income, and your net annual take-home pay is $100,000, then a $30,000 annual out-of-pocket full year of college would require 30% of your net annual income.

High-income families must earn as much as $2 *pretax* to pay for every $1 of college costs. Ironically, because of the higher tax bite for higher income earners, the cost of college today requires a proportionately higher amount of a high-income family's income and assets than that for a lower-income family. If you are in a high tax bracket, as much as 50% of your gross earned income is depleted by paying federal, state, local, Social Security, and Medicare taxes. This means that in order to pay for a $30,000 per year college bill, you need to earn $60,000 in *pretax* dollars. Therefore, funding the entire four years can easily cost a family $240,000 in *pretax* out-of-pocket dollars. Multiply this number by each additional college-bound child in the family, and the education commitment becomes financially challenging. Furthermore, the dollars required for college often skyrocket even higher because of the fact that only 15% of all undergraduate students actually graduate within the allotted four-year time frame. And then there are those students who may go on to attend graduate school.

Most families are not financially prepared to pay for college, and the competition for college financial aid money is intensifying. Colleges, when determining distribution of financial aid awards, have an *expected minimum education savings* amount that families need to meet for *each* child. Specifically, the colleges typically expect families to have saved at least 1.5% of pretax income for *each* year before the child enters college. For example, if you earn $150,000 pretax and have two children, you are expected to have saved $81,000 toward college over the eighteen-year precollege period ($150,000 x 1.5 percent x 18 years x 2 children). In actuality, only 4% of all college families have saved $5,000 or more for college, and a shocking 50% have saved nothing at all to educate their children.

Today's higher college funding costs will force many parents to delay their retirement, to reduce their accustomed standard of living during retirement, or to never retire at all. Many parents delay having children to pursue careers and develop affluent spending habits. Even after having children, they continue to spend most of their current earned income and do not adequately save for college. Furthermore, any savings program for college must be intelligently invested because the lower the rate of return, the more money you are required to save. Remember that every dollar used to pay for the high cost of college diminishes savings being allocated for funding retirement. Even worse, parents are often required to borrow or withdraw funds from their retirement plans or discontinue contributions toward retirement during the college years. When the college commitment ends, trying to catch up with retirement funding requirements is difficult because there is usually too little time left to accumulate sufficient amounts for living a desired retirement lifestyle.

Borrowing more than ever before is required to fund college. College costs have soared, and larger amounts of savings are required to fund attending college. However, parents typically do not save what is required, and the state governments have drastically cut back on subsidized funding to the state universities and colleges, making them less affordable. The inability for families to afford college has caused heavy borrowing to pay for college, an increasing problem intensified by how the federal government subsidizes higher education. Today, the federal government's subsidization of higher education has shifted from that of providing grants that do not have to be repaid to that of offering student loans, as well as providing education "tax breaks," for which most higher-income families do not qualify. The student loans required for attending college can be staggering. According to Federal Reserve data, as of 2020 the typical amount of a student loan outstanding is between $25,000 to $50,000. The following is a true story that illustrates the long-term ramifications of student borrowing, and while sobering is unfortunately less onerous than many other student loan stories.

Audrey graduated from Ohio State University with $3,500 in student loans. Not bad considering that most undergraduate student loan amounts total over $25,000 upon graduation. However, Audrey then married Jim, who had obtained his law degree by borrowing $65,000 in student loans, which is again not bad considering that the average accumulated debt for law students totals around $95,000. So, Audrey and Jim's combined student loans total $68,500. But, the good news is that the federal government allows them the option to repay all of the debt over thirty years at $400 per month. Jokingly, Audrey says, "Let's hope we stay married that long!"

What Will College Cost You?

Here are some important financial planning questions about college costs that you should think about as early as possible.

- How much money specifically will it cost in future dollars to send your children to college?
- How do you plan to accumulate the required amount?
- How old will you be when your youngest child graduates from college?
- How much money specifically will be required in future dollars to fund your secure retirement?
- How do you plan to pay for college and still adequately fund your retirement objectives?

You'll need realistic answers and solutions for these types of questions to avoid stressful money requirements during the college years and to prevent an uncertain financial situation regarding your retirement years. Most families are not able to set aside the required amounts involved. Furthermore, each year that you postpone your college savings and investment program, the financial commitment becomes increasingly challenging. The result is that parents and/or the students will probably need to consider borrowing options for funding college. However, by starting sooner rather than later to plan and save for college as part of a comprehensive and coordinated financial planning process, you can make the college experience more manageable and less daunting. Furthermore, as part of your comprehensive planning process, you'll know how your ability to retire will be affected, and you will be able to prepare an informed retirement funding analysis as well.

"YOUR FATHER ALWAYS TAKES IT HARD WHEN THAT COLLEGE TUITION BILL ARRIVES IN AUGUST."

©Reprinted with special permission of King Features Syndicate.

Affording College Requires Comprehensive *Financial* Planning by Parents and Proactive *Academic* Planning by Students

The college experience can be a very challenging and stressful milestone for both parents and students, especially when the family has not saved enough money. Procrastination and ignorance about the college planning process are why families often can't afford the preferred college of the student's choice. There are important college planning activities that require coordinated action by both parents and students. Parents need to plan financially and the students need to prepare academically for the college challenge. In college planning, timing is everything. Most families wait until the junior year or, even worse, the senior year of high school to start thinking about college. This is a serious mistake. Successful college planning depends upon important student academic decisions and family financial strategies being implemented throughout the entire four years of high school. Furthermore, everyone involved in the college planning process should be aware of each other's responsibilities and should approach the process as a coordinated team effort. The number of college planning activities increases each year as the commitment becomes closer. Many of the activities, if started early, will set the groundwork for a successful outcome. Poor planning, or no planning, makes it impossible to manage everything that needs to be done before and after the critical middle of the student's junior year in high school. Now the big question: How can you properly manage the college commitment and avoid very costly college planning mistakes? First, you should start by assuming responsibility for taking the actions recommended without procrastinating. By parents and students working together to responsibly do what's recommended, the college experience will be more manageable and less stressful.

Parent Responsibilities

Determine your funding commitment, and commit early to a savings program that increases as your income increases. If you don't know where you're going, you won't know how to get there. It's that simple. So, it is extremely important that you realize specifically the magnitude of dollars that will be required to fund the college commitment. Also, appreciate how powerful the compounding interest effect of investing over time is, and that delaying the savings program robs you from reaping its benefits. Go to Investor.gov for a compound interest calculator, which you can use to input your college savings plan, and see first-hand the power of compound interest.

Understand the financial aid system. Financial aid determination starts with the calculation of your expected family contribution (EFC), which is the amount of money you are expected to pay toward college. Using a government-mandated federal methodology formula, the calculation is based upon data about family income and assets, family size, and the number of other college students in the family. The data is submitted to the Department of Education for processing on a form known as the **Free Application for Federal Student Aid (FAFSA).** The first time this form is submitted occurs in January through March of the student's senior year in high school. The requested information includes financial data for both the student and the parents and uses the most current values for assets as well as income tax return information from the just-ended tax year (all of this is subsequently verified when the final tax return is completed). For each year thereafter that the student attends college, a FAFSA renewal form has to be submitted.

QUIET MILLIONAIRE® WISDOM

*The best overview about the financial aid system
and higher education is provided by the Department
of Education's website, www.ed.gov.*

Many private colleges provide substantial amounts of financial aid using their own endowment money. Therefore, they may inquire even further about your financial situation by using the institutional methodology in addition to the federal methodology to calculate the EFC. This entails submitting additional financial information by completing a **Financial Aid Profile (FAP)** application, also known as a **PROFILE** application. By knowing the components and rationale of the EFC formula, high-income families can legitimately plan ways in advance to improve their eligibility for financial aid. For example, income earned by the student and investments in the student's name are much more heavily weighted and penalized under the EFC formula than are the parents' income and assets. Therefore, tax reduction strategies that advocate titling investments in the child's name may backfire in a costly way when financial aid eligibility is being determined. Later, financial aid strategies specifically for high-income families will be discussed.

Understand how a financial aid need analysis is conducted to avoid possibly overpaying for attending college. A need analysis determines a student's eligibility for financial aid at a particular institution using the following formula:

> COA (Cost Of Attendance)
> – EFC (Expected Family Contribution)
> = FN (Financial Need)

The cost of attendance varies according to each school and includes *all* costs encompassing tuition, fees, books, room and board, daily living expenses, and travel costs, all of which cause the financial need to be different for each school. Be aware that financial aid awards can be discretionary and discriminatory regardless of the calculated financial need. Simplistically, suppose a school costs $20,000 a year to attend and your EFC is calculated to be $10,000. According to the need analysis, your eligibility for financial aid is calculated to be $10,000:

$$\begin{array}{l} \$20{,}000 \text{ (COA)} \\ \underline{-\$10{,}000 \text{ (EFC)}} \\ =\$10{,}000 \text{ (FN)} \end{array}$$

However, just because your financial need is $10,000 does not automatically mean that you will be provided $10,000 in financial aid. While some schools might meet 100% of your financial need, other schools might offer far less financial aid regardless of your calculated financial need. For instance, a school may offer a financial aid amount that meets only 50% ($5,000) of your financial need or an even lower 30% ($3,000), or it might offer no financial aid at all. As will be discussed subsequently, this is why part of your college planning process should be to select and apply to a number of schools having the financial resources and the willingness to offer you financial aid. Otherwise, you could end up paying your EFC *plus* a significant portion of your unmet financial need. In effect, any unmet amount can be considered a premium charged by the college for the student to attend.

Develop an intelligent comprehensive financial planning approach for college planning. It's important that high-income families plan for college as part of a comprehensive financial planning approach in order to be aware of the conflicting benefits and pitfalls that can arise when implementing various college planning strategies. For example, good tax reduction planning can often conflict with and harm opportunities for receiving financial aid, and the financial gains from taxes saved must be weighed against the potential effects upon receiving financial aid awards. Chapter Thirteen will discuss further how financial aid strategies interact with tax reduction strategies as well as how they are affected by investment programs involving 529 college savings plans, uniform gifts to minors accounts, and retirement plans.

Shared Parent-Student Responsibilities

Most students lead hectic daily lives, with their time consumed by school, social activities, and family responsibilities. This often causes them to procrastinate and not take time out to plan for matters that are not immediately pressing. The same holds true for parents, and when the time comes to fund and manage major milestones in life such as a college education for their children, there can be emotional distress for the entire family. Keep in mind that managing the college experience can be stressful for both the parents and the student. The student's transition of leaving family and lifelong friends to attend college away from home can be an emotionally unsettling experience. Insufficient planning for these transitional changes can cause the student to fail academically and be unhappy with the college experience and can possibly result in a costly waste of money for the parents. Allowing procrastination and uninformed decisions to dominate the college planning process unquestionably increases the risk for an unsuccessful outcome.

Prepare and support your student for attending college. Part of the parents' college planning responsibility is to help the student prepare academically and socially for college. Remember, the student alone cannot be expected to do all that is necessary without guidance from his or her parents to supplement what the schools cannot provide in preparing for college.

This is a process that should be considered and monitored throughout the student's high school career. Unfortunately, parents are often consumed with managing their own life issues, are uninformed about the college needs of their children, and rely too heavily upon the schools to provide the required guidance. It is extremely important that parents communicate and support their student by working together closely on all college planning activities. This is a team effort, and there is a direct correlation between the student's success and the amount of parent interest and involvement in preparing the student for college.

Start academic planning for college early. Not every student is destined to attend Harvard. Accordingly, there should be a proactive and realistic assessment of the student's intellectual and academic capabilities. Ideally, this assessment should be accomplished by the student's first year in high school in order to determine what coursework should be selected throughout high school and to help avoid frustration and disappointment. Parents should be careful to guide, not direct, the student's decision-making process, and this is where the school's guidance counselor can be helpful. Be sure to fully utilize the resources of the high school's guidance department, and start early by meeting with the guidance counselor before the student starts the first year of high school. In order to best guide the student, it is important that the guidance counselor be familiar with the student's capabilities and education objectives, and often this requires that the parents and the student proactively interact with the counselor.

Review possible career interests and select appropriate college preparatory courses. Many students have no idea what they want to choose as a work career, while others seem to know from a very early age. It is important to stimulate thoughts about possible future ambitions. Open family discussion about the student's possible career interests should begin as early as possible. This enables parents to more intelligently participate with the guidance counselor about which courses should be taken throughout the four years of high school to best prepare the student for college entrance and career qualifications. For example, it would make no sense to load a student up with a bunch of math and science courses if he or she wants to be a journalist, or to load up on art and English courses if he or she is headed toward the medical field. As the student begins to define career interests, have him or her research the qualifications and job activities for his or her career interests and interview people currently working in these areas to help further tighten career choices.

Develop productive study habits, time management, and research and organizational skills. Parents, by providing for their student a study environment without tempting distractions such as television and non-study computer activities, will help assure academic competitiveness during high school. Students need to know how to research, study, and absorb large amounts of information, and then regurgitate the knowledge for understanding and testing. This will pay even bigger dividends when the student is in the more challenging environment of college academics. Often, developing this discipline before college can mean the difference between academic success and failure when attending college.

Student Responsibilities

Participate and assume leadership roles in school and community activities. The message here is to make after-school hours count. By participating in group activities such as sports and clubs, students develop social and leadership skills and learn to both compete and cooperate. Keep in mind that there are many ways to be a "star" and develop talents that exist beyond athletic activities. Colleges take into consideration the importance of the student's background, involvement in well-chosen activities, and leadership roles assumed.

> *"There are two forms of education. One teaches us how to learn,*
> *and the other teaches us how to live."* —**James Adams**

Don't neglect participation in community activities that involve helping others. Not only is this good as a college planning strategy, but also it helps develop the student's appreciation for a more beneficial living situation. This appreciation may also serve to reduce the stress associated with the student's materialistic peer pressure that is often thrust upon parents as well. With respect to controlling materialism and helping the less fortunate, here is a great opportunity for parents to lead by example.

Learn Managing Finances 101. Students need to understand that money accumulation is most often hard earned and needs to be managed intelligently. Unfortunately, many parents may not serve as good examples or role models for intelligent financial management. Furthermore, schools do not teach it effectively, if at all. As a result, many students go off to college and can't even balance a checkbook. Even worse, they typically get inundated with irresponsible credit card offers that can lead to trouble with reckless spending. Early learning of intelligent financial management will benefit the student as he or she transitions to living more independently while attending college and thereafter.

Develop a college entrance exam strategy to achieve the best possible test score results. The college admission process is competitive. Taking college entrance exams often causes the student anxiety and stress. Although the test scores alone do not determine an admission decision, a higher college entrance test score can make the difference in being accepted by a top-choice quality school, as well as being awarded financial aid. This is particularly the situation when the applications coming from students with similar grade point averages and comparable extracurricular activities are reviewed.

There are two not-for-profit college entrance exam sponsors: the College Board, which offers the SAT tests, and the American College Testing program, which offers the ACT test. Students often inquire about the differences between the SAT and the ACT and are usually concerned with how the scores on one test compare to the scores on the other. It's important to understand that some students do better on one test than the other. A student may be better suited to the English and reading sections of the ACT if he or she has strong grammar and reading skills. A student with a stronger vocabulary may find the SAT verbal section easier to handle. Math on the ACT tends to include some basic trigonometry, while SAT math does not go past basic geometry.

The best advice for students is to take both the SAT and ACT tests and determine the best outcome. Sample questions and exams are made available from the organizations that administer both tests. Because most colleges will accept either ACT or SAT scores, it's advantageous for the student to take both exams and submit the best comparative result. For example, if you score 1650 overall on the three-section SAT but a 29 composite on the ACT, you're better off submitting the ACT score. If the high school permits, taking these college entrance exams should ideally start during the sophomore year to gain familiarity with the testing environment and test content.

The Preliminary SAT/National Merit Scholarship Qualifying Test (PSAT/NMSQT®) should be taken in the sophomore year for familiarity and retaken in the junior year. Students attending high school for the full four years before entering college must take the PSAT/NMSQT in their junior year in order to enter the National Merit Scholarship Competition (NMSC). NMSC scholarships are awarded in the spring of the senior high school year. Registration for the test is done by the high school, not the student. Interested students should see their counselors no later than the beginning of their junior high school year to arrange taking the PSAT/NMSQT in October.

The National Merit Scholarship competition finalists have an opportunity to receive scholarship money from three sources. First, there are **National Merit Scholarships,** where finalists compete for a *one-time* $2,500 payment towards the student's freshman year. This is a prestigious scholarship that's awarded on a state representational basis. Second, there are **corporate-sponsored merit scholarships** for children of the company's employees, or residents of a community where a company has operations, or where the finalists have career plans that match what the corporate sponsor wishes to encourage. These scholarships may be either *renewable* for four years of undergraduate study or awarded on a *one-time* basis. Third, there are **college-sponsored merit scholarships** offered by sponsoring colleges to finalists who have been accepted for admission and have informed the NMSC within published deadlines that the sponsor college is their first choice to attend. These awards are *renewable* for up to four years of undergraduate study. Regardless of whether the student takes the PSAT/NMSQT to qualify for the National Merit Scholarship Competition, the student should take both the SAT and ACT tests no later than the fall and spring of their junior year in high school. If necessary, a test preparation course should be taken to improve test score results. Be aware that test scores tend to be better the second time around as a result of increased comfort and familiarity. In any event, the best test results, regardless of when taken, are those used for purposes of college admission.

Diligently compose essays and a personal résumé for college admissions and scholarship awards. Many schools require that an essay be written as part of the application process, with the subject matter and length being specified. This important activity is often not given much effort by the student. It takes quiet blocks of time and a number of revisions to prepare these important written communications. Typically, the essay is a personal statement about a particular life event, a significant period, or a value that has influenced the student's very young life in a heartfelt and honest way. This is not the time to be artificial or contrived just to impress the reader. The structure and content should be well thought out for development and refinement in advance of submission. It sometimes helps the student to start a diary or journal to collect and recall significant life events for these essays. Parents can also help the student brainstorm and compose essay topics, but they must be careful not to taint the creative process by doing too much or going beyond the student's comfort level with their participation. Usually, but not always because of time limitations, an English teacher's or a guidance counselor's involvement can be beneficial in helping with the student's essay.

Select and approach potential providers of recommendations. The student should develop an interacting relationship with at least two teachers for deriving recommendations as part of the college admissions application process. It is also extremely important that the student's guidance counselor become familiar with the student's capabilities and college objectives. Parents would be wise to participate here too.

Hone the student's written and verbal communication skills. Articulate communication is important throughout life. It is a fact that perception and judgment by others is influenced by how well we express ourselves via all means of communication. For students, good communication can improve the "marketing" of themselves in the written college admission requirements as well as in their scholarship opportunities. This will also benefit students during the interviewing process, which many college admissions require. Furthermore, beyond college, these developed written and verbal skills will go a long way toward establishing and advancing students in a successful career.

How to Select the Right College

Because of a lack of knowledge about the college selection process, surveys reveal that only 15% of all college-bound students wind up completely happy with their choice. In addition, consider that students switching to a different school is costly. Choosing the "right" college that fits the student's personality and the parents' affordability is a very important decision. A good decision assures a smoother transition from high school and increases the probability that the student will graduate with an undergraduate degree and a job in four years.

QUIET MILLIONAIRE® WISDOM

*Selecting the right college is a critical decision
in the college planning process.*

Often, a poor college selection is made because it is based upon where friends or a high school sweetheart may be attending. With an inappropriate college selection, some students become so distressed or overwhelmed by the experience that they flunk or drop out altogether. These occurrences are costly in time and money. Even if the student decides to transfer to another school, most likely the earned coursework credits will be lost in the process, which then causes greater amounts of money to be paid for college than is necessary.

Sometimes it's not the student's fault that a bad selection is made. Parents often can adversely affect the decision because of their own preference, lack of knowledge, or disinterest. They may influence the decision because of some form of self-interest that is in conflict with the student's best fit, such as preferring the student to attend a college close to home, to attend their own college alma mater, or to go to the least costly school. While it is important to help guide the student, in the end, it should be the student's decision to make. Parents and students working together on the college selection process in a diligent, intelligent, and informed manner can greatly improve the chances for the college experience to be an academic and financial success.

Start the college selection process as early as possible during high school. It takes time to research and evaluate the many important criteria about colleges that are often overlooked in the selection process. If you wait to start your research until the latter part of the junior year or during the senior year of high school, there is a high degree of probability that you will not make the best college selection both financially and for the student's satisfaction. The following are some selection criteria to consider:

Cost: Although important, it does not have to be the driving force if intelligent comprehensive college planning is done.

Value: Weigh the benefits you expect to receive compared to the price you will pay. Choose an affordable college that feels comfortable and is academically challenging to provide a lifelong learning benefit.

Location: Should the student commute or live on campus? Is the distance from home satisfactory? Is the campus setting right: big city urban or quiet rural comfort in a college town? Warm or cold weather? Etc.

Size: Is the campus size right: large with thousands of students and a high student-to-faculty ratio or small with close personalized student interaction with professors?

Diversity: What are the student body personality, background, and geographic and cultural heritage? Is there a religious orientation?

Academics: What percentage of faculty are PhDs? Does the college offer course majors that interest the student and prepare him or her for graduate school or a career choice? What is the attrition rate of students not graduating? Are there co-op programs? Is there job placement assistance?

Campus Life: What are student activities outside of class? Are living and eating arrangements acceptable? Safety? Alcohol and drug policies? Are there fraternities and sororities?

Athletic Programs: If the student wants to participate in a varsity sport, is it a realistic expectation? If not, is there intercollegiate participation, and are there opportunities for intramural and recreational sports?

Extracurricular Activities: Are there activities offered to meet the student's social interests, personal growth, and career aspirations?

Facilities: What is available? Do they include libraries, laboratories, student center, theater, arts, athletic center, and computer resources? How do they accommodate students with special needs or disabilities?

Financial Aid: What types and amounts of assistance are available? Does the school have money to offer if it wants to attract the student?

There is no single resource or easy way to gather information about the selection criteria. Preliminary information is available by viewing college websites and accessing available published materials and software packages. But, in the end, the only way to complete the criteria evaluation process is by making on-campus visits. Remember that visits take place only after as much screening as possible has been done from home.

Select schools where the student profiles in the top 20% of all applicants with respect to grade point average and college entrance exam results. By choosing schools where your child profiles competitively on an academic basis with other students, he or she will be more suitably challenged by his or her education. The parents may be happier financially too because often schools will compete with money to attract more desired students. This is why some schools will not offer a competitive financial aid package if your student is not in the top 20% bracket.

Visit as many selected schools as possible before deciding whether to apply or attend. Keep an open mind with no preconceived notions about schools. Often, following a college visit, initial top choices drop from serious consideration to no consideration, and secondary or previously unknown choices rise to the top. Many high school students base their initial college desirability upon what their parents, guidance counselors, or friends recommend. College guides, magazines, media sports events, or college teams also may influence them. Regardless of how they initially decide upon their college choices, students must visit the campuses of these schools in order to get a true personal feeling about each school. Spring breaks and summer vacations offer valuable free time to tour campuses, ideally before actually applying. Under no circumstance should a decision be made to attend a school without an on-site visit. Personal dialogue with the admissions and financial aid officers and relevant faculty members should take place. Ideally, getting direct feedback from students currently attending and even arranging an overnight stay on campus can be helpful as well.

Commit to using the four-year college planning checklist to pull the process together and to reduce errors and omissions. Both the student and parents should commit to using the below checklist throughout high school. Notice how the number of activities to be implemented increases throughout high school the closer the student gets to college. So remember to start early to plan and prepare for college using a proactive, comprehensive approach. Failure to develop and activate an intelligent college planning process can prove to be a very expensive mistake causing your out of pocket costs for a college education to be greater than necessary or even beyond affordability.

Four-Year College Planning Checklist

Freshman Year

___**Student and Parents:** Explore possible career and college major interests.

___**Student and Parents:** Meet with guidance counselor for a recommended schedule of college prep courses to be taken throughout high school for careers and college majors of interest.

___**Student:** Establish good study habits and commit to a consistent study routine. Strive for a high GPA, especially in required college prep courses. Manage time effectively.

___**Student:** Learn to use the library effectively, including computer research. Enhance vocabulary skills and writing abilities.

___**Student:** Become involved in school and community service activities for use on the résumé when applying to colleges and for scholarships. Strive for leadership positions.

___**Parents:** Calculate your expected family contribution (EFC) to know whether your child is eligible for need-based financial aid and whether legal repositioning of income and assets to increase eligibility is feasible and warranted.

___**Student:** Update the guidance counselor about your career and college major interests and reaffirm that high school course selections remain appropriate. Formulate your sophomore year college prep course schedule.

___**Student:** Seek summer employment for income and savings for college.

Sophomore Year

___**Student and Parents:** Begin college selection process. Review catalogs and websites of colleges that have preferred attributes and academic course majors of interest. Research their history for providing financial aid.

___**Parents:** Recalculate your EFC for determining and implementing appropriate financial aid enhancing strategies prior to the base year calculation.

___**Student:** Consult guidance counselor about registering for the Preliminary Scholastic Aptitude Test (PSAT). These scores are mandatory to be eligible for the National Merit Scholarship Program and certain other scholarships. Take the PSAT test in October for practice in taking college admission tests and to establish eligibility for scholarships.

___**Student:** Continue to participate in school and community service activities to be a more attractive college admissions candidate and improve opportunities for scholarship awards.

___**Student:** Update guidance counselor about your career and college major interests and reaffirm that high school course selections remain appropriate. Formulate your junior year college prep course schedule.

___**Student:** Seek summer employment for income and savings for college.

Junior Year

September–December

___**Student:** Review your cumulative grade point average for possible improvement. Take advanced-placement (AP) courses.

___**Student:** Register and take in October the PSAT test for the second time to qualify for National Merit Scholarship eligibility.

___**Student:** Obtain schedule for SAT and ACT test dates. Register and prepare to take SAT and ACT tests during fall, spring, and summer—the earlier the better to determine whether a test preparation class is needed to improve test score results.

___**Student and Parents:** Attend college night programs and college fairs. Obtain information about colleges of interest.

___**Student and Parents:** Narrow preferred school choices to between ten and twelve that include at least one resident in-state school, one safe school, one reach school, and six to eight "good" financial aid schools that meet your selection criteria.

___**Student and Parents:** Begin to schedule college campus visits. Research local resources for scholarships and grants through guidance counselor, church, employer, chamber of commerce, and local business organizations. Avoid scams that ask for money and offer guarantees.

___**Parents:** Recalculate your EFC. Last chance to reposition income and assets before the base year for determining financial aid calculations that start as of January 1.

January–May

___**Student:** Strive to achieve high GPA. Graduating in the top 10% of the class can offset lower SAT and ACT scores and improve opportunities for being admitted and receiving financial aid from more schools.

___**Student:** Register to take the SAT and ACT tests in spring and summer if did not take in fall. Take test prep course if concerned about results. Have the scores sent to the schools being considered.

___**Student:** If enrolled in advanced-placement courses, take AP tests.

Summer

___**Student and Parents:** Research and review career interests. Interview people working in the careers of interest. Formulate course curriculum for senior year. Seek summer employment.

___**Student and Parents:** Continue to visit colleges being considered.

Senior Year

September–October

___**Student:** Register and retake the ACT and SAT tests in October if necessary. Submit the highest test results to all schools of interest. Note: This submission involves a fee if not completed at the time of test registration.

___**Student:** Compose essays and a résumé for college admissions and scholarships. Seek out two teacher references, and make sure the guidance counselor is familiar with your capabilities and aspirations.

___**Student and Parents:** Firm up narrowed list of eight to twelve colleges for application. Make sure to include "good" financial aid schools that meet selection criteria and where the student profiles in the top 20% relative to all other applicants. Include at least one in-state fallback school.

___**Student and Parents:** Obtain admission applications and prepare to meet specified requirements for narrowed list of colleges. Determine and be prepared to meet admission and financial aid application deadlines. Start submitting through the guidance department the required admissions package for each school. Be prepared to encounter possible resistance from the guidance counselor for submitting the recommended eight to twelve school applications; guidance counselors typically prefer just two or three.

___**Student and Parents:** Continue to visit college campuses on the narrowed list. Thoroughly explore campus, classrooms, and dorms. Speak with students and faculty. Meet with admissions and financial aid officers. Include, if possible, the experience of a student on-campus overnight stay.

November–December

___**Student and Parents:** Complete and submit admission applications before all filing deadlines.

___**Student and Parents:** Obtain from guidance department the FAFSA and the CSS PROFILE financial aid forms. Prepare preliminary IRS tax return. Preliminarily, prepare the FAFSA and, if required, the PROFILE as well as other school-specific financial aid forms for submission in order to meet all financial aid filing deadlines. Note: The FAFSA form cannot be submitted before January 1.

January–May

___**Parents:** Finalize preliminary income tax return for answers on financial aid forms. Complete and submit the FAFSA and, if required, the PROFILE as well as other school- specific financial aid forms by no later than February 1. Keep copies. Meet all financial aid deadlines starting with the earliest.

___**Student:** Verify that midyear transcripts have been sent to each school receiving your application for admission.

___**Parents:** Monitor mail for the Student Aid Report (SAR) and, if submitted, the CSS PROFILE acknowledgment. Note your EFC amount. Review and make any corrections. Resubmit if necessary. If SAR is correct, retain and submit to your final-choice college for selections.

___**Parents:** Send verification and final IRS tax return to each college requesting verification.

___**Student and Parents:** Monitor mail for college acceptances and financial aid awards.

___**Student and Parents:** Review and compare financial aid offers for possible appeal. If housing deposit is required for more than one school, make sure to make any refund requests within deadline.

___**Student and Parents:** If appropriate, appeal financial aid awards in an intelligent, non-threatening manner.

___**Student and Parents:** Review final financial aid awards and make final college selection by May 1. Send required deposit, signed financial aid award offer, SAR, and final grade transcript when available.

Submit all pertinent loan applications. Notify other colleges of your final decision.

___**Student:** Seek summer employment, possibly at the chosen school's locale.

QUIET MILLIONAIRE® SUMMARY

- **Realize that if you have a college funding problem, then you also have a retirement funding problem.**
- **Be aware of the trends challenging the affordability of college in order to plan successfully.**
- **Take time to figure out early what college will cost you and commit to a savings program.**
- **Start the college selection process as early as possible in the high school career.**
- **Know and implement your responsibilities as a parent in the college planning process.**
- **Know and implement your parent-student shared responsibilities in the college planning process.**
- **Help the student know and implement his or her responsibilities in the college planning process.**
- **Become knowledgeable about how to select the right college—the most important decision of the college planning process.**
- **Make on-site college visits.**
- **Commit to using the four-year college planning checklist.**

CHAPTER 10

Fund Affordably the College Experience

I f you diligently plan in advance to manage the college experience, you're already on your way to reducing the financial stress of funding and affording college with less borrowing. Parents, grandparents, and others who are serious about saving for a child's college education have various options to decide upon, which include both intelligent and *not so* intelligent ways to accumulate money for college.

QUIET MILLIONAIRE® WISDOM

The single most important piece of advice to fund and afford college is to systematically start saving early even if initially it is just a small amount that can be increased periodically. This way your commitment is in place, and the power of investment compounding for growth is underway.

Intelligent Ways to Accumulate
Money for Funding College

529 Plan: Certainly, you should consider taking advantage of 529 plans, named after Section 529 of the IRS code, which codifies the plan and provides legislated tax advantages in order to encourage more savings for college. The plans are individually sponsored by the state governments and more recently by a consortium of private colleges. However, you must be cautious about which of the plans you choose to contribute to because there is a vast difference in the quality among the various state and private college sponsorships. You're permitted to open multiple 529 plans and thereby choose to invest with the plans you deem are best for you. The student doesn't have to attend college in the state where the money is saved, and it's possible to transfer from one state's plan to another. Furthermore, at any time you're allowed to switch the student beneficiaries from one family member to another as college funding needs may change.

529 plans come in two basic forms, and depending upon the state, you can use either one or both types of plans. One type is termed a **guaranteed prepaid tuition plan**, whereby the contributions are placed in an account that the state "guarantees" a rate of return that will keep up with tomorrow's inflated tuition costs. The other type of 529 plan is termed a **college savings plan**, which has investment options for you to select from, but the options do not guarantee a performance rate of return. The contributions can be invested in a restricted selection of mutual funds for potential additional growth that is not guaranteed but that is intended to outperform the guaranteed option. In both types, the contributions grow tax free.

Money invested in a 529 plan is not subject to federal taxation and, depending upon the state, may not be subject to state taxation, provided the accumulated funds are used to pay for any *qualified* postsecondary undergraduate and graduate educational expenses. The expenses are considered *qualified* if the withdrawals are used to pay for tuition, fees, books, supplies, and equipment. Room and board expenses are also allowable if the student is deemed attending on a half-time basis or more. Because there are no earned-income restrictions for contributing to a 529 plan, higher-income families are able to benefit from the tax breaks offered by these plans. This is significant because high-income earners are typically excluded from using most other tax breaks allowable for education funding.

The states compete with each other nationwide for attracting investment funds to their state. Therefore, some states offer *only* their in-state residents a state income tax deduction on contributions, while other states provide matching contributions for investments made by their residents. Some states join with the federal government in not taxing the 529 plan investment gains when the withdrawals are used to pay for qualified expenses for colleges located within that state. Be cautious about the lure of the individual state incentives because they may not be as beneficial as perceived. The 529 plan investment options are limited and vary in quality. Some plans are substandard and have made deals with big-name investment companies to offer the plans through commissioned salespeople, resulting in excessive operating costs that should be avoided. If the investment options perform poorly and the plan's internal administrative costs are high, the incentives and tax benefits may be offset and meaningless.

An advantage offered by the 529 plan is that parents, grandparents, and others can be the owner of the account rather than the child, and therefore they retain control of the investment money. Furthermore, when determining the financial aid awards, the colleges thereby consider the 529 plan to be an owner asset rather than a student asset, which is less penalizing. However, many colleges now are assessing the saved money as a student asset when structuring their financial aid awards regardless of the titling.

The 529 plan is an especially useful estate planning device for removing large amounts of taxable money rapidly from estates. Ordinarily, individuals can exclude from gift taxation only up to $15,000 annually for each student, or $30,000 for gifts made by married taxpayers. However, if the money is contributed to a 529 plan, five years' worth of annual exclusion gifts can be accelerated into one year. This means that married taxpayers can contribute up to $150,000 ($30,000 x 5 years) (up to $75,000 for individuals) to each student within one year without being concerned about a potential gift or estate tax liability. But, *the contributor must be sure not to make any other monetary gifts to the student during the five-year period.* Also, if the contributor dies before the end of the five-year period, the estate would include the prorated remaining balance of the contribution for federal estate tax purposes, but the earnings and appreciation would be ignored. For additional information about 529 plans, go to the College Savings Plans Network and/or SavingforCollege.com.

Coverdell Education Savings Account: The Coverdell Education Savings Account (formerly known as an Education IRA) is named after the late Senator Paul Coverdell, who sponsored the legislation that created the account. Withdrawals from the Coverdell can be used to pay for qualified college expenses as well as qualified elementary and secondary school expenses, both public and private schools. The 529 plan withdrawals can be used to pay for only qualified college expenses. Qualified Coverdell expenses include room and board, tutoring, computer equipment, uniforms, and extended day care program costs. Contributions to the Coverdell are not tax deductible, are limited to $2,000 annually per each student under the age of eighteen, and can be made as late as the April 15 tax filing deadline. Although the contributions are not tax deductible, the withdrawals are tax free as long as the money pays for qualified education expenses. Coverdell funds must be used by the time the student turns thirty, or else the account owner is assessed a 10% penalty and taxed on the investment gains. Allowable contributions to the Coverdell are phased out for married taxpayers with an adjusted gross income between $190,000 and $220,000 and for individual taxpayers with an adjusted gross income between $95,000 and $110,000. Therefore, high-income earners may not be eligible to contribute to the Coverdell but can contribute to a 529 plan, which has no income restrictions. However, if eligible for both, contributing to a Coverdell does not limit your ability to simultaneously contribute to a 529 plan. This ability to contribute to both enables a more diversified investment approach for college savings because the Coverdell does not restrict where the money can be invested as the 529 plan does.

Be aware that in determining financial aid eligibility, the Coverdell account is automatically assessed as a more heavily weighted student asset, whereas the money in a 529 plan can be considered as a less penalizing parent or grandparent asset. Furthermore, control of the money in a Coverdell is automatically transferred to the child at age eighteen, whereas control of the money in a 529 plan is never relinquished by the adult owner. With respect to financial aid planning, if the student is not expected to receive need-based financial aid, and if you are eligible to contribute, then the Coverdell account should be considered for use as a college savings vehicle because the contribution amount is limited to only $2,000 per year for each student. Therefore, the relatively small amount of money accumulated in a Coverdell account will have little influence upon any financial aid determination that is not based upon need. For more information about Coverdell ESAs, go to SavingforCollege.com.

Taxable Investment Account (not tax deferred): The investment gains and income earned in a taxable account are subject to taxation each year and are not tax deferred. However, with intelligent investment and tax management, the annual tax consequences for a taxable account due to capital gains, dividends, and interest can be kept low and sometimes can be a better way to save for college than saving in either a 529 plan or a Coverdell account.

This is because money in a taxable account that is in the name of a parent, grandparent, or business, instead of in the student's name or designated as a college savings vehicle, can have a lesser negative effect upon financial aid award determinations. Furthermore, an appeal can be made to the financial aid office that the use of the money in a taxable account is necessary for retirement or for purposes other than college funding, which cannot be a valid appeal for money in a 529 plan or Coverdell. Certainly, your investment program for college funding should include taxable accounts for this reason, and it gives you flexibility to use the money for any purpose, including college if required.

Roth IRA: The Roth IRA is primarily intended for use as a retirement savings account, and every effort should be made to keep Roth money for use during retirement and not use it for college funding. However, the Roth IRA can be an effective savings tool for college funding, and money inside a Roth does not affect financial aid awards. Certainly, anyone who earns less than the modified adjusted gross income (MAGI) eligibility requirements to contribute annually to a Roth IRA should consider contributing annually the maximum up to $6,000 if under age 50; $7,000 if over age 50. For the tax year 2020, the MAGI must be under $139,000 for single filing, under $206,0000, for married filing jointly. With respect to making withdrawals from a Roth IRA to pay for college expenses, because the contributions are made on an after-tax basis, the *principal* (the amount contributed) portion of the withdrawal is tax free and penalty free at any time. Similarly, with respect to the *investment gains* portion of the withdrawals from a Roth IRA, there are also no taxes or penalties for paying college expenses if the Roth has existed for at least five years from January 1 of the year you made your first contribution and you are at least 59½ years old. Otherwise, the investment gains portion (only) of the withdrawals for paying college expenses is taxed as income, but the 10% penalty for early pre-59½ withdrawals is waived. You should be aware that parents can contribute an amount up to $6,000 a year to a Roth IRA for their college-bound student, provided that the student earns a comparable amount up to $6,000. This is worthwhile because if the Roth money is not used by the student to pay for college expenses, up to $10,000 can be withdrawn both penalty free and tax free for a first-time house purchase, or, alternatively, the money can be allowed to grow forever tax free and be used by the student for future retirement.

Traditional or Regular IRA: A traditional IRA can be used the same way as a Roth IRA to fund college and with the same restrictions. However, there is a significant disadvantage in using the traditional IRA because the contributions made to a traditional IRA are usually done on a pretax basis instead of on an after-tax basis as is done for the Roth IRA. This means that the *entire* pretax amount of any withdrawals from a traditional IRA is subject to income taxes, while only the *investment gains* portion of taxable withdrawals from a Roth are taxed.

Not So Intelligent Ways to Accumulate Money for Funding College

There are some not so intelligent ways to save for college that should be avoided because they can harm your chances for receiving financial aid or because they are not the best type of savings vehicle for college or any other long-term accumulation purpose.

Uniform Transfers to Minors Act (UTMA) or Uniform Gifts to Minors Act (UGMA) Account: A minor's account is a way to maintain control of money for minor children until they reach the legal age of *maturity* at eighteen or twenty-one, depending upon state law. Often, the motivation for opening a minor's account is to accumulate money in the child's lower tax bracket with less income tax consequences. However, you have to be aware of the "kiddie" tax that comes into play until the child reaches age fourteen. As of 2020, the "kiddie" tax rules allow a child under age fourteen to receive $2,200 in investment income (interest, dividends, or capital gains) free of any income tax. Any investment income above that for the child is taxed at the parents' higher income tax rate. Using a minor's account to reduce taxes can backfire on financial aid planning strategies and in the end can be more costly than the tax savings gained. This is because college financial aid awards are more negatively affected by accumulated money being titled in the student's name rather than in the parents'. In essence, the attitude of the school is "Spend the child's money first, and then we'll talk to you about financial aid." Another major disadvantage of a minor's account that often causes regret for parents is that the money in the account legally becomes the child's at the lawful age of maturity—age eighteen or twenty-one, depending upon the state. The child is free to take the money without parental consent and spend it any way he or she desires. In fact, there are instances where children have sued parents who have refused to give them their gifted money. Often parents are not aware of these disadvantages associated with a minor's account. When considering putting money in the minor's name, all of the pros and cons must be knowingly measured and weighed. Money that is already in a minor's account can be transferred to a 529 plan, although it could be considered a taxable gift and should not be done without professional guidance.

Annuities: Annuities are sold by insurance companies mainly to accumulate savings on a tax-deferred basis for retirement income. However, the financial use of annuities is sometimes misused and abused by annuity salespeople by being sold as way to save for college without reducing financial aid awards. Their rationale is that annuities are deemed a retirement asset by the colleges and therefore are not considered in the financial aid determinations. While the argument used to frequently work, the college financial aid offices have become wise to this practice, and they now often reduce their financial award amounts by the dollar amounts tucked away in annuities. Some salespeople even suggest that you save for college using an annuity, yet they know that you will have to make penalizing withdrawals to pay for college by incurring income taxes and a 10% early-withdrawal penalty on the growth of the money. The misguided rationale used is that the benefits of tax-deferred investment growth and the limited impact of the accumulated money upon financial aid awards offset the income tax and penalty consequences. However, be very careful about using this approach as a college funding strategy because, as mentioned, the colleges are wise to this maneuver for financial aid purposes. The result is that the cash invested in an annuity for college will probably be considered as being available to pay for college; therefore, you accomplished nothing beneficial. As discussed, there are more intelligent ways to save for college than using an annuity. In fact, annuities do not usually merit being used as a savings vehicle for college, retirement, or any other purpose, and they should be avoided because of their high costs and the better investment alternatives that exist.

Life Insurance Policies: Life insurance policies that accumulate *cash value* inside of them (whole life, universal life, and variable life insurance) are commonly known as "permanent" insurance policies as opposed to "term" insurance policies that are in force for only a specified number of years. Here again, as with annuities, insurance salespeople are motivated by the higher commissions earned by selling permanent policies as compared to the much smaller commission amounts derived from less costly term insurance policies, which have lower premiums for the same size death benefit. For college planning purposes, the claim for cash value life insurance is that the cash built up inside the policy accumulates in a tax-sheltered environment, is available for use without penalties whenever you want it, and will not be factored into the financial aid formulas. As with annuities, cash value life insurance policies have questionable merit for use as a college savings vehicle. Instead of using permanent life insurance to save for college, it is better to institute a less costly term insurance program whereby you can increase the amount of cash flow available to go toward college savings because of the lower premiums while also providing an even larger death benefit for family survivors. When combining a need for life insurance with a need to save for college, buy term insurance and invest the money from the lower insurance premiums (the difference) in a combination of the previously discussed intelligent ways to save for college.

U.S. Government Series EE Savings Bonds: U.S. Government Series EE savings bonds earn interest that can be tax-free if the bond is used to pay for qualified education expenses or rolled over to a 529 plan. However, the interest earned on EE bonds does not keep up with the increasing college costs.

Bank Certificates of Deposit and Savings Accounts: Bank CDs and savings accounts similarly earn low rates of returns just as U.S. Government Series EE savings bonds do, plus they have the added disadvantage of the interest earned being taxable, regardless of your income level. Low-interest-paying bank accounts should be utilized only for funding short-term cash needs of less than one year and not for a longer-term college savings program that requires more growth.

Alternative Ways to Make College Affordable If You Have Not Saved Enough

Attending college is expensive. Saving enough to cover the entire cost is a challenge, even for high-income families. However, there are alternative ways to help make college more affordable that enable you to avoid borrowing excessively or affecting your retirement objectives.

Attend a community college or a state university. A student can attend a community college or a state university for the first two years, and then transfer to a preferred choice or more expensive college to complete the four-year undergraduate degree. This alternative can reduce college costs and still enable the student to receive a degree from a preferred school. However, there are downside risks. If the student does not attain high grades in transferable course credits while attending the community college or state school, the course credits may be lost with the transfer. This would cause an additional expense to obtain the undergraduate degree and offset intended cost savings. Furthermore, schools often do not offer their best financial aid packages to transfer students. Keep these risks in mind when using this strategy.

Attend a college that offers a cooperative education program. Approximately nine hundred colleges and universities offer cooperative programs whereby the student while attending college alternates periods of full-time classroom study with periods of full-time employment. The cooperative employers are college approved and offer intermittent periods of full-time employment in job fields that the student is interested in pursuing upon graduation. The student usually makes enough money to pay for a good portion of the college costs and often has a preferred opportunity for employment with the cooperative employer upon graduation. The downside to the cooperative education approach is that the full-time employment periods typically extend the graduation time to five or more years. Cooperative education programs should not be confused with the government-sponsored work-study financial aid programs that provide students with part-time jobs on campus or in the local community.

Have the military pay for college. There are two military options you can consider. The first option is the Reserve Officer Training Corps (ROTC), which has branches at many colleges. To qualify for a ROTC scholarship, the student must apply in the senior year of high school and should also have a satisfactory grade point average as well as above-average test scores on the SAT and ACT exams. ROTC scholarships usually cover full or partial college tuition and provide a monthly spending allowance in exchange for required military service after graduation. The second option for having the military pay for a college education is by attending one of the service academies. However, gaining acceptance is extremely competitive. To apply, the student must have excellent grades and high test scores on the SAT and ACT exams. The student must pass the physical requirements and have a recommendation from a congressman or senator. If all of this is accomplished, the student can receive a free college education in exchange for required military service upon graduation.

Attend Advanced-Placement (AP) or College Level Examination Program (CLEP). Students can obtain a four-year undergraduate degree in less time by participating in the Advanced-Placement (AP) and the College Level Examination Program (CLEP). The AP program enables the student to earn college credits by taking advanced courses in high school that are acceptable toward degrees at most colleges and universities. AP courses also allow the student to explore in depth a universe of knowledge covering nineteen subject areas that might otherwise remain untaught in the high school curriculum. This helps the student to gain an edge in college preparation, stand out in the college admissions process, and broaden intellectual horizons. The CLEP provides students of any age or grade level an opportunity to show college-level achievement by taking exams in undergraduate college courses. The student can satisfy a proficiency requirement by demonstrating a mastery of the content of required degree courses such as basic math or a foreign language. Passing CLEP exams can jump-start obtaining required college credits and is also beneficial for dual-degree candidates or students just a few credits shy of college graduation requirements. There are 2,900 colleges that grant credit for advanced standing by passing CLEP exams.

Information about both the AP and CLEP programs can be obtained from the high school guidance department and the website www.collegeboard.com. In conjunction with these programs, a way to further reduce college time and cost is for the student to take extra course loads during each semester and, if necessary, attend summer sessions offered by the college.

Purchase a rental property located where the student attends college for income and tax benefits. The student has to live somewhere, so purchasing rental property near the college provides the student a residence and rental income from other students and derives tax benefits for owning rental property. If the rental property appreciates in value, it can be subsequently sold at a profit, which can then be used to help pay for the cost of college.

Hire the student if you own a business. As an employer, you can pay your student up to $12,000 income per year without incurring income taxes and can deduct it as a business expense. In addition, you can contribute up to $6,000 a year to a Roth IRA in the student's name.

Take advantage of education tax credits. There are two forms of tax-reducing education tax credits available to help offset the costs of higher education, the American Opportunity Tax Credit (formerly Hope Credit) and the Lifetime Learning Credit. Be aware that both credits can't be taken simultaneously for the same student in the same tax year, so there may be times when you have to determine which credit is more advantageous to use in any given tax year. Furthermore, both of these tax credits are entirely phased out if your modified adjusted gross income (MAGI) exceeds $180,000 for married taxpayers or $90,000 for individual taxpayers. In addition, if any free scholarship money is received, then this will also stop any eligibility for taking either of the credits. Keep in mind that the various education tax breaks are loaded with interactive restrictions, and knowing how to use them optimally is confusing. The American Opportunity Tax Credit allows eligible taxpayers to claim a maximum annual credit of $2,500 per eligible student for qualified college expenses paid during the student's four years of college. The Lifetime Learning Credit allows taxpayers to claim an annual tax credit equal to 20% of the first $10,000 in total qualified college expenses for all eligible students in the family up to a maximum of $2,000.

Take advantage of education tax deductions. Education Tax Deductions are allowable for interest paid on education loans, up to a maximum of $2,500 per year provided your income is under certain limits. For additional information about education tax credits and deductions, go to IRS.gov.

Consider college distance learning. College distance learning is becoming more prevalent. With college populations rising, it is becoming impossible to place all college-inspired students physically on campus. Distance learning, where the student and teacher are connected by Internet technology rather than the classroom, is becoming a very viable alternative. This enables more students, especially many part-time working students, to obtain a college education and not to be burdened with a lot of debt to repay after getting their college degree.

How to Get Maximum Financial Aid

Now that you have learned about the ways to save for college and make it more affordable, it is time to proceed to the next step—getting financial aid from the colleges. Knowing about realistic financial aid planning strategies can help you narrow the funding *gap* between what you have accumulated for college and what needs to be paid out of pocket in order to make college more affordable. For high-income families in particular, this is challenging but doable if the financial aid planning process is started early and approached intelligently. The increasing number of students attending college is causing many colleges and universities to expand their faculty and facilities, which is straining the operating budgets and financial resources of the schools. To make matters worse, the federal and state governments have also reduced their subsidies for higher education. In addition, the type of financial aid being provided today is more in the form of loans that have to be repaid rather than grants and scholarships that do not have to be repaid. This combination of circumstances means that there is less money available today for an increased number of students seeking financial assistance, while simultaneously the costs to attend college are rapidly soaring.

Focus on comprehensive college planning strategies and don't waste time and energy searching for private scholarships. Private scholarships account for only 1% of all financial aid money, and they come mainly from local companies, organizations, associations, and employers of family members. Inquire with the high school guidance counselor about which local scholarships might be available and apply to those first. Be aware that private scholarships are often taxable and can jeopardize the financial aid awards provided directly from the school. The other 99% of financial aid comes from the federal government, your resident state, and the schools to which the student applies. Most scholarships provided for high-income families are derived from the colleges directly. Therefore, if you are serious about receiving financial assistance, it makes more sense to spend your time and energy going after the 99% rather than the long-shot 1%. It is also important that you determine each school's policy regarding the receipt of outside scholarships. Some schools will consider the receipt of any outside scholarship money as a replacement for the scholarship money that they were going to award. Alternatively, other schools may instead allow outside scholarships to replace the financial aid loan money instead of their scholarship money.

Select colleges that use financial aid to attract students who do not need it. The determination for need-based financial aid awards is primarily based upon family income levels, and this means that most high-income families are deemed to make too much money. However, because of the increased need and demand for larger amounts of financial aid, some colleges prefer to allocate their financial aid resources to attract students from high-income families who require less financial aid. The result is that students from high-income families who can afford to pay more for college sometimes have an edge in receiving financial aid over equally qualified students who have more of a financial need. While this may not seem fair, keep in mind that operating a college is, in essence, like operating a business, which is meant to be profitable—if it is not profitable, it will go out of business. In fact, there is a new profession that has erupted on the college campuses called the enrollment manager, whose job it is to enroll the most desirable students for the least amount of cost to the college. The more richly endowed *private* colleges use the term "professional judgment" to offer money to students they want to attract, which means that it is possible for many high-income families to receive financial aid awards that enable the student to attend a higher-priced college for an out-of-pocket amount comparable to that of attending the less financially endowed public universities. Moreover, the colleges will compete for a student they want to attract by offering non-need-based financial aid. However, for this to happen, an informed college planning and selection process must be implemented.

Know where the student profiles academically relative to other school applicants. In order to improve financial aid opportunities, you should pick schools where your student profiles as being in the top 20% of all the incoming freshmen with respect to grade point average (GPA) and SAT/ACT scores. You can usually obtain this information from the school's admissions information and website. Although schools offer financial aid based upon need, they definitely give preferential treatment (i.e., more free money, fewer loans) to students who profile in the top 20% of the incoming class. This is done to attract the academically better students to their school. Be sure to use this to your advantage and include schools in your search where your student profiles high academically relative to other like applicants.

Apply to a sufficient number of schools to include those considered good potential providers of financial assistance and those motivated to use it to attract your student. All colleges are not financially equal and generous. Higher-priced private colleges typically have more money to attract students than do the lower-priced state-supported schools. You should research the historical financial aid track record of the colleges to which your student is applying. The College Board (www.collegeboard.com) publishes a College Cost and Financial Aid Handbook, which itemizes the costs to attend each college as well as its financial aid history, typical financial aid packages awarded, average percentage of need met, average student debt, etc., for more than 3,000 two- and four-year colleges. However, be aware that this data is generalized. If the student profiles high academically and the school wants the student to attend, more money can become available even from schools that supposedly have poor financial aid track records. Therefore, you must select and apply to a diversified array and adequate number of schools in order to shake the award money loose. Every school to which the student applies is shown on the financial aid FAFSA application submitted to the processing center. As a result, all of the schools know whether they have to compete financially to attract the student. The student should apply to six to twelve schools that meet criteria for academic major, geographic location, size, etc., and should include as many as possible of those schools having a good financial aid history. This should be done even if the student has a predetermination to attend a particular school in order to generate competing financial aid awards. Furthermore, very often the student's top choice will change during the selection process. Be prepared to meet resistance from the high school guidance departments about processing applications to more than a few colleges. This is because they have a limited amount of time to devote to this activity, and they do not always understand the beneficial outcomes for the student. You may have to be assertive to obtain their cooperation. In the end, it is not the guidance department but the student who has to be happy with the school selected, and it is the parents who have to manage the financial commitment for college.

Apply for financial aid even if you think that you will not qualify. The variables that influence financial awards are numerous, and high-income families should always apply for financial aid. Let's look at an example of a how a college might award financial aid to a high-income family that is determined by a school to have no financial need.

$$\begin{array}{l} \$25{,}000 \text{ (cost of attendance)} \\ -\ \underline{\$50{,}000 \text{ (expected family contribution)}} \\ \$0 \text{ (financial need)} \end{array}$$

Does this mean that the high-income family will not receive any financial aid and might as well not even apply for it? Definitely not! You should apply because each college can award discretionary "professional judgment" money that goes beyond the formula's financial need results. The professional judgment decision may be based upon a multitude of criteria such as the student's ethnic and cultural profile, athletic ability, grades, or geographic background. Some combination of the criteria is what motivates the school to attract the student to attend by offering financial aid regardless of need. However, *financial aid forms must be submitted in order for the colleges to make offers of non-need-based money designed to attract the student.* Many high-income parents do not fill out the financial forms because they assume that it will be a waste of time. This can be a costly mistake.

Understand early how your financial information is evaluated by the colleges. High-income families can also benefit by understanding early on how their financial information is evaluated. The way that assets are titled and which family members earn how much income can make a significant difference in the EFC calculation and can influence the amount of financial aid offered on a professional judgment basis. Specifically, investments titled in the student's name and income earned by the student are weighted much more heavily than if in the parents' names.

- **Assets**: After allowing for an exclusion of a certain amount of assets, the parents' assets are assessed at a low graduated rate between 2.6% and 5.6%, while the student's assets are assessed at a much higher fixed rate of 35%, with no asset exclusion allowance. Assets owned and titled in the name of a business count less heavily in financial calculations than do those titled as personal assets. Furthermore, certain assets are not included at all in the financial aid formulas. For example, the FAFSA does not ask questions involving the value of the personal residence, retirement plans, annuities, and cash values inside life insurance policies. Be aware that tax reduction planning may often conflict with financial aid planning. Many tax advisors do not understand the conflicting interaction of the tax laws with the financial aid rules. For example, you may be advised to title investments in your child's name using a uniform minor's account to reduce parent tax liability. While this advice may help reduce taxes, it can seriously reduce potential financial aid awards in an amount greater than the dollar amount saved on taxes. Furthermore, the tax laws prohibit the child's money in a minor's account from being taken back by parents or anyone else who gifted the money. You should seek the advice of a tax advisor before any money is withdrawn from a minor's account in order to improve financial aid eligibility.

- **Earned Income:** Parents are allowed to exclude a greater portion of their earned income from the financial aid calculations than the student can. Furthermore, the parents' income is assessed at a lower graduated rate ranging from 22% to 47% versus the student's income being assessed at a higher fixed rate of 50%. Always be aware of how the various financial and tax planning transactions affect levels of income, and know that good income tax planning may harm financial aid opportunities. For example, with the increasing graduated assessments being applied to parent income, converting from a traditional IRA to a Roth IRA during the student's base year for the EFC calculation should be avoided. This is because the amount of the converted traditional IRA is shown on the tax return as additional taxable income occurring during the year. While this might be a smart tax and retirement planning maneuver, it will often require explanation to the college financial aid office and could reduce financial aid awards.

- **Investment Income:** As with earned income, investment income is assessed at the different rates as shown above for parents and students. Furthermore, income occurring from gains on the sale of profitable investments during the initial base year for financial aid calculations can adversely impact awards. It is better to wait until either before or after the base year to liquidate profitable taxable investments having gains. This is because the financial aid formulas penalize income more heavily than investment assets being held.

- **Financial Position:** Even if you do not qualify for need-based financial aid, you should position your finances in a manner that allows professional judgment to be used. For example, the college financial aid office may be better able to justify using professional judgment if investment assets are titled and deemed for meeting parents' needs rather than for use by the student. However, make certain that all positioning of assets and income for financial aid purposes is carefully implemented in a manner that is both legal and ethical.

Fill out financial aid applications correctly and do not miss college submission deadlines. The starting point for processing financial aid requests to the colleges is your completion of the **FAFSA** form, which is used to submit your family and financial information through a central processing center operated by the federal government's Department of Education. The FAFSA application has a section for you to list all of the schools where you want the central processing center to forward your processed information. In addition to completing the FAFSA, some private schools will require you to also fill out a **Financial Aid Profile (FAP)**, also known as a **PROFILE** form, as well as their own financial aid forms requesting specific financial information they may want to see. The FAFSA is not available for completion until January 1 of each year. However, it must be processed promptly in January in order for the processing center to get your information to each of the schools in time to meet their financial aid application deadlines. Each school has a specified deadline for submitting financial aid requests. You must be prepared in advance to complete and submit all the required forms within very short allowable time frames in order to be considered for financial aid. Generally, the colleges that have the most financial aid money typically also have the earliest submission deadlines. When completing the FAFSA, the school that has the earliest financial aid deadline dictates the timing for completing the FAFSA processing. Even though current income tax information is requested on the forms, waiting until the tax return is completed may cause you to miss a substantial number of early deadlines. Accordingly, the required tax information must be assembled and submitted on the financial aid forms before the return is prepared. Then, when the final tax return is completed, it is sent to the colleges that request to see it for verification of the data you previously submitted on the financial aid forms.

Mistakes made in completing these forms can cause processing delays and missed deadlines.

One of the major reasons critical financial aid deadlines are missed is because more than 90% of the FAFSA forms are sent back by the processing center because of seemingly harmless errors and inconsistencies in the answers. Minor mistakes such as correcting application errors with Wite-Out and omitting Social Security numbers can cause costly delays in the processing of your information. Other costly mistakes occur in deciding what assets to include and what values to use on the financial aid applications. For example, when valuing your real estate property, are you properly valuing your residence and any other real estate such as rental property? While the FAFSA form does not request information about the primary residence, most of the other financial aid forms do inquire about how much equity value is in your home. Often, home values are overstated on the financial aid forms because families are not familiar with an alternative form of market valuation using an approved "housing index multiplier" formula. The housing inflation index calculates your home's market value based upon the original purchase price and the date of purchase. You might be better off using the "multiplier" value on the financial aid forms instead of providing an estimated value based upon real estate comparables. Of course, if special particulars to your house warrant stating a lower market value, that valuation should be used as long as it can be substantiated.

Follow-up after submitting the completed college financial aid forms. If the FAFSA form is submitted properly during the first go-round, you should receive within approximately four weeks a multipage document from the federal processing center titled the **Student Aid Report (SAR)**, which is a computerized printout of all of the personal and financial information answered on the FAFSA form. The SAR shows your calculated **expected family contribution (EFC)** number, which is the amount that you are expected to pay toward the student's college education. However, the EFC amount shown on the SAR is *not* the number that many private colleges use in their calculations for making financial aid awards. Private schools instead often use the "institutional methodology" rather than the "federal methodology" to calculate your EFC, which typically results in a higher EFC number. The SAR printout information should be reviewed, and you should make corrections to any wrong information that you find on the report. In addition, if you used *estimated* income and tax information when originally submitting the FAFSA, the actual final tax return numbers can be submitted on the SAR. You should return the corrected SAR to the processing center and should also contact the financial aid office at each of the schools that received your original FAFSA information to find out how they want you to submit the corrected SAR information to them. Within two to four weeks after you submit the corrected SAR to the processing center, you should receive an updated SAR reflecting all of your changes. Review the SAR again to make sure the information is correct, and also contact the schools to confirm that they have all of the information required for them to send you a financial aid award letter. Some schools will require you to send them a completed copy of your tax return before they will offer you a financial aid package. Therefore, it is recommended that you prepare your income tax returns as early as possible. Furthermore, some financial aid forms are randomly selected for "verification," which is the equivalent of being selected for an audit by the IRS. If you are selected for verification, you will be asked to supply a copy of your tax returns and additional documentation confirming the income and assets you listed on the financial aid forms. Do not be concerned if you are selected for verification; it is a commonplace activity for determining financial aid awards. By adhering to the above, everything should proceed satisfactorily, and you can expect to receive financial aid award letters during March and April of the student's senior year in high school. May 1 is the usual final date on which the student must decide whether to accept the financial aid award and attend the college.

Determine the school's financial aid policy about providing assistance during the entire four years. While no school will ever provide a four-year financial aid guarantee, the initial award at most schools usually establishes what can be expected unless the family's financial circumstances change significantly. However, some schools award students a higher amount of financial aid for the first year in order to attract them to attend. Then, in years two, three, and four, they offer a much lower package. The school figures the student will be reluctant to transfer after having attended the school for the first year. It could also become a serious problem if family financial circumstances change after the first year and the school will not adjust a student's financial aid package. You should ask the school about its policy for making adjustments if financial adversity should occur for the family or when other younger family members subsequently attend college simultaneously. Knowing what to expect up front can avoid difficulty later. Sometimes it makes sense *not* to apply for financial aid during the first year if proper planning for improving financial aid eligibility has not been done. However, this could backfire because many schools have a policy of giving priority financial aid consideration to incoming freshman and to students who are already receiving financial aid. If this is the case, you may be excluded or may receive an insignificant amount relative to what might have been awarded with intelligent advanced planning.

Don't reject federal work-study awards. The federal work-study program is a form of financial aid that provides part-time jobs for students to help pay for their educational expenses. A set amount of federal funds is made available by the government to the school for disbursement at its discretion to pay for student work. Some schools do not like to see a rejection of their work-study offer, and this can influence their decision about offering other forms of financial aid. The jobs can be on campus working for the school or off campus working for the community with a private nonprofit organization or public agency. However, some schools may have federal work-study arrangements with private for-profit employers, but the jobs must be judged as relevant to the student's course of study. The earned income is not taxable and is not included in the financial aid calculations as earned income by the student. For parents concerned about the work-study program affecting their student's academic achievement, studies reveal that students actually do better academically because they develop more efficient time management and study habits. Furthermore, when assigning work hours, the financial aid administrator and employer consider class schedule and academic progress, and there is a limit as to how much time can be committed because the amount earned cannot exceed the total federal work-study dollar amount awarded.

Don't apply for an "early decision" acceptance and thereby lose your leverage for appealing financial aid awards. By applying for an early-decision acceptance from a college, the student must sign a binding agreement to attend if accepted. Not only does it commit the student to enroll at the college if accepted, but the student must also agree not to apply anywhere else and to withdraw all other applications if accepted. Because the school knows that there are no other colleges in competition for the student, it can allocate its financial aid money to attract other students that remain uncommitted. Therefore, it can be a very costly decision to apply for an early-decision acceptance from a college and lose leverage to appeal for the most possible financial assistance.

Be prepared to appeal financial aid awards. If a school that your student is interested in attending has not offered a competitive financial aid package, be prepared to appeal mis-awards and under-awards from the colleges. Most parents assume that the initial amount of financial aid awarded by a school is final. However, if a school has financial aid resources and really desires the student to attend, it will offer tuition discounts and other forms of financial assistance to attract the student. However, the school will probably not be motivated to compete beyond its initial award unless you can show more generous award letters from other academically competitive schools. This is why it is important to research and apply to a number of schools that are likely to offer your student financial aid. An informed selection process can also help you determine whether a particular school has offered a mis-award or under-award and whether an appeal for increasing the school's initial financial aid award is warranted. The appeal process must be approached intelligently and in a nonthreatening manner. If you have selected colleges with financial resources and a desire to compete for the student, there is often an opportunity to increase the amount of money provided.

Use special family circumstances to increase financial aid awards. There are special circumstances when a family situation does not fit into the "norm." This includes divorced or separated parents; parents owning a business or farm; parents being unemployed, disabled, or deceased; minority students; gifted students and athletes; students qualifying as "independent" students without parent financial support; or families burdened with excessive medical expenses. Many families, in one way or another, do not fit into the statistical norm, and they should be aware of how this affects their opportunities for financial aid. The following are explanations of the special family circumstances that can affect the amount of financial assistance received:

- **Divorced or separated parents:** If the student's parents are divorced or separated (or will be soon), there are a few key things they should know before completing financial aid applications. Only the financial information for the custodial parent with whom the student lives for the majority of the year should be provided on the financial aid forms. This can be done even if the custodial parent does not claim the student as a dependent on his or her income tax return. Custody, rather than financial support, determines financial aid eligibility. For planning purposes, it might be beneficial having the student reside the majority of the time with the parent who has a less favorable financial situation according to financial aid calculations. Private colleges may request information about the income and assets of the "other" divorced parent. While this can impact the amount of the school's own funds awarded, it will not reduce the amount of federal financial aid awarded. If the parent with whom the child resides remarries, information about the income and the assets of the new spouse must be included as if he or she were the biological parent. This may not seem fair, but it is the way the financial aid system works. Putting a financial commitment to fund college for children in a divorce decree can prove harmful to financial aid awards. While this financial assurance cannot always be avoided because of mistrust between ex-spouses, any legal commitment to pay for college is part of the questioning on the financial aid forms. Obviously, this can negate the perceived need for financial aid by a custodial parent to whom the college funding commitment is made.

- **Parents owning a business or farm:** When determining financial aid awards, business assets and farm assets are given less weighting than personal assets. Therefore, it may be beneficial to retitle certain personal assets such as taxable retirement accumulation investment accounts and investment rental properties into a business entity such as a corporation or limited liability company (LLC). Furthermore, as a business owner or farmer, you have an ability to control the amount of your income shown during the years that your student is in college. This income flexibility can increase your financial need amount.

- **Family loss of income because of unemployment, disability, or death:** If the family's breadwinner becomes unemployed, receives notice about potential unemployment, or if as a business owner experiences adversity, you should inform the college financial aid office about the change in financial circumstance. The same applies when a parent becomes disabled or dies. If the school has financial resources and is motivated for the student to attend, extra help may be provided during the period of financial hardship. Expected income, rather than the levels of earnings, will be used to calculate the EFC and the amount of the financial need.

- **Academically gifted students:** High-achieving students academically are always a preference for colleges, and many private schools try to attract top students by offering academic scholarships and grants. Qualifying for a National Merit Scholarship can serve as an announcement to the colleges of an academically gifted student and can provide financial scholarship support that does not decrease the amount of other financial aid awards.

- **Athletes:** Athletic scholarships are tough to come by and should not be relied upon. In most instances, athletic scholarships do not pay for the entire cost of college and should be sought after only as a supplement to other forms of financial aid. That being said, the student does not have to be at top Division I sports caliber to be awarded a scholarship. Division II or III schools will also offer preferential financial packages. Make certain to contact the athletic department and meet with the appropriate coach at each college you visit. Also, have the student's high school coach write letters of recommendation to each college. Keep in mind, however, that there is life after sports for the student, and the academic quality of the school should not be ignored.

- **Minorities:** If your child is African American, Hispanic, Native American, or any other deemed minority, contact the colleges and find out about the availability of scholarship programs for minorities. Although there is controversy over awarding discriminatory types of scholarships, there are some colleges that offer them, and these types of scholarships should be taken advantage of if the student qualifies.

- **Independent students:** An independent student is awarded financial aid based upon his or her financial situation as opposed to that of the parents. Before thinking you will make your child appear to be independent, here are the criteria you must be able to overcome:

  Is the student going to be twenty-four years of age or older before December 31 of the first year of college?

  Is the student a veteran of the armed forces?

  Is the student an orphan or ward of the court?

  Does the student have legal dependents?

  Is the student a graduate or professional student?

  Is the student married?

  If the student's situation does not fit into any of the above questioned circumstances, then he or she can't be considered independent. The schools will look to the parents' financial data even if the student is entirely out on his or her own financially.

- **Excessive medical and disability expenses:** Some families are burdened with high medical bills that take a disproportionate amount of earned income. The financial aid office may take medical hardship into consideration in determining how much money to award, and the circumstances should be brought to the office's attention.

QUIET MILLIONAIRE® WISDOM

Financial aid reduces college out-of-pocket costs and thereby increases the amount of money available for funding other financial goals.

Don't underestimate the financial impact of college upon your ability to adequately meet other financial needs and objectives in life. You must be diligent about your college planning in order to reduce your financial commitment and make college more affordable. Most high-income families do not receive financial assistance without including financial aid planning as part of their comprehensive college planning process. Every family situation presents different financial aid generating opportunities, and you need to plan accordingly. The discussion thus far has been about the best ways to save for college and alternatives to make college more affordable if you have not saved enough, as well as how to get financial aid. However, it's likely that you still have a *gap* to fund, which is the amount of money you owe the college beyond what you have saved and received in financial aid.

How to Fund the "Gap"

When all of your college planning activities, accumulated savings, and financial aid awards in the form of "free money" grants and scholarships are still not enough to pay for college, you have what is termed a funding "gap." Paying out of current cash flow to fund the gap may be an option for some high-income families but often does not make financial sense when low-interest-rate student loans can be used as an alternative. Most families end up having to borrow money to finance college today. Borrowing the wrong way can add thousands of dollars of interest costs to the financial burden of paying for college. Intelligent choices must be made about the best ways to borrow and who does the borrowing—the student or the parents. Loans in the student's name usually have more favorable interest rates and repayment terms. The student can borrow from both the government and "alternative" private loan sources to finance the funding gap of a college education. Federal- and state-sponsored student loans are the least costly way to borrow for college, but they often are not sufficient to cover the entire funding gap and need to be supplemented with borrowings from private lenders. The following is an overview of all of the government and private loan options available to students and parents.

© Reprinted with special permission of King Features Syndicate.

QUIET MILLIONAIRE® WISDOM

The most intelligent borrowing strategy for college funding is to borrow in the student's name and for the parents, if able and warranted, to help repay the student loans.

Student Loans for College Funding

Federal Loans to Students: The federal government lends students two types of college loans (Perkins and Stafford) that have low interest rates and do not require credit history or collateral.

Perkins Loan: The money for Perkins loans is funded by the federal government but is disbursed at the discretion of the colleges to undergraduate and graduate students having *exceptional* financial need, and therefore most families are not eligible. The interest rate is fixed at 5%, and the government subsidizes (pays) the interest costs until nine months after the student graduates, when the loan repayment period begins for as long as ten years. The Perkins loan amount that the student can borrow is determined by the school's financial aid office. For undergraduate students, the amount can be up to $5,500 per year with a cumulative maximum of $27,500; for graduate students, the amount can be up to $8,000 per year with a cumulative limit of $60,000 for the combined undergraduate and graduate Perkins loans.

Stafford Loan: There are two forms of Stafford loans: subsidized or unsubsidized (by the federal government). The **subsidized** Stafford loan is approved for students determined (by federal formula) to have a financial need, and therefore the federal government subsidizes (pays) the accruing interest costs for the student while attending school. The **unsubsidized** Stafford loan is approved for students determined *not* to have a financial need, and therefore the federal government does *not* subsidize (pay) the accruing interest costs while the student is attending school. However, the student can defer paying the accruing interest costs until the loan repayment period begins after graduation by letting the accruing interest be added into the unsubsidized loan amount. The Stafford loan interest rates are relatively low while the student is attending school as well as during the repayment period after graduation. After graduation, all of the individual Stafford loans (subsidized and unsubsidized) can be consolidated into one loan with repayment options from ten years up to as long as thirty years. Stafford loans are worth considering even if you don't need to borrow for college because during the time that the Stafford loans are outstanding you may be able to leverage a higher investment rate of return than the lower tax deductible lower percent interest rate charged.

Unfortunately, the allowable borrowing amounts for Stafford loans are relatively small. Undergraduate students can borrow a combination of subsidized and unsubsidized federal Stafford loans as follows: freshman year $2,625, sophomore year $3,500, junior year $5,500, senior year $5,500, with a cumulative limit of $23,000. Graduate students can borrow $18,500 per year, with a cumulative limit of $65,500 for subsidized loans, which is a combined limit for both the undergraduate and graduate Stafford loans. There are very limited circumstances when the graduate student can borrow additional amounts each year, with the combined cumulative limit being increased to $138,500.

Eligibility for Stafford loans is made automatically by completing the FAFSA form, which is used to apply for all forms of financial aid. Depending upon the determined need for subsidization, the full allowable Stafford loan amount can be divided between subsidized and unsubsidized portions. Even though the unsubsidized Stafford loan is available to all students regardless of financial need, you must still submit the FASFA form in order to be eligible for any Stafford loan money. Furthermore, if additional private student loans are needed, it is required that the Stafford loan be obtained first in order to receive supplemental private student loans. Stafford loans can be obtained either directly from the federal government or through an approved lender. The financial aid office of the college that the student is attending will direct you as to where and how to process the paperwork for the Stafford loan. Upon graduation, the student has the option to use the Federal Consolidation Loan program to consolidate all accumulated

Stafford loans into one low-interest-rate loan with a variety of extended repayment schedules available, which makes repayment more manageable. Keep in mind that the Federal Consolidation Loan program consolidates only Stafford loans and does not include any supplemental private-lender student loans.

State Loans to Students: In addition to providing free money grants and scholarships on a limited basis, many states offer low-interest-rate student loan programs, primarily to finance and retain in-state resident students who plan to pursue certain careers such as social work, medicine, law enforcement, and teaching. Part of the borrowing and financial aid seeking process should include contacting your state's higher education agency to determine what special financial assistance programs may be offered to in-state resident students. However, keep in mind that most of the financial assistance offered by the states is done mainly by supporting state universities and colleges directly in order to provide lower tuition costs for the in-state resident students.

Private Loans to Students: Private-lender student loans, also termed alternative student loans, are uncollateralized loans that typically have higher interest costs than student loans offered by the federal and state government. However, the interest rates and repayment schedules are usually more attractive when compared to the loan options that parents have available for borrowing. Applying for these loans is easy. The Internet offers numerous website sources of private student loans, which can be applied for online. However, it is very important to compare private student loan lenders for the lowest interest rates and loan fees available. Remember that private student loans are not available without first having submitted the FAFSA form to obtain the federal Stafford student loan. The private loans combined with the Stafford loans can be used to finance 100% of an undergraduate and graduate college education. Private student loans accrue interest, which can be added into the loan (capitalized) while the student is attending college. Repayment of the private loans is deferred until after the student graduates, at which time the accumulated private loans can be consolidated into a single loan for one monthly payment amount. The private loan consolidation process is entirely separate from the Federal Consolidation Loan program.

Parent Loans for College Funding

Federal Loans to Parents: Parent Loan for Undergraduate Students (PLUS): Parents can borrow up to 100% of the cost to attend college from the federal government with the Parent Loan for Undergraduate Students (PLUS) program. PLUS loan interest starts to accrue immediately and cannot be added back (capitalized) into the loan amount. The interest rate is fixed at varying relatively low rates, and up to $2,500 of the interest costs is tax deductible annually even if you don't itemize. Repayment of borrowings usually begins sixty days after each disbursement of funds is made to the school. However, some PLUS lenders may permit loan repayment to be deferred until after the student graduates. The repayment term can be up to ten years, but this is not recommended because parents should be striving to have the PLUS loans repaid in full before their retirement. PLUS loans are the financial responsibility of the parents, not the student. Unlike loans to the student, the parents must be creditworthy. If parents are denied a PLUS loan for credit reasons, the student becomes eligible for higher Stafford loan limits. PLUS loans show up on the parents' credit report and could cause interference with their other borrowing needs such as mortgage and auto financing. Therefore, federal loans in the student's name with lower interest rates and more extended repayment terms are recommended instead of the parents borrowing to fund college. Parents still have the option to repay the college loans in the student's name if they are able and if it makes financial sense.

Private Loans to Parents: College Funding Loan: Private loans approved specifically for parents to fund college (also known as alternative loans) are really not any different from other types of credit rating–based loans. These loans should not be used to finance college because they show on your credit report and interfere with your ability to borrow for other purposes such as financing a house or an automobile purchase. As already discussed, it is more desirable that all borrowing for college funding be done in the student's name. Furthermore, if the parents do borrow for college funding, the PLUS loans discussed above or the home equity line of credit, which is discussed next, are preferable alternatives, but neither is recommended.

Home Equity Line of Credit (HELOC): Home equity lines of credit can be used to finance any funding need, including college. The interest costs for home equity loans are tax deductible with limits if you itemize deductions on Schedule A of Form 1040. However, borrowings under the line are not tax deductible if used to pay for the same college expenses paid by another tax-deductible interest borrowing such as a student loan. In other words, there is no double tax deduction benefit for the same college expenses.

Retirement Plan Loan: If your group retirement plan at work permits (not IRAs), you can borrow for college up to 50% of your vested interest in the plan, up to a maximum of $50,000 by law. However, this could present a costly problem if you leave the company under any circumstance with loans outstanding. All borrowings from a retirement plan must be immediately repaid with funds outside the plan or else the loan is considered a distribution subject to all taxation and penalties that would normally apply for withdrawals. Retirement plans are intended to fund retirement, and every effort should be made to avoid using that money to pay for college expenses.

Where to Find Competent Guidance
for College Planning

Determining how to intelligently plan for college, how to select the right colleges, and how to minimize your out-of-pocket costs for college is a complicated process. There is a lot to learn and understand about the "business" aspect of college, how colleges approach filling their student enrollment quotas, and how financial aid is given out. Both the student and parents must be savvy about college planning. Parents also have to be knowledgeable about comprehensive financial planning and tax strategies to make college more affordable. If managing the college experience is done improperly, it usually causes the student to select the wrong school to attend and the parents (and/or the student) to pay unnecessarily large amounts of money out of pocket to fund college at the expense of achieving other financial objectives.

Guidance Counselors: Guidance counselors can play an important role in helping the student structure an academic program to prepare for college. They can assist in identifying colleges of academic interest and coordinate the college application process to include high school transcripts and letters of recommendation. Guidance counselors can also serve as an advocate for the student when the colleges want additional background information about the student and the high school's curriculum. Accordingly, it is very important that both the student and the parents establish an ongoing interaction with the guidance counselor in order for the counselor to be an informed and willing advocate. Don't expect or rely upon high school guidance counselors to provide the comprehensive college planning that is required to make college more affordable. Although most guidance counselors are willing to assist in any way possible, the guidance departments are too busy with many other roles beyond college counseling. This limits the amount of proactive and personal assistance they can provide. Furthermore, they are not knowledgeable about all of the complex financial planning, tax planning, and financial aid planning strategies that require a coordinated comprehensive approach for achieving the best results. The high school's financial aid nights provide too little information too late with respect to financial aid planning. The most that can be expected is merely a last-minute overview of completing the financial aid forms. Unfortunately, this limited instruction is not very effective because more than 90% of the financial aid forms submitted for processing are returned because of errors and omissions. As a result, financial aid deadlines for submitting applications are often missed. There is much more to be done besides just filling out the requested information on the financial aid forms and waiting for your award letters from the colleges. This approach is very costly, and the high schools do not have the time or the training to help you with *all* of the necessary college funding and financial aid strategy needs.

College Financial Aid Officers: Don't rely upon the college financial aid officers at the colleges to help you apply for financial aid. Asking the financial aid officer to help you get more money from the school is like going to the IRS and asking it to help you save money on your taxes. It's not in the college's best interest to show you how to get the most money from the school. It has a limited amount of funds to give out to a large number of students who request financial aid.

Professional College Planners: Many families mistakenly believe that they can manage the college experience on their own. But parents lack knowledge about the enormity of the college planning process, which requires comprehensive and coordinated activities being taken on by both the student and the parents. They also don't realize how costly mistakes can be. Doing it yourself using free advice may be cheap, but paying for competent, good professional advice can be a wise investment. You probably would not hesitate to pay a tax advisor for help to lower your tax liability or pay a lawyer to avoid losing money from a lawsuit. So, why would you not consider using a qualified college planning professional to help lower your out-of-pocket financial commitment for college—especially because the financial commitment to attend college can be as much as $25,000 to $50,000 a year? By starting the college planning process early and relying upon the *right* kind of guidance, the fee charged should more than pay for itself many times over by costs saved.

What should you look for in a professional college planning advisor? Unfortunately, college planning advisors are an unregulated group, and some are loaded with defrauding schemes to take your money in exchange for providing suspect results. These advisors have different forms, and one can be a commission-hungry insurance agent whose college planning agenda centers on selling you a cash value life insurance policy or an annuity as a way to exclude accumulated money from being calculated in the financial aid formulas. This agenda is lucrative for them and costly for you. Another such advisor comes in the form of financial aid and scholarship search companies that promise and "guarantee" to obtain money for families with college-bound students. These firms are typically not reputable and use official-sounding names in order to appear professional and legitimate. Just about all families with a college-bound student receive unsolicited enticing letters saying "Your student has been selected" or "We guarantee to get thousands of dollars in financial aid and scholarships." They typically require that an up-front fee be paid and offer a full money-back guarantee if the promised results are not produced. However, in the end, these supposedly reputable firms either vanish or do not deliver on anything, including their guarantee to return your money. *Never pay anything to anyone making these kinds of offers.*

As discussed, a comprehensive financial planning approach is required for effective college planning. That is what you need to look for in a college planning advisor: one who is a *fee-only* advisor and not biased with advice that is motivated to push financial products to earn a commission. Also, be aware that the term "fee-based advisor" implies fee-only and can be misleading. Fee-based means that the advisor charges fees but is also licensed to sell financial products and receive commissions as well. Subsequently, you will be shown how to find a competent financial advisor who can guide you with a comprehensive financial planning approach, which includes the college planning process. Once you get through managing and paying for the college experience, it is all too short a time before the reality of retirement comes into focus. The next two chapters will cover how to manage, afford, and enjoy your retirement experience where you can feel financially independent and secure about not running out of money when you stop earning an income.

QUIET MILLIONAIRE® SUMMARY

- Use the 529 college savings plan, Coverdell education savings account, Roth IRA, and taxable investment account to intelligently save for college.
- Avoid using the minor's account, annuity, cash value life insurance, U.S. Government EE bond, bank certificate of deposit, and savings account to save for college.
- Consider the alternative ways to make college more affordable if you have not saved enough.
- Apply to a sufficient number of schools.
- Don't apply for early-decision acceptance for college.
- Understand the financial aid system and how it applies to you, and then plan and apply for financial aid accordingly.
- Use student loans, not parent loans, to fund the "gap" between the cost of attending college and what you have saved and received in free financial aid.

- Know where to find and use a competent and comprehensive college planning professional if you are not fully prepared and willing to knowledgeably complete the process on your own.
- Don't jeopardize funding your other lifetime objectives such as retirement by paying too much for college.

CHAPTER 11

Make Working or Retiring Optional

Do you know that prior to the twentieth century, people typically worked until the day they died? Retirement as a way of life didn't exist! Then, by the 1950s, 50% of all workers were able to stop working to retire by age 65. By the 1990s, the percentage of workers able to retire by age 65 had increased to 84%. However, retirement trends are changing again. Now, an increasing percentage of people over age 65 are continuing to work. Some by choice, but for many others, it's to maintain their standard of living or just to survive financially. The meaning of "retirement" is different for all of us. What does retirement mean to you? Being free to do what you want without working and without worrying about money? Being financially independent and feeling secure enough about not outliving your money? Being able to do something that you really want to do by starting a new and exciting second career? Maybe you'll never retire per se. If so, hopefully it'll be for the right reasons. Unfortunately, ill-fated retirement outcomes are becoming more and more common, but can be avoided with some intelligent retirement planning. However, when it comes to planning for retirement as well as other financial objectives, people seem to make costly and unnecessary mistakes through ignorance and procrastination.

QUIET MILLIONAIRE® WISDOM

People don't plan to fail, they fail to plan.

Failing to plan and start early to save enough for retirement are the main reasons that most people cannot afford to retire. They dream and wish and hope rather than set specific goals and seriously work a plan to achieve them. The quiet millionaire knows that the failure to plan and save for retirement can become an overwhelming mistake because it is usually impossible to play "catch up" during the accumulation stage for retirement and there is no turning back once the actual retirement decision has been made. Keep in mind that retirement can be made by choice as planned or by circumstance, which may not always be on your terms. Unfortunately, many high-income earners are irresponsible, extravagant spenders who typically allocate only a relatively small portion of each paycheck for retirement savings. They foolishly believe that the cost of not planning and saving for retirement is small and that it will take only a little bit of extra effort in the future to make up for lost time. Not knowing what needs to be done (lack of knowledge) and putting off what needs to be done (procrastination) make up a deadly combination that steals potential wealth. This chapter reviews the reasons and the dynamic trends affecting the affordability of retirement. Knowing these trends will alert you to the mounting obstacles and pitfalls associated with retirement planning and why you must start intelligent planning earlier and more diligently than previous generations of workers. You will also be shown how to determine whether you will be able to quit working when you want to and not run out of money.

Dynamic Trends Affecting the
Affordability of Retirement

Pension income retirement plans are being replaced by employee contribution retirement plans. Historically, the pension *benefit* retirement plan funded by the employer provided the employee a lifetime of *certain* retirement income. Today, it is being replaced with the employee *contribution* retirement plan being funded primarily by the employee, which provides the employee an *uncertain* amount of retirement income. It used to be commonplace that people remained with the same employer for their entire working life and in return the employer funded a pension income retirement plan, which provided the employees with income for their entire retirement life. The amount of the retirement income benefit was defined based upon the employees' length of employment and income level, and accordingly the pension plan in technical terms is referred to as a *defined benefit plan*. Today, the structure and funding of retirement plans have changed to an employee contribution retirement plan because employees typically make multiple job changes and because the pension funding requirements have become too costly for employers. Instead, it is now the employees who are primarily responsible for funding their own retirement income needs by contributing a defined amount of their earned income to a retirement plan such as a 401(k), 403(b), SEP-IRA, or SIMPLE-IRA plan, which in technical terms is referred to as a *defined contribution plan*. Unfortunately, most workers do not sufficiently save for their retirement. Furthermore, the employee contribution retirement savings plans often offer limited and underperforming investment options from which to select. Moreover, even when employees are offered worthwhile investment options, many plan participants make poor selections for achieving the required growth. Worst of all, some retirement plans encourage or require that employee investments be concentrated in the employer's company stock. This lack of diversification can be very risky even if the company stock is of a large publicly traded company.

People are living longer during retirement and, therefore, need to accumulate more money than ever before to last a lifetime. Today, a 65-year-old male can expect to live another 16 years on average, while a female at age 65 can expect to live another 19½ years. This means that there will be an increasingly large widowed population, especially when you consider that most wives are younger than their husbands. Therefore, women are even more likely to experience the consequences of inadequate savings for retirement. Most workers are not making the maximum contributions allowable to their retirement plans. Even if they are saving the maximum allowable in their retirement savings plan, that amount alone will usually be far from sufficient to meet many accustomed standards of living. Supplemental saving for retirement must also be done beyond just retirement plans and IRAs. However, research shows that the savings rate for average American workers as a percentage of their income is near zero. In other words, they spend what they make. Most pre-retirees and retirees do not understand how fast increases in the cost of living, income taxes, estate taxes, and a catastrophic illness can wipe out even substantial retirement saving accumulations. You need to account for these things to plan and save adequately so you can know for sure when you can quit work.

Because of poorly structured investment management programs, it will take a longer time and require larger amounts of money to be accumulated to fund a secure retirement. For overly aggressive investors, greed often turns to grief when stock market adjustments cause devastating losses. Alternatively, for overly conservative investors, their money is often not working hard enough to grow and keep pace with inflation. By intelligently structuring your investment portfolio in accordance with your risk tolerance comfort level, you can let your money work harder for you instead of you working harder for your money.

Social Security alone will no longer be a reliable source of adequate income for retirement security. Social Security started in 1935 and was greatly liberalized between 1950 and 1975. Since then, the demographics have changed so that today the ratio of retirees collecting Social Security checks is increasing relative to the number of current workers who are contributing to the system. This has made the financial future of Social Security become uncertain and unsound unless restructuring and additional funding is implemented. Social Security presently represents about 40% of the retirement income that the average retiree lives on. However, Social Security is becoming the primary source of retirement income for the increasing number of baby boomers who are retiring. This is because the private pension income retirement plan is disappearing, and the amount of savings being set aside by workers for adequately funding their retirement income needs is insufficient. As a result, the present structure of the Social Security system will be challenged by the increasing demographic and financial demands being made upon it. There have been various proposals made for fixing the Social Security system. One proposal is to increase the eligibility ages for collecting benefits. This would result in a lesser funding liability because of a longer contributing period by workers and a shorter withdrawing period by recipients. Although it is only a partial solution, it is reasonable because people are living longer and staying healthier, and more of today's jobs do not require physical labor. It is possible that Social Security benefits will become indexed according to the retiree's total income level and financial need, which would phase out benefits entirely for the more affluent retiree. In fact, the current taxation of Social Security income benefits has already been rendering the benefits received insignificant for many high-income retirees. In addition, personal Social Security retirement accounts have also

MAKE WORKING OR RETIRING OPTIONAL

been considered for younger workers whereby a portion of their payroll taxes could be allocated by them for placement in growth investments to achieve a higher (and lower as well) expected return. However, this proposal places more risk on the worker for receiving income from Social Security during retirement. Poor investment choices made by the worker and/or generally poor investment performance could ultimately require the government to fund in the future a costly bail-out of the Social Security system and the desperate plight of retirees requiring income to merely exist.

College funding costs for educating children will delay or destroy retirement plans for an increasing number of families. Americans typically do not save enough for funding future major milestones such as college and retirement. Trying to catch up because of a delayed start usually does not work. Each year of delaying savings dramatically impacts your ability to meet future needs. Taking advantage of long-term *compounding* investment returns is a compelling reason for starting early and intelligently structuring a disciplined investment program for retirement. The challenge many families face to save enough for retirement is made difficult because parents have to divert money to pay for educating their children, and then try to make up for lost time when that commitment is done. If you have children to educate, how old will you be when your youngest child graduates from college? Will you have to rob your retirement savings to pay for college? Remember, your retirement plan savings alone is probably not enough to financially secure your retirement. It is going to take a lot of money to retire. Do you know how much? By following the cost-reducing college planning strategies discussed previously, you will be able to allocate more money for retirement that otherwise will have to be used for college funding.

Failing health, rather than choice, will become the primary reason for retiring. An increasing number of people are working to age sixty-five and beyond for various reasons such as to retain their group health insurance coverage until they are eligible for Medicare at age sixty-five, to survive financially, or just because they enjoy working. As a result, many people continue to work until they physically can no longer commit to maintaining employment. This uncertainty of how long you can physically remain in the workforce before failing health forces retirement can complicate the financial planning analysis and cloud what preparation is required for adequate funding.

Long-term-care expenses, out-of-pocket prescription costs, and other medical expenses are becoming a major financial factor for accelerated depletion of retirement savings. Long-term care can devastate retirement resources. Most people do not incorporate quantified "what if" medical expense scenarios into their retirement cash flow analysis. A fact of reality is that more women than men will suffer the consequences of not planning for high medical expenses during retirement. This is because wives are more frequently the surviving spouse, and furthermore the husband may have already seriously impacted the family's savings with a costly illness prior to death.

Retirees will have higher levels of debt than previous generations to repay out of their retirement cash flow. Credit cards did not exist for previous generations of retirees, and auto and consumer credit loans were not available to anyone without earned income. Furthermore, it was considered intelligent retirement planning to pay off a mortgage before retirement. However, during a low-interest-rate environment, this may not be the best strategy to implement. If the mortgage debt interest rate is low relative to the expected rate of return on investments, maintaining a mortgage during retirement could be an intelligent leveraging strategy for additional retirement capital. In addition, the mortgage interest deduction can offset the income tax liability incurred as money is being withdrawn from tax-deferred retirement plans. Using low-interest-rate borrowed money that a mortgage can provide enables you to utilize the spread or differential in interest rates. This is what skilled lenders such as bankers do very profitably, and for pre-retirees and retirees, it is an opportunity to utilize the lender's money for a more profitable retirement. With a fixed low-interest-rate mortgage, the monthly repayment amount remains the same (significantly, a mortgage payment does not increase with inflation) while the interest cost steadily decreases each month. Meanwhile, the residence's market value continues to appreciate whether or not there is a low-interest mortgage loan outstanding. The home equity money becomes available for investment instead of being dead or wasted retirement capital, which, outside the house, could be providing compounding investment growth in order to extend the length of time before retirement money might run out. Furthermore, if desired, the invested home equity money is available to reduce or pay off the mortgage balance at any time. Caution: This intelligent mortgage leveraging approach should be done only with the careful guidance of a comprehensive financial advisor. As with all debt management, there are many planning considerations that need to be discussed and evaluated, and it is not recommended as an appropriate strategy for everyone.

Extracting cash from home equity with a *reverse mortgage* and from a permanent cash value life insurance policy with a *viatical* or *life settlement* will become more prevalent as a source of supplemental retirement income.

- **Reverse Mortgage:** Many retirees have a large amount of money that is tied up in their home equity that they could use to provide them with additional retirement income. However, using traditional mortgage financing to extract home equity for cash to pay for living expenses during retirement might be either not affordable or not available at all. Alternatively, if the house is sold to obtain cash, they still have to live somewhere. Therefore, another form of mortgage, termed a reverse mortgage, is becoming readily available for retirees. A reverse mortgage enables retirees to continue living in their home and access the equity value that is tied up in the house in order to use it for living expenses. The roles of lender and borrower are *reversed* from that of a traditional mortgage; the lender pays you instead of you paying the lender during the life of the mortgage. You remain the owner of your home, and are responsible for paying property taxes, homeowner insurance, and maintenance expenses. The amount of money advanced depends upon the borrower's age and the value of the home equity. There are financing fees and ongoing interest costs, which are added to the loan balance and repaid when the loan is over. The loan is over when the last surviving borrower dies, sells the home, or permanently moves out of the home. The amount owed equals all the loan advances, plus all the interest that has been added to the loan balance. If the total amount owed is less than what the home is worth, then you (or your estate) keep whatever amount is left over. Furthermore, you can never owe more than what the house is worth at the time that the loan is repaid, and the reverse mortgage lender cannot seek repayment from your income, other assets, or your heirs. To determine whether a reverse mortgage is appropriate for you, be sure to work with a reputable independent financial advisor to help you evaluate the merits and pitfalls and direct you to a trustworthy reverse mortgage provider. Additional information about reverse mortgages can be found at www.reversemortgage.org or www.aarp.org.

- **Viatical and Life Settlements:** While reverse mortgages can be used to extract money from home equity for retirement income, it's now also possible for retirees to use viatical settlements and life settlements to extract a lump sum cash amount from their life insurance for use during their lifetime. Viatical settlements are offered to the terminally ill, while life settlements are offered to those people who are still healthy. In essence, both of these financial tools provide the retiree a discounted lump sum cash advance against their insurance policy's death benefit. In exchange for the cash advance, the future proceeds from the death benefit are assigned to the company or individual that makes the death benefit advance. The amount of cash advanced is determined by the size of the death benefit available and how long you are expected to live, but typically the advance against the death benefit is severely discounted. For example, a $1,000,000 life insurance policy might provide a lump sum cash advance of only $300,000. Upon the insured's death, the cash advance provider, which has been assigned the life insurance policy's death benefit proceeds, receives the full death benefit amount regardless of whether the death happens in one month or thirty years. Whenever the death occurs, survivors receive none of the life insurance proceeds that would have otherwise been available. In both instances, you have to watch out for scams and abuses when considering a viatical or life settlement, and they should be considered only as a last resort. In order to be certain whether either is appropriate for you, be sure to work with a reputable independent financial advisor who can help you evaluate the merits and pitfalls and direct you to a legitimate provider.

Multigenerational living patterns will become a more prevailing way of life, returning to the way it used to be before financially independent retirement living became feasible. Today, an estimated 22% of the American population is categorized as the "sandwich generation," meaning they are parenting their own children and taking care of their parents at the same time. Some estimates project that in the next ten years, nearly two-thirds of working families will be required to take care of an elderly parent. This can cause major stress on family finances, emotions, and relationships and can affect the sandwich generation's ability to plan and accumulate money for their own secure retirement. Fortunately, research also shows that for the majority of families that establish multigenerational co-residency households, with good communication and cooperative family dynamics in place, several generations under one roof or nearby can provide positive outcomes. The benefits experienced include enhanced well-being and better care for grandchildren as well as for grandparents, more love and caring responsibility being exchanged through chores and activities, and the joy of family closeness, which has been lost in recent generations.

Ways to Save for a Secure, Worry-Free Retirement

Any method that you use to save for retirement is good; the main thing is to do it and start early. Many people work for employers that sponsor a group retirement savings plan such as a 401(k), while other people have no group plan offered by their employer and instead have to save for retirement using an individual retirement savings vehicle such as an individual retirement account (IRA). Some people also save beyond their retirement plan by investing money in an individual taxable investment account. Most people will have to use some combination of group and individual retirement savings plans as well as individual taxable investment accounts in order to accumulate enough for having a secure retirement lifestyle. This section discusses all of the different options that are available to save for retirement, some of which are better than others.

Group Retirement Savings Plans

Group retirement savings plans are sponsored by employers and should be the starting point for a retirement accumulation program, especially if the employer makes some form of matching contribution to the employee's contribution. There are certain employer-sponsored group plans that are approved by the IRS as *qualified* for certain favorable tax benefits and savings incentives, while others are termed *nonqualified*, with less tax benefits and incentives for the employee to save for retirement. As mentioned before, the structure of today's employer-sponsored group retirement plans has shifted the responsibility to have enough money for retirement from the employer (pension income plan) to the employee (retirement savings plan). If your employer sponsors and makes committed contributions to a pension income plan on your behalf, you are one of a decreasing and fortunate few. Today, employers more typically make some form of matching contribution to a group retirement savings plan such as a 401(k) or 403(b), and/or the employer makes a discretionary contribution to a profit sharing plan if the company's profitability warrants it. It's a "no-brainer" that as an employee you should contribute to a retirement savings plan whatever amount is necessary to receive your employer's matching contribution if there is one. Not all employers make matching contributions, but if they do, it is a gift of money that you should always take advantage of.

Regular 401(k) and 403(b) retirement savings plans (pretax contributions, tax-deferred investment growth, taxable withdrawals). In simple terms, the 401(k) plan is a group retirement savings plan sponsored by a private company employer, while the 403(b) plan is a retirement savings plan in the form of a tax-sheltered annuity (TSA) sponsored by a nonprofit organization employer. Employees are allowed to contribute money via payroll deduction on a pretax basis, which increases the amount you can save and reduces your taxable income. There is an annual dollar limit on the employee's contribution amount, which as of 2020 is $19,500 and is adjusted upward annually for inflation. In addition, some 401(k) and 403(b) plans permit a federally legislated "catch up" provision, which allows participants that are age fifty or older to contribute an additional amount, which as of 2020 is an additional $6,500, and this too is adjusted for inflation annually. Employers may choose to match up to as much as 50% of the employee's contribution, but many offer a much smaller match or no match at all. As stated before, if the employer does match a portion of the employee's contributions, the employee should always contribute enough to receive the full match amount, unless he or she does not expect to be with the employer long enough (usually three to five years) to have a vested interest in the match amount. The pretax contributions made to a 401(k) or 403(b) retirement savings plan are allowed to grow tax deferred until being used in retirement, at which time the withdrawals are fully taxed at ordinary income tax rates. Accordingly, the more you take out in order to keep up with the increasing living costs during retirement due to inflation, the higher the dollar amount of taxes you will pay. This double-barreled threat of inflation and taxes is often misunderstood and not properly accounted for in many retirement analysis projections, causing eventual financial hardship for retirees. Therefore, any retirement cash flow analysis must include assumptions about inflation and taxes as shown subsequently in the retirement projection example at the end of this chapter.

Roth 401(k) and Roth 403(b) retirement savings plan (after-tax contributions, tax-free investment growth, tax-free withdrawals). The IRS permits employers at their discretion to offer 401(k) and 403(b) plan participants the option of designating their contributions as *after-tax* Roth contributions instead of *pretax* regular contributions. The Roth designated contributions, unlike the regular, will not be taxed when the money is withdrawn during retirement because the contributions were made on an after-tax basis. The value of this Roth feature being added to the 401(k) and 403(b) is because unlike the Roth IRA, which has earned-income limitations for being eligible to contribute, there are no such earned-income limitations for contributing to the Roth 401(k) and 403(b). As a result, high-income earners can now also participate in the ability to invest money that will not be taxed during retirement or ever again. You should consider this the 401(k) and 403(b) Roth option instead of the regular pretax option if you anticipate a higher income tax bracket during retirement either because of high dollar amounts of annual withdrawals or because the current relatively low income tax levels will increase in the future. The quiet millionaire® is willing to give up the pretax benefit on the "seed," or the smaller contribution amount, in order to gain the tax-free benefit of paying no taxes on the "harvest," the larger dollar amount coming out during retirement.

Simplified Employee Pension Plan (SEP-IRA) (pretax contributions, tax-deferred investment growth, taxable withdrawals). A SEP-IRA retirement plan is a form of a profit sharing plan that is especially appealing for small business employers because the use of readily available IRS-approved prototype plan documents is permitted. Therefore, setting up the plan is easy, and the administrative costs are kept low because of reduced paperwork and minimal ongoing reporting requirements to the IRS. The employer's annual profit sharing contribution depends upon the company's profitability and affordability. Therefore, each year the employer can use its discretion on whether to make a profit sharing contribution directly to the individual employee's SEP-IRA retirement account, the amount of which can vary each year or be discontinued at any time. The contribution made for each employee is based on a percentage of annual pretax income, and the percentage rate must be the same for all plan participants. For example, if the percentage of pretax income contribution rate is determined to be 10% in a given year, the employee who earns $100,000 receives a $10,000 contribution, while the $25,000 employee receives $2,500. In another year, the determined rate could be reduced to 5%, whereby the contribution amounts would be $5,000 and $1,250, respectively. Some SEP-IRA plans also allow the employee to contribute annually in addition to the employer's profit sharing contribution. However, by law, there is a maximum allowable contribution amount that can be made for each plan participant. The combined annual contribution by both the employer and employee can be no more than 25% of the employee's pretax income, with a maximum allowable dollar limit of $57,000 per year (as of 2020 adjusted annually for inflation). Because each employee has his or her own separate tax-deferred retirement account, he or she can choose among the plan's available investment options in accordance with individual tolerance for risk. The investments grow tax free, and all accumulated amounts can be rolled over for continued tax deferral to a regular IRA if the employee leaves the company for any reason. Any withdrawals are subject to the same restrictions and taxation as regular IRAs, and borrowing against the account is not permitted.

SIMPLE-IRA Plan (pretax contributions, tax-deferred investment growth, taxable withdrawals). The SIMPLE-IRA is similar to the SEP-IRA in that it is simple to set up and administer. However, its sponsorship by employers is limited to companies with fewer than one hundred employees. The contributions to a SIMPLE-IRA plan are made primarily by the employee, who may contribute 100% of his or her annual pretax income up to a maximum of $13,500 per year as of 2020, and an additional $3,000 annual "catch-up" provision became available for participants who are age fifty or over. In addition, the employer has options to provide matching contributions. Plan participant accounts are always 100% vested immediately, which includes the salary reduction amount and the employer's matching contribution. The employee can choose from the plan's available investment options as he or she sees fit. Loans are not permitted. For additional information, go to IRS.gov.

Individual Retirement Savings Plans

Employer-sponsored group retirement plans are not always available for individuals to save money toward their retirement. Furthermore, if a group retirement plan is available, the contribution amounts allowed are limited by law and are not adequate to fund a financially secure retirement. Therefore, accumulating enough money for retirement often requires using *individual* retirement plans, which can be done on both a tax-deferred or taxable account basis.

Regular or Traditional Individual Retirement Account (IRA) (pretax or after-tax contributions, tax-deferred investment growth, taxable withdrawals). A regular IRA allows contributions that are tax deductible, and the investment earnings can grow on a tax-deferred basis until retirement, at which time the withdrawals are subject to federal income tax. There are no income limits for making contributions to traditional IRAs. Annual contributions allowed for the regular IRA are limited to a maximum of $6,000 or 100% of your annual earned income, whichever is less. A total of $12,000 can be contributed per married couple, provided at least that amount of income has been earned by one or both of the spouses. Furthermore, each person age fifty or older may make a "catch-up" contribution of an additional $1,000. Generally, high-income earners who participate in employer-sponsored group retirement plans are not permitted to make tax-deductible contributions to a regular IRA. Withdrawals from a regular IRA without penalty can start at age 59½ and are subject to ordinary income taxation. Withdrawals made before the age of 59½ will be subject to an additional 10% early-withdrawal penalty fee except where certain allowable exceptions apply. Withdrawals are required to begin no later than April 1 of the year following the year in which you reach age 70½. The rules for regular IRA withdrawals are complex and loaded with pitfalls, and it is recommended that you seek the advice of a qualified professional to avoid a costly mistake. Be aware that even if you contribute each year the maximum allowable pretax contribution amount to a regular IRA during your entire working career, the financial accumulations probably will not be sufficient to fund a desirable retirement lifestyle. Other supplemental savings must be done.

Roth IRA (after-tax contributions, tax-free investment growth, tax-free withdrawals). The Roth IRA, named after the late Senator William Roth, has a powerful tax advantage over the regular IRA when withdrawals are made during retirement. Although the investments inside both types of IRAs can grow without taxation, withdrawals made from a Roth IRA are not subject to taxation, while withdrawals made from a regular IRA are taxed as ordinary income. Unfortunately, higher income earners typically can't contribute to the Roth IRA because of earned income limitations, unlike the regular IRA. As of 2020, the limitations are modified adjusted gross income $139,000 single filing, $206,000 married filing jointly. The maximum amount of annual contributions allowed for the Roth IRA are the same as for the regular IRA described above.

Individual Annuity (pretax or after-tax contributions, tax-deferred investment growth, taxable withdrawals). Individual annuities are offered by insurance companies and by some banks. For federal income tax purposes, individual annuities are classified as either qualified or nonqualified. The investments inside both can grow on a tax-deferred basis, but an individual *qualified* annuity is subject to the same regulations and restrictions as the regular IRA and therefore qualifies for pretax contributions. Accordingly, when the annuity owner makes withdrawals, both the contribution amount and the investment gains are taxed as ordinary income and are subject to a pre-age 59½ 10% early-withdrawal penalty as well. An individual *nonqualified* annuity does not qualify for pretax contributions, and therefore the contributions are made with after-tax dollars and are not tax deductible for federal income tax purposes. Accordingly, when the annuity owner makes withdrawals, only the investment gains, not the contribution amounts, are taxed as ordinary income, and the 10% early-withdrawal penalty is applied only to the investment gains. Unlike the qualified annuity, the nonqualified annuity does not have limits for eligibility with respect to earned income or contribution amounts.

QUIET MILLIONAIRE® WISDOM

Annuities are costly, high commission insurance products that are misleadingly sold as safe investments, and should be avoided.

Annuities are particularly popular with commission paid, financial and insurance salespeople. You should avoid purchasing annuities, most especially for investment purposes. They typically have high internal costs, which harmfully reduce your investment growth and offset the proclaimed tax-deferral benefits. Furthermore, withdrawals from annuities are taxed at the higher ordinary income tax rate instead of at the lower capital gains tax rate. Moreover, heavy penalties and surrender charges are incurred for making early withdrawals. For these reasons, although there might be special circumstances that are appropriate for buying an individual annuity, most times they do not merit being used as a savings vehicle for retirement or any other purpose. In particular, IRA annuities should be avoided because of their high internal administrative and mortality costs, which can be eliminated by using the non-annuity regular IRA instead.

Taxable investment account (after-tax contributions, taxable investment growth, taxable withdrawals). In some instances, making pretax contributions and deferring taxes when saving for retirement may not be as beneficial as saving in a taxable account. This is because capital gains tax rates are lower relative to higher ordinary income tax rates. Therefore, withdrawals from retirement plans, which are taxed at ordinary income tax rates, could be double the amount of taxes paid on a taxable investment account, which can be managed to pay the lower capital gains tax rate. Certainly, you should always contribute an amount to a retirement savings plan that takes the maximum advantage of any employer's match. Never forego that gift money. However, because a taxable growth investment portfolio can be structured in a tax-efficient manner, it should be part of an intelligent savings program. Moreover, as described previously in the taxes chapter, harvesting investment tax losses can offset investment capital gains, which can effectively further lower the already lower capital gains tax rate. In addition, an ongoing, proactive, tax-efficient investment program, which emphasizes capital appreciation more so than dividend and interest income, helps keep taxes lower. Furthermore, not only can money invested in a taxable retirement account be structured for lower tax consequences when making retirement withdrawals, but also the money is more readily available without IRS penalties in the event of taking an early retirement prior to the age of 59½. In order to avoid a 10% IRS-imposed penalty for pre-59½ retirement withdrawals from a retirement plan, a customized IRS-approved periodic distributions program has to be established. Otherwise, the added 10% penalty on top of the ordinary tax can cause a nearly 50% hit on every retirement dollar withdrawn. This big difference between 50% and the lowest 15% capital gains tax rate is another compelling argument for balancing your retirement savings program between tax-deferred and taxable accounts.

Net Unrealized Appreciation (NUA) rule: (pretax retirement plan contributions, tax-deferred investment growth, retirement withdrawals taxable at lower capital gains rates). There's a little known and seldom used tax-reduction strategy, whereby your employer's company stock that's highly appreciated and concentrated within your tax-deferred retirement plan can be taxed at lower capital gains rates upon your retirement. It may be beneficial for investment diversification and tax reduction purposes upon your retirement to withdraw the company stock from the plan and pay lower capital gains taxes on the increased value, instead of rolling over the company stock portion of the plan to an IRA for subsequent higher taxation at the ordinary income tax rates. This can be done by using the IRS net unrealized appreciation (NUA) rule for retirement plan assets consisting of highly appreciated employer company stock.

In summary, there are a number of informed choices you have to make to save and preserve money for a worry-free retirement. Furthermore, there are very costly and unforgiving mistakes that can be made because of all of the IRS rules and regulations that you must address correctly. Therefore it might be wise for you to work with a qualified fee-only financial advisor to guide you on how to abide by the cardinal rules for tax-deferred and taxable accumulations for retirement.

Four Cardinal Rules for Tax-Deferred and Taxable Saving for Retirement

Rule 1: Always contribute to an employer-sponsored group tax-deferred retirement plan enough to get any company match. It's free money!

Rule 2: Never contribute *after*-tax dollars to a non-Roth employer-sponsored group tax-deferred retirement plan, regular IRA, or insurance company sponsored annuity.

Rule 3: If eligible, always contribute the maximum allowable amounts to a tax-deferred Roth IRA. This money will never be taxed when withdrawals are made if you abide by the rules.

Rule 4: If you are in a lower tax bracket during the retirement accumulation period than you expect to be during the retirement withdrawal period, then evaluate saving in a taxable account vs. a tax-deferred retirement account. This increasing tax bracket circumstance can occur if an increasingly affluent lifestyle is occurring and will not decrease during retirement.

QUIET MILLIONARE® WISDOM

Know how much money you'll need for retirement
to live according to your accustomed standard
of living and not run out of money.

Most pre-retirees have no idea when they can actually retire, and they don't know how much they need to live on and not run out of money. Without specifically quantifying their retirement objectives, pre-retirees often aren't aware what amount is required for funding a wishful retirement and living the life they want. Moreover, the combined negative effect of inflation and taxes during retirement is often underestimated. The following story about Grandma Jo illustrates the devastating effects of inflation and taxes:

> *Grandma Jo did not want to take any risk with her money. Like many retired seniors, she thought that banks were the safest place for her money with their FDIC "guaranteed" protection. So, she bought five $100,000 CDs at five different banks, which paid an average rate of 4% interest. In addition to the interest earned on her CDs, Grandma Jo also had retirement income from Social Security, two pensions, and*

an IRA, which combined put her in a 25% tax bracket. This meant
that the effective after-tax rate on her bank CDs was actually 3%.
Accordingly, with her living expenses going up 5% every year because
of inflation, Grandma Jo's CDs are losing money because of a yearly
negative 2% loss in purchasing power as follows:

4%	$500,000 annual CD interest	**$20,000**
–1%	Annual taxes (25% tax bracket)	**– 5,000**
3%	Net after-tax annual interest	**15,000**
–5%	Annual inflation	**– 25,000**
–2%	Annual loss	**– $10,000**

This means that after twenty years, Grandma Jo's $500,000 in CDs
has lost $200,000 in purchasing power ($10,000 x 20 years), and
her $500,000 becomes worth only $300,000 in purchasing power
without her having spent a cent. In effect, the low-interest-rate CDs
have effectively built in a –40% (–$200,000) guaranteed total loss of
principal, which is a sure way for Grandma Jo to run out of money
during her retirement.

QUIET MILLIONAIRE® WISDOM

Annual increases in the costs of living and taxes
present a higher risk for retirement security
than is often anticipated by pre-retirees.

The Department of Labor's published inflation rates are a myth compared to reality. The Consumer Price Index (CPI) indicates that the inflation rate has averaged about 2.25% for the past twenty years and is currently in the 2.3% range. Calculating the actual inflation increases for basics such as food, housing, energy, automobiles, gasoline, and health care reveals that the CPI is a dangerous and financially damaging statistic to use for the retirement planning process. The following are several examples of high inflation big ticket expenses affecting many families adversely:

- Health Care Costs: The Centers for Medicare and Medicaid Services (CMS) projects that overall health care costs, including all private and public spending, will increase by an average of 5.5% per year over the next decade.

- Health Insurance Costs: The U.S. Bureau of Labor Statistics states that as of 2020 the Consumer Price Index for health insurance costs is 10.7%.

- College Tuition Costs: According to FinAid.org, college tuition will continue to increase at an historical average rate of 8% per year. This means that the cost of college doubles every nine years.

Why would the government misrepresent the true rate of inflation? One very big reason is that the annual cost of living increases for federal employee pensioners and Social Security benefits are based on the CPI. If the government was honest about inflation, the annual increases for these government-funded retirement programs should have more than doubled. Financial advisors typically use 3% to 4% as the average annual rate of inflation in their retirement planning assumptions. On the basis of the true inflation rate, even those assumptions are too low. It's more prudent to use a 5% inflation factor in preparing retirement cash flow projections and thereby leave room for any margin of error with that higher presumed inflation rate. Better to err on the side of caution and have an excess of cash than to come up short at the end. And if the retirement cash flow analysis works successfully on paper, you know that it's more likely to succeed in actuality.

Now think about this: If the cost of living keeps going up during retirement and you expect to maintain your accustomed standard of living, how does this affect the amount of taxes you pay during each year of retirement?

Remember that all pretax contributed money inside of a tax-deferred retirement plan has never been taxed. So, *all* the money that you withdraw will be subject to ordinary income taxes. Accordingly, as the cost of living goes up each year, it follows that you'll have to withdraw more money in order to keep up, and this will create a *higher* tax liability each year, which is contrary to most people's common belief. This double-barreled blast of inflation and taxes is destructive to retirement cash flows.

Of course, no one can accurately project with 100% certainty what will happen in the future. Fortunately, today's computer technology enables experienced retirement planners, using appropriate assumptions and intelligent data input, to improve the predictability for achieving desired retirement objectives. If retirement is doomed for failure, it's better to find out in advance on paper and plan for success rather than live with flawed expectations and run out of money. However, be aware that data put into a computer can produce false expectations, and this is a risk you can't afford. Be realistic, honest, and accurate with your numbers. Furthermore, be cautious about relying upon the results produced from using do-it-yourself computer retirement programs because they are too simplistic and therefore are not accurate enough for such an important decision that can't be reversed once the retirement commitment is made.

For a reliable confirmation of your retirement cash flow analysis, you should consider seeking professional guidance from a competent financial planning professional. However, be diligent about who you select because selecting the wrong advisor can also put your retirement security at risk. You'll probably be best served by working with an independent, comprehensive, *fee-only* financial advisor whose advice is not biased with motivation to sell you an annuity or some other form of financial product for a commission. Don't wait to plan for your retirement until you are ready to retire. In order to ensure a worry-free, financially independent retirement, you need to correctly position yourself and then monitor and adjust your planning as both personal and external dynamics continue to change during your lifetime.

QUIET MILLIONAIRE® SUMMARY

- Intelligently plan for retirement and other milestones.
- Understand and know your own retirement plans provided through your employer and any group savings plans, as well as the pros and cons for all the various ways to save for retirement.
- Know the realistic dynamic trends affecting the affordability of retirement in order to plan and manage your finances intelligently.
- Become familiar with the Social Security system as well as with long-term health care possibilities.
- Use the Cardinal Rules for successful retirement.
- Understand the effects of college planning, failing health, and long-term health care on your retirement plans.
- Learn how to overcome the double-barreled negative effects of inflation and taxation both before and during retirement.
- Understand and utilize the various retirement savings plans.
- Periodically (at least annually) perform a detailed retirement cash flow analysis to determine and monitor whether you will run out of money during your lifetime.

CHAPTER 12

Preserve and Transfer Maximum Wealth

I n retirement, the primary financial objective for most people shifts from accumulating and growing their wealth to preserving, protecting, and transferring their wealth. However, the quiet millionaire® knows that it is just as important during retirement to still grow assets as well as to preserve and protect them to keep up with the increasing living costs and to manage the uncertainties that can occur with today's long retirement duration. The biggest uncertainty of all is how long you are going to live. Some people might have an unrealistic estate goal of "bouncing the last check." The quiet millionaire® has a more ambitious intention to instead transfer the maximum possible amount of remaining wealth to survivors. The only way to control achieving this goal is to plan in advance. This also makes certain that the transfer will be smoother, and ensure that the wealth is distributed in accordance with the way one intended. The previous chapter discussed how to make certain you accumulate enough wealth to live the life you want during "retirement," whether or not you choose to work. This chapter discusses some of the best ways to grow, preserve, and protect your wealth during "retirement," and then transfer the remainder for maximum value during the estate settlement process.

QUIET MILLIONAIRE® WISDOM

Successfully accumulating and keeping wealth requires knowledgeable planning and timely implementation.

You can't allow procrastination, false beliefs, and negligence to happen. Without proactive intelligent planning, your retirement wealth will become very costly taxable income while you're living and burdensome estate taxation upon death. In addition, you'll cause unnecessary and upsetting hardship for the people you care about the most.

Best Ways to Grow, Preserve, and Protect Your Accumulated Retirement Wealth

Proactively develop a comprehensive retirement funding game plan that optimally coordinates tax minimization strategies while utilizing retirement money from all your financial sources. The amount of taxation for money that you use during retirement depends upon your work career and how you accumulated the money for retirement. Some retirees have their money in tax-deferred retirement accounts and annuities that have never been taxed but that will be subject to costly taxation as withdrawals are made. Many retirees also will receive taxable income from Social Security, and some will receive taxable income from a company pension plan as well. Retirement money that is located outside of tax-deferred retirement plans in taxable accounts, rental properties, and business interests is also subject to taxation when withdrawn. Taking money from all the various sources of retirement funds requires a well-thought-out optimization strategy or else a significant amount of accumulated wealth can vanish because of taxes both during and after your lifetime. For example, the IRS has a required minimum distribution (RMD) schedule that forces you to withdraw money from tax-deferred retirement plans and IRAs (except Roth IRAs) starting at age 70½ for the remainder of your expected lifetime. If you should die before completing the IRS required schedule for lifetime withdrawals, the federal and state governments will be there to collect the remaining income taxes owed on the deferred money as well as any estate or inheritance taxes owed. It *is not* in your best interest to remain on cruise control when traveling the complicated and confusing road of retirement and estate taxation because as much as 90% of your wealth can be lost to taxes, leaving only 10% for you and your survivors to use. It *is* in your best interest to work with a professional advisor who can safely guide you through and around all of the financial road hazards you may encounter before it is too late to avoid them.

Account for catastrophic long-term-care costs in your retirement cash flow planning analysis and determine how you will manage and pay for this risk. A major threat to your security during retirement is the financial devastation that catastrophic long-term-care costs can cause your investment portfolio. One of the most important parts of any retirement cash flow analysis is to include performing a "stress test" for catastrophic long-term-care expenses. This is done by hypothesizing specific "what ifs" for your retirement cash flow analysis that compare the different investment portfolio outcomes that might occur *if* you:

- Use your investment portfolio to pay premiums for long-term-care insurance to fully or partially limit your exposure to the potential out-of-pocket costs for catastrophic long-term care and protect your financial security.
- Use your investment portfolio to fully or partially self-insure your exposure to the potential out-of-pocket costs for catastrophic long-term care. Going broke and relying upon Medicaid (medical welfare) is not an acceptable option for the quiet millionaire. If your retirement

cash flow analysis reveals that your investment portfolio is more financially secure by paying affordable insurance premiums, then you should avoid shouldering the financial risk of long-term care and pay the premiums to insure.

Maintain a well-diversified investment portfolio that will continue to keep you ahead of inflation. The reduction of your money's purchasing power as a result of inflation is an investment risk you can't afford at any time and especially during retirement when you're living off of your investment portfolio. Having a bank certificate of deposit (CD) mentality during retirement erodes the value of your money for paying living expenses. Another valuable aspect of the retirement cash flow analysis is the process of inputting various assumptions for investment rates of return to determine how detrimental it is by getting too "safe" with an investment program during retirement. Remember, as discussed in the previous chapter, you must keep your eye on the net after-inflation, after-tax investment rate of return in order to make your retirement money last longer.

QUIET MILLIONAIRE® WISDOM

With a diversified investment portfolio, you don't have to be right about every decision you make 100% of the time (only most of the time) for it to be well protected and grow.

By having a well-diversified investment portfolio during retirement that grows faster than the rate of inflation, you lessen the risk of running out of money. Furthermore, with a well-structured investment portfolio, you can comfortably withdraw money to live on when difficult investment performance periods occur without permanently harming the portfolio's overall value. The advantage to this circumstance is that no matter when money is taken out, there are always some parts of a diversified portfolio to access that are performing relatively well and having their "time in the sun," and the more downtrodden portions of the portfolio do not have to be invaded. Then, when the clouded portions shine again, they are intact to regain value and make a major contribution to overall growth. Strategically, during difficult investment times, certain asset classes such as the fixed income portion of an investment portfolio can be made somewhat over-weighted in order to steadily anchor the portfolio and defend it against downside risk. Then, when economic and investment conditions improve and regain momentum, certain other asset classes can become strategically over-weighted in order to capture maximum growth opportunities. This is not market timing; rather it is asset class "tuning" to make sure you "win by not losing."

Understand annuities and their pitfalls and how to manage them for best results. An annuity is an insurance product that is the reverse of a life insurance policy and is sold as a tax-deferred investment vehicle that provides income. There are two basic types of annuities: fixed and variable. The money placed in fixed annuities is invested and managed by the insurance company in a fixed-income bond portfolio that pays interest, which is adjusted at least annually. Alternatively, with variable annuities (VA), the money is invested by the owner of the annuity in a diversified array of mutual funds sponsored by the insurance company. VAs are intended to provide more growth than fixed annuities but with more consumer responsibility and risk than fixed annuities. When issuing a *life insurance policy*, the insurance company determines how long you are expected to live and accordingly charges a premium for underwriting a *death benefit*. With an *annuity*, the insurance company also determines how long you are going to live and, according to how much money you invest, will *guarantee* to pay you a fixed *income benefit* for the remainder of your lifetime from the time that you start the income payments (annuitize). However, there are pitfalls if you choose a lifetime fixed income payment (annuitize). The payment amount always stays the same and does not keep pace with inflation, and if you die after receiving as little as one income payment, the insurance company gets to keep all of the remaining money you invested. With life insurance, you "win" if you die early, while with an "annuitized" annuity, the insurance company wins if you die early. Neither arrangement seems good.

Depending upon the annuity policy, there may be other alternatives besides a "guaranteed" lifetime fixed-income benefit that you can select. One option might be to elect a fixed-income benefit for an *agreed certain period* of time such as five or ten years. This way, if you die before the agreed income period is up, your survivors will receive the benefit amount still owed for the remaining unused period. Another option is to instead *withdraw* your money as needed from an annuity without being "guaranteed" a stipulated fixed-income amount. The advantage to making the withdrawal election is that you can be flexible about how much and when you take money out. The pitfall is that you give up any form of "guaranteed" fixed-income benefit, but the positive side is that by letting the invested money inside the annuity continue to grow, you may be able to take out larger payments as needed and better keep up with inflation. Another advantage to the withdrawal program is that the annuity's survivor beneficiary(s) does not lose receiving any investment amount remaining inside the annuity if you die before using it all. In most instances for reasons already discussed, the withdrawal program is usually the best option to elect. However, be aware that an un-annuitized annuity in the withdrawal mode can present an income tax hardship for the named survivor beneficiaries, which can be avoided by investing money instead in a taxable account and forgoing the tax-deferral benefit. This is because any money remaining inside an annuity does not "step up" for income tax purposes to the value at the date of death, and therefore survivors have to pay income taxes on the gains that have been tax deferred over the years, whereas survivors inheriting a taxable account do not have to pay any taxes on the gains because the investment value is "stepped up" to the dollar value that exists at the date of death.

Annuities are often sold by financial salespeople as being a great tax-deferred savings vehicle for retirement and/or college funding. What they do not tell you is that annuities have high fees and internal costs and onerous surrender charges and penalties, and they also do not tell you that they get paid an exorbitant commission for selling them. One of the biggest travesties involving annuities is the sale of an IRA annuity, which is entirely unwarranted because a less costly non-annuity regular IRA already offers the same tax-deferred investment benefit. So if people attempt to sell you an annuity as an investment for retirement, college funding, or any other reason, just remember that they win and you lose.

The best decision is not to purchase an annuity in the first place, but if you already have an annuity, there is a transaction you can do to improve your situation. Specifically, it is an IRS-approved transaction termed a "1035 tax-free exchange," which allows you to transfer the money from one annuity to another without income tax consequences. But you have to be careful because this transaction is often abused by persons selling annuities in order to gain another commission being paid on the money being transferred, and there may be costly early-surrender charges incurred for the annuity being replaced. Therefore, if you already own an annuity and choose to do a 1035 exchange, be sure to fully understand how to make sure it's in your best interest. Also, make sure you realize all of the costs involved and make sure that you're moving to an annuity that pays no commissions (no-load), has no surrender charges, and is immediately available for you to use any time you want your money. Annuity pitfalls can be ugly, but the storyline for buying them can sound beautiful.

Consider and evaluate converting a regular IRA to a Roth IRA. If you have money situated inside a regular IRA and in any given tax year your modified adjusted gross income (MAGI) is less than the Roth income limitations (see IRS.gov), you should evaluate whether converting your regular IRA to a Roth IRA makes financial sense for you. In particular, during retirement, without any earned income, you might be able to plan your income flow in order to stay under the MAGI threshold. Be aware that if you convert your regular IRA to a Roth IRA, it can be done either on a full or partial conversion basis in order to control the amount of income taxes you are required to pay on the dollar amount converted. Regardless of whether you decide to convert all or part of your regular IRA to a Roth IRA, it's important that you pay the taxes owed with money from outside the regular IRA to avoid paying additional taxes and possible penalties. If you use the regular IRA funds to pay the taxes incurred on the conversion, that amount used to pay the taxes is considered a withdrawal and is also subject to taxation, which reduces the conversion benefits. Even more costly is if you are under age 59½ and use the regular IRA funds to pay the taxes because that amount used is considered to be a premature distribution and is also subject to a 10% early-distribution penalty. Retirees who determine that they will not need to use all of their regular IRA money during their lifetime will find the Roth IRA conversion opportunity to be especially attractive. This is because once the money is converted to a Roth IRA, you are no longer forced to start making withdrawals at age 70½ as the IRS mandates be done with regular IRAs. Making it even more attractive is the fact that neither you nor the beneficiaries you name for the Roth IRA will ever have to pay taxes on withdrawals once the conversion process is completed. Invested money can grow and never be taxed again, and you will never have to be concerned about income tax rates going up in the future. Doing the Roth IRA conversions the right way can be tricky, but gaining from the potential payoffs can be a wealth building and preservation bonanza. It's probably best to seek fee-only professional guidance as part of a comprehensive financial planning process.

Best Ways to Transfer Your Estate's Wealth for Maximum Value and in the Most Private, Least Difficult Manner Possible

Estate planning is a financial area where many costly, negligent errors occur and therefore remains an important topic to consider in how to transfer the most amount of wealth to survivors with the least amount of hassle for them. The following are some of the major activities that should be done to accomplish that objective.

Legally prepare, execute, implement, and maintain proper estate planning documentation. Most people don't want to think about their own mortality, which is an uncertain certainty. When in good health, everyone expects to live a long life, but it does not always turn out to be that way. Estate planning is not just for the ultra-wealthy, and documentation must be established during your lifetime in order for your intentions to be legally effective upon your incapacity, incompetence, or death. As a basic minimum, everyone should have a simple will prepared by an attorney, and it should definitely not be a do-it-yourself document. If there is no documentation, there is no family control of the estate settlement process. Rather the process is in the control of a probate judge who has no idea about your true desires and who abides by a set of state laws that might not match your actual intentions. Often, family members who were once close are torn apart by disputes, frustration, and greed. In other words, you left a confused mess resulting in unnecessary hardship. No family is immune to the consequences of money disputes. Another important aspect of estate planning that is often neglected by not having prepared a valid will is what happens to minor children in the event that both parents are tragically gone. Without proper documentation, a judge will have to decide issues such as who will have custody of the children and who will be responsible for the children's money and welfare. It might not produce the same decisions you would have made, and this could mean additional hardship for the children.

Other important documents to have in place include a living will and durable powers of attorney for health care and financial decisions. Your attorney, in conjunction with the will preparation, should also prepare these documents. In addition, all beneficiary designations for life insurance, retirement plans, IRAs, etc., should be reviewed and kept up to date for accuracy. If you have a potential federal estate tax liability (remember all of your life insurance counts in the estate tax calculation), then you should also have a revocable living trust to increase the amount of assets that can be distributed estate tax free. In addition, having trusts in place keeps the estate settlement process private because the court-supervised probate process can be avoided.

It's very important for you to be aware that your trust documents are just worthless pieces of paper until you execute them and actually complete the titling and funding of assets in the trust's name. Furthermore, in order to avoid or reduce potential federal estate taxes, you need to make sure that the funded trusts have assets that are properly balanced in value between the spouses. Unfortunately, some attorneys are not diligent about properly funding trusts and balancing asset values once the trust documents are prepared and signed. So, make certain that you hire only an attorney that will diligently follow up for completion of the implementation required after the trust documents are signed.

All documentation must abide by the state laws where you legally reside. If you relocate, the documents must be reviewed again to assure they conform to the laws of the new state of residence. You should also maintain an up-to-date *non*-legal document termed a "final letter of instructions," which details such things as funeral arrangements and the location of important documents, insurance policies, investments, cash, safe-deposit boxes, etc. Because life is full of unexpected events, it is important that there be open and detailed communication with ultimate survivors even if the need for their estate settlement role is expected to be a long way off. There are also other numerous complex estate planning issues and strategies too comprehensive for the scope of this book that require many specific forms of legal documentation to implement. The purpose of bringing this up now is to make you aware that having even the basic documentation is very beneficial and to recommend that you initiate action with a comprehensive financial advisor working together with a competent estate planning attorney. This should be done even if you don't have a potential estate tax liability in order to remain in control of the distribution of your assets and to clearly and legally communicate your intentions to survivors. Moreover, family survivors who will be responsible for settling your estate should be introduced to your financial advisor and attorney during your lifetime in order for the family to be more prepared in the event that something happens.

Stay up to date with changes in the federal income and estate tax laws and update your tax reduction planning strategies throughout the year. Federal estate tax laws are continuously in disarray, which requires constant monitoring to stay updated and informed about any necessary adjustments in estate planning strategies. As of 2020, most relatively simple estates (cash, publicly traded securities, small amounts of other easily valued assets, and no special deductions or elections, or jointly held property) do not require the filing of an estate tax return. A filing is required for estates with combined gross assets and prior taxable gifts exceeding $11,580,000 in 2020. However, estate tax filing requirements are a politically fickle moving target that must be monitored to help protect your accumulated wealth from potentially onerous taxation. The dollar amount filing requirements for federal estate taxes have been substantially lower in the past, and quite possibly might be much lower again in the future. Moreover, be aware that most states also impose an inheritance tax on remaining estate assets, and with much lower dollar filing requirements.

Have sufficient estate liquidity for paying all taxes owed at death. If your estate plan does not provide enough cash to cover final expenses such as outstanding debt and taxes owed, then valuable assets may have to be sold immediately and frequently for much less than their actual market value. Planning should be done in advance in order to avoid this scenario that robs survivors from retaining hard-earned accumulated family wealth. One planning tool can be life insurance that provides proceeds for the required liquidity at death. In addition, life insurance proceeds are not generally subject to income taxes and when properly structured in advance may not be subject to otherwise applicable estate taxes.

Establish a lifetime gift-giving program to reduce taxes and provide income. As of 2020, an individual can gift each year up to $15,000 (adjusts for inflation) to any person without incurring federal gift tax. Married couples can gift up to $30,000. This is a good way to reduce the value of your estate and transfer it over time. For parents and grandparents who may want to reduce the size of their estate and educate children, the college savings 529 plan offers a unique opportunity because it enables them to accelerate five years' worth of the annual exclusion amount into one year. Best of all, the 529 plan is the only estate planning device available whereby a monetary gift is considered an irrevocable completed gift for estate tax reduction purposes, but in fact the gift can be revoked in the event the money should be subsequently needed or if the student becomes unworthy of the gift. However, if the money is taken back, there is an income tax liability and 10% penalty incurred on the earnings and appreciation. The 10% penalty is waived if the student beneficiary becomes disabled or is deceased. It is also waived if the student receives a scholarship and the withdrawal of funds equals the amount of the scholarship. The family limited partnership

(FLIP), grantor-retained interest trust (GRIT), grantor-retained annuity trust (GRAT), and the grantor-retained unit trust (GRUT) are some of the other estate and gift tax reduction entities used to maximize the transfer of wealth to family members. A discussion of the best ways to effectively use these techniques is extensive and beyond the scope of this book, but you should be aware that they exist and may warrant your consideration.

Use appreciated investment assets to make monetary gifts. One way to use this strategy is to shift a tax liability from a higher to a lower income tax bracket by gifting an appreciated asset such as a stock or mutual fund to someone who is in a lower tax bracket than you. This way, the appreciated asset can be sold without any tax liability to you and with a smaller tax liability being incurred by the person receiving the gifted appreciated asset. For example, the lower tax liability can be created when a grandparent makes a gift to a grandchild. However, watch out for something called the "kiddie" income tax, which occurs when the child is under age fourteen. Also, be cautious to abide by the limited $15,000 gift tax exclusion to avoid possible gift tax consequences.

Even more tax beneficial is to gift an appreciated asset to a charitable or religious organization or to any other IRS-approved nonprofit entity that is excluded from having to pay any tax on the gain in value for the donated appreciated asset. Making gifts to a charitable or religious organization with appreciated investments instead of cash can leverage the size of your contribution while at the same time reducing your tax liability. For example, assume that you own a mutual fund that you paid $10,000 to purchase and that it has grown in value to $30,000. If you were to sell it, you would have to pay a capital gains tax. If you wanted to donate the net proceeds to a charitable organization, you could, but there is a better way. Instead, donate the appreciated $30,000 mutual fund to the charity, let it sell the fund tax free, and remove all your tax liability. In addition, the amount of your contribution is increased, and your income tax deduction is larger as well. A more sophisticated planning idea using this appreciated asset planning concept is to establish a charitable remainder trust (CRT), which provides you the added benefit of receiving lifetime income, the amount of which depends upon the size of the contribution amount. Sometimes, business owners having a highly appreciated value for their business use the CRT to avoid paying a huge tax on the gain business value and to reduce their estate tax liability, get a large charitable deduction, and create a source of lifetime income for their retirement.

Plan Smartly to Advance Confidently in the Direction of Your Dreams

Would you just jump into a car or take an airplane and go wherever the driver or pilot decided without planning your trip? If so, you would likely wind up somewhere other than where you intended if you had planned your course. Nevertheless, this is how many people plan their travel through life. In essence, they're counting on a miracle to reach their desired destination.

> *"If one advances confidently in the direction of their dreams,*
> *and endeavors to live the life which they have imagined,*
> *they will meet with a success unexpected in common hours."*
> **—Henry Thoreau**

Your financial success is not in the hands of some "fickle finger of fate" or fortunate changes in the economy; it's completely up to you to plan and manage the course of your life and to fulfill your dreams.

QUIET MILLIONAIRE® WISDOM

The future is now for managing your financial life.

You need to discover the true you and to define specifically what the important achievements and goals are for your life. This will form a solid and motivating base from which to plan and manage your finances. Intelligent financial management will enable you to accumulate money for financial security and independence and to maintain control of your path through life. Here's how to make sure that your destiny isn't a matter of circumstance, but rather a matter of choice and achievement:

- Overcome procrastination. Plan and follow through, properly informed.
- Know where you are today relative to where you want to go. Don't be uninformed about your situation and what it will require to get to your destination.
- Set specific goals for where you want to go. A goal remains only a dream if it is not specific. We all should have dreams, but to be terrific, you must be specific!
- Formulate and implement workable strategies for achieving your goals. Carrying out successful strategies requires making informed decisions about issues such as tax reduction, investing for growth in a comfortable risk tolerant manner, purchasing financial products, and evaluating which financial products are most appropriate and from whom to purchase them.
- Manage your financial plan both proactively and responsively to your dynamically changing personal circumstances, i.e., changes in employment, earned income, health status, and family life transitions such as education funding commitments, retirement, etc.

- Adjust to shifting external events such as changes involving economic conditions, tax laws, inflation, and investment returns, etc.

- Monitor and measure the progress relative to your plan's assumptions and expected outcomes. For example, are your assumptions about investment rates of return and inflation increases holding up? Are you maintaining the discipline to accumulate the amounts required for meeting your specified financial goals? Stay alert for when and how to best fine-tune and adjust for any changes in your personal circumstances and outside events.

Do It Yourself or Hire a Financial Advisor?

When planning and managing your finances, you have an important decision to make. Should you do it on your own or with the help of an objective and competent professional advisor? Either way, there are all sorts of resources available to you. Many might seem convincingly reliable and trustworthy, but actually could do irreparable harm. You might not even realize that financial damage has been done until it's too late, when you're required to make unexpected, anxious adjustments and realignments to your lifestyle. Therefore, it's important that you discern good advice from bad. Here are some suspicious sources:

- Mass media noise from television, newspapers, magazines, the Internet, etc. These resources can be especially harmful because they indicate credible communications. However, too often it's unregulated hype that's more intended to attract your attention and sell wares than to provide you with intelligent solutions. At best, the mass media offer rules of thumb and generalities that may not be applicable or appropriate for your particular situation.

- Subscription newsletters that play upon greed and ignorance with enticing claims about secret strategies for easy financial success. Warning: There are no get-rich-quick schemes to replace an intelligent, ongoing financial management program. At best, the scheme maybe works for a designated period that the schemer chooses to show you for substantiating the claim of success.

Even if you're able to discern the good advice from the bad, think about this. Would you build a house that you intend to live in without a contractor? Similarly, would you build a financial house that you intend to live in without a financial advisor? While you could try to build either on your own, the final construction may be shoddy, the required maintenance may be unmanageable, and therefore the outcomes may not be the best ones for you. For these reasons, maybe you might seriously consider working with a qualified professional who possesses the necessary tools and the right skills to advise you on how to build and maintain your complete financial house. It's for you to decide as you learn from this book what's required to do the job right. This is not intended to be a "how to do it yourself" book. Rather, this book provides "blueprints" to use yourself and/or to show an advisor to help you with the construction of your financial house. Furthermore, if you decide to use a financial advisor, you'll also become aware of how to find and hire one that's qualified and worthwhile for you.

Hiring a Professional Advisor for Guidance Could be Either Your Best or Worst Investment

The quiet millionaire® realizes that "good advice is seldom free" and that "cheap advice is likely cheap in value." Often, advice can be self-serving for the provider. It can also be downright incompetent and inappropriate. Moreover, don't be foolish enough to believe that the descriptions for financial service providers as "big" and "well known" and "reputable" will ensure that you're getting the best direction for your situation. This is why there are so many regulatory watchdogs required to guard the financial terrain.

On the other hand, if you work with the right advisor, it takes only a few tidbits of good, sound advice to make a professional fee worth paying. Consider this: If during a down market, your $500,000 investment portfolio would have dropped 25% ($125,000) under your control, but because of the investment advisor's structure, it decreased only 10% ($50,000), would a $5,000 annual investment advisory have been a cost or a good investment? Furthermore, if while you are withdrawing money for funding retirement, the same advisor, included in the same fee, showed you ways to reduce taxes by $5,000 a year, plus provided other value-added financial planning and management services, would paying the $5,000 annual fee for such comprehensive advice be worthwhile to you?

This book advocates the merits of working with a *fee-only* advisor because the commission-only and fee-based advisors can be biased and motivated by commission compensation to sell financial products as part of their agenda. Also, be realistic about working with investment consultants or advisors employed by well-known and, therefore, perceived reputable brokerage firms and banks. Realize that they too can be biased to direct you toward the financial products and services offered by the firms they represent rather than objectively representing you as their deemed employer. Although they may be book experienced, they might not be practically experienced.

Unbiased advice is more likely to be received from an entrepreneurial, independently owned and operated, *fee-only* advisory firm. Furthermore, the advice is usually superior to that received from commission-earning salespeople and from salaried employees representing large, multilayered bureaucratic financial firms. Importantly, receiving unbiased, competent professional advice also helps you to avoid making uninformed or emotional financial decisions. However, the method of compensation does not guarantee advisor competency, and you should go through a careful due diligence advisor search and interview process. This process, if done properly, should produce a successful advisory working relationship that lasts a lifetime.

Be cautious about relying too heavily upon references. While they're important and should be a part of the search process, it could turn out to be a situation of "what is good for the goose might not be so good for the gander." Furthermore, advisors are going to provide you with only references that they know will respond positively to your inquiry. You need to evaluate objectively and first-hand the competency, trustworthiness, and rapport with the prospective advisors produced by your search process. Any concluding decisions about which financial advisor to hire should be made by *both* spouses in a married household, even if one spouse usually takes the lead in the family's financial decision making. The deferring spouse may turn out to be the survivor who then must assume more responsibility for the financial situation.

QUIET MILLIONAIRE® WISDOM

*Know for certain that a financial advisor is qualified
and trustworthy before you hire them.*

How to Find and Hire a Financial Advisor That's Right for You and Be In Control of Your Life as a Quiet Millionaire®

- *Visit the CFP Board website CFP.net to locate a Certified Financial Planner™ in your local area.*

- *Visit the National Association of Personal Financial Advisors (NAPFA) website www.napfa.org for a listing of fee-only advisors located in your local area.*
- *Visit the financial advisor's website.*
- *Contact the financial advisors under your consideration for a free, no-obligation introductory interview.*
- *Make a final selection for establishing a working advisory relationship.*

Work to discover the true you and to define specifically what the important achievements and goals are for your life. This will form a solid and motivating base from which to plan and manage your finances. Intelligent financial management will enable you to accumulate money for financial security and independence and to maintain control of your path through life. Your destiny should not be a matter of circumstance but rather a matter of choice and achievement.

QUIET MILLIONAIRE® SUMMARY

- Know and implement the best ways to grow, preserve, and protect your retirement wealth.
- Learn how to transfer your estate's wealth for maximum value and in the most private, least difficult manner possible.
- Legally prepare, execute, implement, and maintain proper estate planning documentation.
- Determine whether you'll take action on your own or with the help of a financial advisor.
- Conduct an informed due diligence search process to find a trustworthy and competent financial advisor who is right for you.
- Be in control of your life and Be the Quiet Millionaire®.

ABOUT THE AUTHOR

 **Brett Wilder** is a Certified Financial Planner™ who with more than forty years of professional experience has guided thousands of people to achieve the aspirations and lifestyles they dream of. *The Quiet Millionaire* concisely explains step-by-step proven ways to build and retain wealth, whether on your own or by working with a properly qualified financial advisor. Brett's expertise has been published in major publications such as Wall Street Journal, Financial Advisor, Investor's Business Daily, The NAPFA Advisor, and Working Wealth Magazine as well as online at major sites such as Entrepreneur.com, TheStreet.com, and YahooFinance.com. He has appeared as a featured guest expert on numerous television and radio programs throughout the United States.

Brett founded in 1989 Total Wealth Planning, a highly-acclaimed, fee-only, financial planning and investment advisory firm registered with the Securities and Exchange Commission. In 2015, he sold the firm to devote time to writing, consulting, and traveling extensively throughout the world. Brett and his wife Sandy divide time residing in Miromar Lakes, Fl and Cincinnati, OH. He lives the life he advocates for readers of *The Quiet Millionaire* to strive for and plan to achieve: *"To do whatever you want, whenever and wherever you want, regardless of whether you want to work or not!"*